BODY FLEX~ BODY MAGIC

ANJA LANGER

WITH BILL REYNOLDS

CB

CONTEMPORARY
BOOKS

CHICAGO

Library of Congress Cataloging-in-Publication Data

Langer, Anja.
    Body flex-body magic / Anja Langer with Bill Reynolds.
       p.   cm.
    Includes index.
    ISBN 0-8092-3930-2 (paper)
      1. Bodybuilding for women.   2. Weight-training for women.
  3. Physical fitness for women.   I. Reynolds, Bill.   II. Title.
    GV546.6.W64L36   1992
    646.7′5′082—dc20   92-28690
                                      CIP

Photographs by Simianer & Blühdorn

Published by Contemporary Books, Inc.
180 North Michigan Avenue, Chicago, Illinois 60601
Manufactured in the United States of America
International Standard Book Number: 0-8092-3930-2

Contents

Acknowledgments

· ·

I would like to extend my gratitude to the company Candy Jay Sportswear, which has always equipped me with sportswear during my years of training and for photo productions.

A thank-you also goes to the company Reebok, Germany, which supported me through its sponsoring contract.

And finally I would like to extend my sincerest thanks and deepest appreciation to Bill Reynolds for his professional guidance, steadfast dedication, and enthusiasm for this project. I'm proud that *Body Flex–Body Magic* is a part of his legacy.

1
Introduction

As a child, I found that my talents and strengths were in physical activities. My first passion was for gymnastics. At eight years old, I became an active member of the gymnastics association and participated, more or less successfully, in several competitions. I also competed in show for a horseback-riding club. Riding was a natural choice for me, as my family owned two horses. From early in my childhood, physical activity was an important and rewarding part of my life. My need for variety also became apparent at this time.

During my teenage years, other sports captured my curiosity. I tried diving when I was 14. Within a year I was able to dive off the 10-meter platform and, my curiosity about diving having been satisfied, I took up jazz dance.

I was filled with enthusiasm for jazz dance. I loved the music, the motion, the expression, and the performing. It was during this period that I met my first love and the boy who introduced me to bodybuilding. Armin is now a very good friend of mine, and I am grateful to him for providing me with a solid foundation in the basics of bodybuilding.

In 1980, at the age of 15, I started training. At that time, I was the only girl in the gym, which didn't bother me at all. The guys were amazed at how strong I was.

Step by step, I started working out. From the first six months, I trained twice a week. I stepped up my training to three times a week, then four times a week, and so on until my first competition, the Baden-Württenberg, in 1981. I placed second to last. Rather than becoming discouraged, I trained even harder, allowing my enthusiasm and ambition to take over. I studied up on dieting and getting the most from my workouts and applied what I learned to my training. A year later, in the same local competition, I won second place.

At this point, bodybuilding was still a hobby for me, and my parents were making sure it stayed that way. In secondary school, I took the first public examination, which allowed me to leave school and put that part of my life behind me—which I did gladly. I was ready to take on the world, but I hadn't yet reached 18. Since my parents were against my bodybuilding, I was forced to prepare for competitions secretly—a situation that only fueled my determination. It wasn't until much later that my parents recognized that bodybuilding is part of my life philosophy and that my positive outlook is a direct result of my participation in the sport.

From 1983 to 1986 I studied graphic art. I have enjoyed graphics since childhood and found it a fulfilling program of study. While in school, I continued training and competing on the side. In 1983 I placed fourth in the German championship. The following year a partner and I came in second in a couple-posing competition in Madrid, Spain. I became the Junior World Champion in Australia in 1985 and, in 1986, won both the German championship and the European championship.

When I finished my education, I decided to make my hobby my profession. The next year was a difficult one because my father died. I managed to win second place in Toronto and fourth place in the Ms. Olympia competition. I won second place in the Ms. Olympia in New York City in 1988.

After the Ms. Olympia, I decided to put pro-competition on hold for a year. My goal was to win the Ms. Olympia title in 1990, and I was going to use all my power and ambition to achieve it. As often happens, mother nature had something else in mind.

So in 1990 I began preparing for a different, though no less exciting, competition: motherhood. I continued training and followed a special diet, and in January 1991 I gave birth to my son, Elija.

I'm still in training, only not competitively right now. But who knows what the future will bring?

For me, the most important part of bodybuilding is working out regularly to maintain a solid base level of strength. This foundation is necessary for both physical fitness and bodybuilding competition. In life as in bodybuilding, it is important to build a foundation of strength. In my own journey through life, there is undoubtedly a parallel between strength of body and strength of mind.

Done properly, training can continue throughout pregnancy

2
First Steps

· ·

Lao-tzu, the father of Taoism, once said that a journey of a thousand miles must begin with a single step. By implication, hundreds of thousands of steps must be taken in order to walk a thousand miles.

The object of this chapter is to make your first steps as a weight trainee good ones. You'll get off on the right foot by learning everything you need to know before you walk into a gym for your first resistance-training workout.

You will learn about bodybuilding goals, weight-training jargon, which pieces of equipment to use in order to reach your weight-training goals, the importance of physical exams, age factors, heredity factors, existing-injury factors, resistance progression, correct exercise form, rest intervals between sets, how to breathe correctly while pumping iron, workout frequency, rest and sleep/awake cycles, when to train, where to work out, what to wear, appropriate starting weights, repetition ranges, basic nutrition, break-in procedures and muscle soreness, warm-ups, safety rules, record keeping, self-evaluation, and optimum physical condition.

If you are a beginner in weight training, consider reading this chapter more than once. To work out safely and productively, you need to master every topic covered here. Beginners usually are a little confused by all of the topics they need to understand. You may find that two or three readings of this chapter will help dispel any lingering confusion about basic training with free weights and other types of resistance equipment.

Possible Goals

· ·

Women who weight train do so for at least one of the following seven reasons:

1. To gain general muscle-mass weight, particularly in parts of the body that are considered to be too skinny
2. To firm up and reduce the size of selected body parts that are too big for total body harmony
3. To strengthen and rehabilitate an injured area
4. To increase strength to handle everyday tasks
5. To improve sports performance

6. To enter competitive weightlifting or power-lifting meets

7. To become a competitive bodybuilder

As is clearly apparent from the foregoing list, weight training can have a variety of effects on a woman's body. When you cross-train by combining weight workouts with stretching and aerobics sessions, you can achieve even greater changes in your body. For a maximum effect on your body, you can incorporate into your cross-training some of the nutritional strategies outlined in this chapter and in Chapter 11.

Because weight training can be used for so many purposes, it has become one of the most popular fitness activities among men and women. Surveys have shown that 35 million Americans train regularly with free weights or resistance machines. Bodybuilding ranks as the 34th most popular sport among television viewers, ahead of gymnastics and many other sports that you might consider to be even more popular.

In Germany, where I make my home, the percentage of individuals who weight train is probably comparable to that in the United States, although no studies have been made of how many men and women here use resistance training. What you really need to understand is that weight training has become a very popular fitness activity in industrially developed societies—even in some underdeveloped countries—and it is increasing in popularity every year.

Weight-Training Jargon
. . . .

A full glossary of weight-training terms can be found at the end of this book, but several basic terms should be introduced before you read further. If you master and use these terms, you'll immediately sound like a veteran weight trainee. Of course, it will take several months before you

look as if you pump iron, but you'll immediately understand the activity's basic terminology.

Weight training is working out with free weights or with machines that place resistance on selected skeletal muscles over their full range of motion. Weight training is sometimes called *progressive resistance training.*

If you combine weight training with specific nutritional practices to change the appearance of your body, you are a *bodybuilder.* You are a bodybuilder even if you don't compete as one. Actually, competitive bodybuilding is such a difficult sport to master that only a small percentage of women bodybuilders go on to compete as amateurs let alone as professionals, and an even smaller percentage of women go on to excel at the sport.

Women compete in two types of weightlifting—each of which has a variety of weight classes—to determine who is the strongest athlete in a competition. The first of these is called *Olympic lifting,* so named because men compete in this style in the Olympic Games every four years. It consists of two lifts: the snatch and the clean and jerk; both require a high degree of strength, speed, and skill in hoisting the weight. Although women don't compete in the Olympics, they do compete nationally and internationally in Olympic-style weightlifting.

The second type of competitive weightlifting is called *powerlifting.* It consists of three lifts: the squat, the bench press, and the deadlift, each of which requires a moderate degree of skill and a huge amount of strength. Women compete in powerlifting nationally and internationally. Women's powerlifting has been an international sport much longer than Olympic lifting.

Doing a *workout* means that you are doing a session of weight training. A workout can also be called a *routine, program,* or *training schedule.* These four terms also refer to the written list of what you actually hope to do in your training session.

Each individual movement performed in your routine is called an *exercise*. Every individual count done of each exercise is called a *repetition*, or *rep* for short. A distinct group of reps is called a *set*. Each set is followed by a predetermined *rest interval* lasting 30–120 seconds, depending, in general, on the size of the body part being worked. Each rest interval is followed by another set of either the exercise done in the previous set or a different movement.

These are the most fundamental expressions used in weight training. Once you have mastered this basic jargon and fully understand these terms, go on to the next section in which you will learn some terms that refer to the various types of equipment you will use in a workout.

Equipment Orientation
· ·

The most basic piece of weight-training equipment is a *barbell*. An illustration of a barbell with all of its parts labeled can be found in Figure 2-1 below.

The *bar* of a barbell is made of either steel or another resistant metal. When counting up the weight on an *adjustable barbell set*, you must count the weight of the bar and its *collars*. Most exercise bars are five feet long, but some are four or six feet in length. With collars in place, a barbell weighs approximately five pounds per foot of length.

The middle part of a barbell bar is usually covered with a *revolving sleeve*, which is a metal tube that rotates in a weight trainee's hands when the barbell is lifted. Crosshatched grooves in the sleeve (or in the bar itself, if it is not encased in a sleeve) are called *knurlings*. The knurlings help you to grasp the bar firmly even when your hands are damp from perspiration.

Cylindrical *collars* are slipped over the bar, and their *locking screws* and/or *set screws* are tightened so the collars are locked onto the bar. *Inside collars* have set screws that lock the collars in place to keep the *plates* from sliding inward toward your hands. *Outside collars* have a locking screw that clamps the collar outside the plates to keep them from falling off the end of the bar.

Several fitness companies market spring-set collars, which look somewhat like clothespins and lock onto the bar by expansion and then contraction of the spring clip. This type of collar is rather new; if you run across it, keep in mind

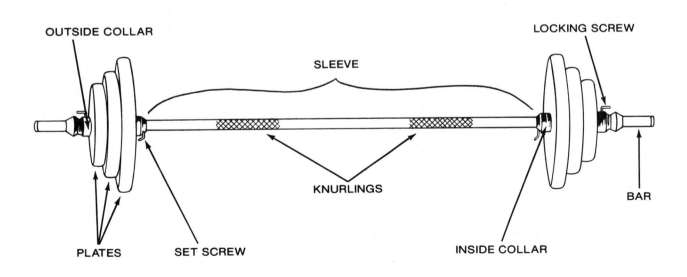

OUTSIDE COLLAR   LOCKING SCREW
SLEEVE
KNURLINGS
PLATES   SET SCREW   INSIDE COLLAR   BAR

that it is dependable only for light weights and only as an outside collar.

Plates are flat discs usually made of cast iron or cold-rolled steel. Some plates are made from concrete and are encased in vinyl to keep the concrete from crumbling. Vinyl-covered plates are widely advertised as being easier on wooden and linoleum floors, but they are comparatively thicker than metal plates, and you can't load as heavy a weight using them.

Most home gyms have an adjustable barbell set on which you can add or subtract plates to change poundage. In organized commercial gyms, you will find *fixed barbells* graduated in weights from about 15 pounds (7 kilograms) to more than 100 pounds (45 kilograms). Fixed weights are arranged on storage racks; be sure to return the bar to the appropriate rack at the end of your set.

If you are doing heavy lifts such as squats, bench presses, or bent-over rows, you'll want to use an *Olympic barbell*—the type of barbell used in weightlifting competitions. An Olympic barbell weighs 45 pounds (or 20 kilograms), and each collar weighs 5 pounds (or 2½ kilograms).

Dumbbells are short-handled barbells that range in length between 10 inches (30 centimeters) and about 16 inches (50 centimeters). Dumbbells are held one in each hand for most upper-body exercises. You can count a dumbbell bar and its collars as 5 pounds (2½ kilograms). Dumbbells are fixed weights in large commercial gyms, where you will find pairs of them ranging from 5–10 pounds (2½–5 kilograms) up to more than 100 pounds (45 kilograms) each. Dumbbells should also be stored in appropriate racks between sets.

Commercial gyms have a wide variety of *exercise benches*, set at diverse angles, which are used primarily for exercising upper-body muscles. *Flat benches* have the padded part of the bench set parallel to the gym floor, while *incline* and *decline benches* are set at an angle. On in-

cline benches a bodybuilder's head is at the upper end, and on decline benches the head is at the lower end. Home gyms usually have a bench that can be used flat or adjusted to form either incline or decline angles.

Some flat benches used for bench presses have a *rack* attached to the head end. The barbell rests in cups at the upper end of the rack supports. You lie back on the bench, set your grip, and simply straighten your arms to remove the barbell from the rack. It's best to have a training partner standing at the head end of the pressing bench to help you rack the weight after you have completed your set. Incline and decline benches also usually have support racks.

Squat racks are used in placing a heavy weight across your shoulders and behind your neck for a set of squats. To use such a rack you need only to step under the barbell, balance it across your shoulders behind your neck, and straighten your legs to remove the bar from the rack. Step back one pace and do your set of squats. Obviously, you have to rerack the barbell at the end of your set, which might require the help of a training partner or two if the weight is particularly heavy.

A variety of *pulleys* can be found in large commercial gyms. Pulleys are used to work mainly the upper-body muscles, although many leg exercises also can be done with pulleys.

Chinning bars are used to work the upper-back muscles as well as the abdominals. In contrast, *dipping bars* are used to develop the pectorals, anterior deltoids, triceps, and sometimes the abdominal muscles.

Leg extension machines are used to develop the frontal thigh muscles, while *leg-curl machines* are used to stress the rear thigh muscles.

A wide variety of *exercise machines* is available in commercial gyms. Most can be used to work only one muscle group at a time, so a large range of machines can usually be found in big gyms. There are scores of companies that currently manufacture resistance exercise machines.

Physical Exams

All women who plan to begin pumping iron should first schedule a complete physical examination with a physician. If you are over 40 or have been sedentary for more than 2–3 years, a stress test electrocardiogram (ECG) should be included in the exam to be certain that your heart and circulatory system are in good condition.

If you have certain types of physical problems, your physician will advise you to avoid specific exercises or higher intensity levels in your weight workouts. You should always follow a physician's advice concerning exercise, particularly if you are training with weights. Weight training is extremely intense exercise that puts dramatic stresses on your body.

Age Factors

Women of any age can work out with weights. Only light weights, however, should be used by prepubertal girls and women over 50 years of age. I have seen both children under 10 years of age and women in their 70s happily pumping iron in the Stuttgart gym where I do my own workouts.

If you are over 40 but under 50 and have been sedentary for 1–2 years or more, you should train with lower intensity until you have conditioned your body sufficiently to stand up under the very high intensity of all-out weight training. The same rule applies if you are under 15 years of age.

Heredity Factors

Particularly if you intend to become a competitive bodybuilder, you should be aware that heredity has a bearing on what degree of physical development you can ultimately achieve. Almost everyone has at least one muscle group that responds easily to resistance exercises and another that seemingly will not respond at all, despite the great amount of training intensity you might place on it.

Both excesses and deficiencies of heredity *can* be overcome if you take an intelligent approach to training. To give you a personal example—my lower body and deltoids have been very easy to develop; my chest, back, and arms have been more difficult to build up. The approach I took to balance my own development was easing up on the faster-developing muscle complexes in order to save my training energy to expend in highly intensive workouts for the more stubborn body parts.

This technique is called *muscle priority training*, and it is used by serious bodybuilders all over the globe. It will be discussed in depth in Chapter 5.

Even women with more modest physical goals than physique competition can use muscle priority training quite successfully. You should not be surprised, however, to discover that you will have to rotate your high-intensity sessions, going from one body part to another in a cyclical sequence. Most women discover that once they have improved a lagging muscle group to the degree they desire, some other body part then looks weak.

Existing Injuries

Life is full of bumps and bruises, and many adults contend with long-term joint problems from sports injuries and/or other mishaps in their youth. Sensible weight training is actually good for many joint injuries. You may find that your joint problems become a thing of the past once you are working out regularly with weights.

If you have a serious existing injury, you might well find exercises that allow you to work around that injury. With informed choices of resistance movements, you may work various parts of your body and not place undue stress on an injured area. One of the biggest advantages of training with weights is that the exercises are specific. Regardless of where you wish to direct exercise stress—and which parts of your body you want to avoid stressing—you will undoubtedly be able to select exercises that allow you to reach your workout goals.

Resistance Progression

Weight training works wonders on a woman's body because it is solidly based on a concept called *resistance progression*. When you place a greater-than-normal stress on a skeletal muscle, that muscle responds by increasing in *hypertrophy*. This means that the muscle becomes better toned, grows stronger, and increases in mass in order to handle larger overloads of resistance in the future.

A muscle increases in hypertrophy only enough to accommodate the overload. It will not increase in hypertrophy again unless you progressively increase the degree of overload placed on it. Therefore, you must gradually and steadily step up the resistance you place on a skeletal muscle to increase its hypertrophy.

If you look at the end of Chapter 4, you will see suggested training programs listed as "Routines." Look at the column marked "Reps" (which is short for "repetitions"). You will see a range of suggested reps, e.g., 8–12. The numerals 8 and 12 are called *lower* and *upper guide numbers*. In simple resistance progression, you start off by doing the lower guide number in repetitions, and then you add 1–2 new reps at each successive gym session until you are at the upper guide number. Then you add 5–10 pounds of resistance to the bar, drop back to the lower guide number, and begin to build up again.

An example of simple resistance progression can be seen in Figure 2-2.

Figure 2-2. Simple Resistance Progression

	Mon.	Wed.	Fri.
Week 1	60 × 8	60 × 9	60 × 10
Week 2	60 × 11	60 × 12	65 × 8
Week 3	65 × 9	65 × 10	65 × 11
Week 4	65 × 12	70 × 8	70 × 9

Note: In this example, "60 × 8" means that eight repetitions are to be performed with 60 pounds.

Figure 2-3. Complex Resistance Progression

	Mon.	Wed.	Fri.
Week 1	100 × 8	100 × 10	100 × 10
	100 × 8	100 × 9	100 × 9
	100 × 8	100 × 8	100 × 9
Week 2	100 × 11	100 × 12	100 × 12
	100 × 10	100 × 12	100 × 12
	100 × 9	100 × 10	100 × 11
Week 3	100 × 12	110 × 9	110 × 10
	100 × 12	110 × 8	110 × 9
	100 × 12	110 × 8	110 × 8
Week 4	110 × 11	110 × 12	110 × 12
	110 × 10	110 × 11	110 × 12
	110 × 10	110 × 10	110 × 11

Most weight-training routines involve doing multiple sets of each movement. In that case, you must reach the upper guide number for reps on each set before adding weight and dropping back to the lower guide number again.

Assuming you are doing 3 sets of 8–12 reps on a movement, you could follow the example of complex resistance progression seen in Figure 2-3 above.

Progression is a lot like building a brick house. You gradually lay down brick after brick until you finally have constructed a home. In the same manner, you gradually work upward in reps, and then add weight and begin to work upward time after time. Eventually you will have developed a terrific-looking body using this step-by-step process.

Exercise Form

Correct exercise form is essential for beginning and intermediate weight trainees because it prevents injuries and transfers all of the beneficial stress to the muscle group that is targeted with a particular exercise. A loose, cheating form can be used profitably by advanced bodybuilders because they know how to cheat to make a set harder to do. Beginners and intermediates tend to cheat only to make a set easier to complete.

Correct form involves using only the muscle group that is stressed by a particular movement. You must not kick with your legs, move your torso forward or backward, or swing the weight upward to the finish position, because any kind of excess body English robs the working muscles of some of the beneficial stress they should be receiving.

Good exercise form also involves moving the weight over its full range of motion on every rep, from complete extension of the muscle being targeted to complete contraction of that muscle and then back again to complete extension. Short, choppy movements definitely allow you to lift more weight, but they can cause injuries; and they fail to stress a muscle group as intensely as is possible when strict body mechanics are used.

Rest Intervals

During an aerobics session, runners run continuously, but it is practically impossible to weight train continuously. Distinct rest intervals are required between sets so you can catch your breath and allow your muscles to partially recover from the last set before attacking the next one. You don't need to rest longer than 1½–2

minutes between sets, however, even when you are working on larger muscle groups like legs, back, or chest, which take plenty of oxygen and energy to fuel contractions.

A normal rest interval for most body parts is 1–1½ minutes, although some of the smaller muscle groups such as biceps and triceps can be trained faster, with rests of only 30–60 seconds between sets. The object of taking these little pauses is to allow you to lift relatively heavy poundages in your workouts while avoiding a cooling down of your body between sets. Long rest intervals would allow your body to cool down excessively, making it more susceptible to injury.

We have already discussed the two main ways in which you can add progressive resistance to an exercise—increase the reps and increase the weight on the bar. There is a third way of increasing training intensity placed on a working muscle, and that is to keep the weight and reps consistent while gradually reducing the length of rest intervals between sets.

Many competitive bodybuilders increase intensity by shortening rest intervals, and they do it that way to help etch in deeper cuts between the muscles prior to a competition. This technique is called *quality training*. By combining quality training with a calorie-deficient diet and a regular aerobic program, it is possible to walk onstage at a bodybuilding competition with a physique that appears to be almost devoid of stored body fat.

Breathing Patterns

One question I am always asked when coaching novices in weight training is, "How am I supposed to breathe during a set?" This is a valid question, and it needs to be addressed before you pick up bad exercise habits, which always are difficult to change.

To understand when to breathe during each repetition, you need to understand that the upward cycle of each rep is called a *positive movement*, while the downward cycle is called a *negative movement*. You should inhale as you do the negative part of each repetition and exhale while accomplishing the positive cycle of the movement.

The foregoing rule is used for training with moderate weights. With truly heavy poundages, you will probably discover that you take in several panting breaths in the top part of the movement and then hold your breath as you lower and then raise the weight. This can be dangerous, however, because holding your breath can cut off the flow of blood to your brain, causing you to pass out. With heavy weights, go ahead and breathe at the top of the movement, but exhale throughout the rest of it, usually by vocalizing something like "ahhhh" or "goooo." By following this procedure you will prevent any interruption of oxygen-rich blood flowing to and from your brain.

Workout Frequency

Each time you have trained a particular muscle group, you need to rest that body part for at least 48 hours before attacking it again. During this resting time, your muscles will recover fully and then increase in hypertrophy. For this reason, beginning weight trainees are instructed to train their entire bodies on three nonconsecutive days each week, a scheme that allows for full recovery between workout days.

The more advanced you become, the longer you will rest between training days. Most serious bodybuilders nowadays follow a split routine in which they divide their bodies up into either two or three groups of equal mass and then train either four days each week (twice for each half of the body) or three consecutive days followed by a day of rest and a repeat of the three-day cycle. Indeed, the three-on/one-off split routine is very popular among competitive bodybuilders, and it is the type of split I personally follow.

A few bodybuilders—particularly those who are over 40 years old—follow a six-day split routine in which they work each muscle group once a week. This type of split routine gives a bodybuilder plenty of recovery time between workouts, which induces accelerated increases in hypertrophy.

The Recovery Cycle

It is axiomatic in weight training and bodybuilding that a muscle does not increase in hypertrophy until *after* it has thoroughly recovered from its preceding workout. Therefore, it's important for you to understand those factors that enhance recovery ability.

Sleep and rest periods are the times when your body recovers most quickly. During the time you are asleep, your body is recovering and secreting natural human growth hormone, and your muscles are gaining in hypertrophy.

Length of sleep periods is an individual matter. If you are training hard enough and your diet is under control, it will be easy to fall asleep each night. An average woman needs 8 hours of sound sleep in order to recover between workouts, but I have known several top women competitors who have consistently slept for only 5–6 hours each night. At the other end of the spectrum, many bodybuilders need 10–12 hours of sound sleep each night in order to wake up feeling fully rested and ready to take on the world.

You should experiment with sleep periods of varying length in an effort to discover how much sleep you need in order to be fully rested and recovered from the previous workout. You might even consider taking a short nap in the late afternoon when most people seem to have low

Before I was 22, I had captured the German, European, and Junior Amateur World Bodybuilding Championships, as well as second place in both the IFBB Pro World and Ms. Olympia competitions.

energy levels. Thirty minutes of sleep during the late afternoon will work wonders for you if you are fatigued.

Once you have determined how much sleep you need each night, be absolutely sure that you sleep for that long. I know that going to a party is tempting, but it can be counterproductive and will not allow you to get the most out of your weight-training sessions.

Resting during the day is also a valuable way to increase the rate of speed at which your body recovers from a workout. Try scheduling a couple of 15-minute breaks during the day when you

either lie on your back resting or sit comfortably at your desk in a resting posture.

The rate at which you recover between workouts is influenced by both your diet and the volume of your training sessions. In Chapter 11 you will learn how and what you should be eating consistently day in and day out in order to help your body recover between workouts. Until you get to that chapter, you will profit from following a few commonsense rules for bodybuilding nutrition that you will find in this chapter.

Overtraining can also cause you to recover more slowly than under normal circumstances. The topic of overtraining is discussed in detail in Chapter 5.

If you are interested in making the fastest possible recovery between workouts, you will have to regiment your life. You should actually write out a schedule for each day and then stick to it, particularly in terms of how much rest and sleep you get. That way you will be on top of the world in nothing flat.

When to Train

Weight trainees and bodybuilders can be found in large gyms or in their own home gyms pumping iron at all hours of the day or night. I personally like to train at about 1:30 in the afternoon, when the gym is the emptiest and I don't have to wait on someone who is drifting through a workout and happens to be camped on a piece of equipment that I need. Almost invariably, I have instant access to any type of equipment I require.

While it doesn't matter when you train, you should be careful to work out at the same time every training day. If you can stick to a set time each day, your body and mind will soon begin to reach peak energy levels at that particular time. In the long run, this will lead to harder and more productive workouts.

Where to Train

Every moderately big town these days seems to have a commercial weight-oriented gym. Some bigger cities have as many as a dozen great gyms. If you happen to be in a city with several gyms close to where you live, take a trial workout at each one and then decide which has the best equipment and best general atmosphere. If possible, you should pick a gym that has outstanding bodybuilders and other athletes training in it. That way you can occasionally get advice from people in the gym who have more experience than you have.

YMCAs, YWCAs, recreation centers, and schools often have superior weight-training equipment. It doesn't cost as much to train at one of these places as it does to train or work out at a commercial gym.

Many women prefer to train in their own home gyms. By doing so they avoid the potential embarrassment they might experience in a big gym if they aren't in good shape and have to try to figure out how to dress for a workout in order to best hide their physical condition. They can also train at any time of the day or night at home, unlike at gyms, which have set hours and are often closed for holidays.

A modest cash outlay will get you an adjustable barbell/dumbbell set and a multipurpose bench. For a couple of hundred dollars you are in business, and you don't need to worry about gym dues that have to be paid on a yearly basis. Once you have sufficient equipment to work out on in your basement, garage, or exercise room, it won't cost you any additional money.

If you plan to set up a home gym, ask around to find out who else in your neighborhood trains with weights in their own home gyms. If you meet the right person, you can pool your equipment and end up with a better home gym. You will also have someone to train with, so you can do some heavier work without worrying about getting stuck under the bar.

What to Wear

What you wear to work out should reflect both function and your innate sense of style. Your workout clothing must be nonbinding, allowing you to move your limbs freely over their complete range of motion in all directions. Your clothes must also keep you warm when the weather is cold, and cool when the weather is warmer than usual.

From a fashion standpoint, there are scores of workout-wear manufacturers with a broad range of both designs and colors from which you can choose personal gym garb. These manufacturers advertise in a variety of muscle magazines, but most prominently in *Muscle & Fitness* and *Flex*, both published by Weider. If you happen to live in Europe, you might look for some of my own clothing designs on sale in gym boutiques across the continent.

Wearing several thin layers of clothing instead of a thick layer or two will keep you much warmer when the ambient temperature is lower than what you are used to. Thin layers are also preferable because they allow you to easily adjust the amount of clothing you have on—you can remove one layer and then another as you get thoroughly warm during a hard training session.

I personally prefer, at a minimum, a pair of tights to cover my legs and a leotard for my upper body. Over these articles of clothing, you can add—depending on how much cold you will have to endure when doing your workout—leg warmers, a tight T-shirt, a looser T-shirt, and a full tracksuit. If it's extremely cold in the weight room where you intend to exercise, you will probably want to wear at least one pair of gloves, because bare skin can freeze almost instantly on very cold steel barbell or dumbbell bars.

Most bodybuilders these days wear either leather or neoprene "rubber" gloves to protect their hands from becoming rough and callused, as bare hands do if they come into contact with the weights during training. Almost all gyms sell workout gloves these days, and you can also find them widely advertised in weight-training and bodybuilding magazines.

On very hot days in the gym, it's actually better to wear one loose and/or absorbent layer of clothing than merely donning short shorts and a tank or tube top. Your body's natural cooler is your skin, which becomes sweaty and cools as the perspiration dries. By wearing absorbent clothing, you actually can conduct heat out of your body and into the surrounding air more efficiently. Surprisingly, wool or cotton works much better as a body-heat radiator than synthetic materials, and you can no doubt find a few sets of tights and leotards made from natural fibers for use on particularly steamy days.

One piece of equipment you should never go without in a gym is a good pair of training shoes, which are worn over thick, absorbent socks. You should never train in your bare feet or while you are wearing rickety sandals, because your arches can be harmfully compressed if you don't have a good arch support in your footwear. You might also bruise or injure your feet if you drop a barbell plate on them when they lack the protection of shoes and socks.

The best weight-workout shoes are cross-training shoes, which are widely available in athletic footwear shops. These have both a solid arch support and a good tread for gripping a calf block with your feet when you are working your lower legs. Even a good pair of running shoes will satisfy these two requirements, but the cross-training footwear has more sturdy uppers, which both support and protect the feet from dropped equipment. Running shoes are a little less expensive than cross-training shoes, and you get what you pay for in training footwear.

One last vital piece of weight-workout equipment is a leather or synthetic fabric lifting belt, which is worn tightly cinched around your waist when you do heavy leg work, overhead lifts, and heavy back movements. This type of belt will support your midsection, the weakest link in your body when you are doing the three categories of exercises just mentioned. A good training belt will also keep you from straining the walls of your stomach, which could eventually lead to a rupture of the abdominal wall and which would need to be surgically repaired.

When you are holding a heavy barbell across your shoulders for a set of squats, or you are holding it out straight at arm's length overhead when doing standing barbell presses, the muscles of your midsection (i.e., the *rectus abdominis*, *external/internal obliques*, and *erector spinae*) are not able to fully stabilize the middle of your body, which forms a bridge between your legs and torso. A lifting belt largely eliminates this problem of instability, because when the belt is tightly buckled around your waist, it adds considerable stability to this otherwise weak and shaky bridge.

Most women need a belt also to protect their lower abdomen, which can protrude and be injured. After a few weeks, you will probably discover that your lifting belt has become a mental crutch and will wear it most of the time as you perform your workouts.

Originally, weightlifting belts were made from stiff, tough leather cut from cowhides. Many belts are still made from leather, but they are normally worn only in competitive weightlifting and powerlifting meets. International rules specify that a belt used in competition can be a maximum of 4 inches (10 centimeters) across the widest part of the belt.

There is no width restriction on training belts,

which are commonly 6–8 inches (15–20 centimeters) in width at the back of the belt. The newest and nicest belts are made from a tough synthetic-fiber fabric, which has Velcro fasteners. There are now wide varieties of colors and designs in fabric belts. There are even designer belts available, and you can have your name embroidered across the back at little extra cost if you like.

I have personally used both leather and fabric belts over the years and prefer fabric belts for every type of exercise except perhaps for squats. I've seen many women squat with quite heavy weights using fabric belts, but I'd personally feel too insecure through my lower back and abdomen if I wasn't wearing my old, trusty, well-worn leather belt. Perhaps if I'd started out using fabric belts—which are a recent innovation—I would have no reservations about using them for any exercise.

While they are sturdier, leather belts are difficult to break in properly. They are so unyielding that when you first wear one you might find that it painfully pinches your sides or lower abdomen. If you first soften the belt by soaking it in water, however, you will find that it quickly conforms to the contours around your waist. If you're looking for a colored belt to match the new blue leotard you just bought at the gym pro shop, you won't find it in leather; only fabric belts come in teal and other designer colors.

Some companies these days are making leather belts with snakeskin or some other type of reptile skin bonded to the basic leather. A few of the snakeskin belts come dyed in basic colors and can be quite striking. Still, I'd rather stick with a pair of fabric belts that cost less than one reptile-skin belt.

Appropriate Starting Weights

Which starting weights will be appropriate for you to use will vary over a moderate range of poundages, the correct weights depending on both your body weight and your recent physical-activity levels. The heavier you are, the more muscle you will have naturally, and the more you can lift. The more physically active you have been prior to taking up weight training, the stronger you will be at first.

I have coached so many young women starting out in weight training and bodybuilding workouts, however, that I can give you very appropriate "averages" or "norms" for starting weights in various exercises in the first suggested routine in Chapter 4. These weights are expressed as a percentage of your body weight (% Bwt.).

Simply multiply the percentage given with each new exercise by your body weight to arrive at the correct starting poundage in the break-in routine. If you come out at something between normal 5-pound (2½-kilogram) increments, round *down* to the nearest 5-pound increment rather than up.

Despite the fact that I have been able to discover norms for most women, there will still be some women who are above or below these standards. So if the weight feels too heavy for you (and you have to struggle to complete the assigned number of repetitions), you should drop the weight by 5 pounds during the next workout. If the suggested starting weight is too easy for you, then feel free to adjust it upward by 5 pounds for the next training session.

These suggested starting weights are applicable only in the first week or so of workouts, after which you will have to keep at least a mental record of what poundages you are using (a written diary would be much better). That way you can keep track of your weight increases in successive workouts.

Repetition Ranges

The appropriate rep ranges for each movement are suggested in all recommended training routines in this book. These are listed under the "reps" column as a range, e.g., 6–10, 8–12, 10–15, 15–20, 20–30, and so on.

In general, the lower reps are best for upper-body movements in which you press a weight upward (bench presses, standing barbell presses, and so on). The range of 8–12 repetitions is best for most other upper-body movements, while 10–15 reps works best for lower-body exercises, particularly those for the upper legs, both the quadriceps and biceps femoris. Reps in the range of 15–20 usually are done for calf and forearm movements, while repetitions higher than that are intended for the midsection muscle areas.

With a little time and observation, you will discover for yourself which rep ranges are best for your various body parts. These ranges may vary from one training cycle to another. In the off-season, when you are trying to build up mass in your upper-body groups, you might do reps in the range of 6–10, while prior to a competition, when you are trying to achieve maximum muscular detail, you might perform reps in the range of 10–15 for the same muscle groups on which you did 6–10 in the off-season building phase.

Basic Nutrition
. . . .

In Chapter 11, as I've mentioned, bodybuilding nutrition will be discussed in considerable detail. For now, you have so many details to master and call up mentally during a workout that I want to provide you only with basic rules of a good bodybuilding diet.

Most champion bodybuilders—myself included—believe that nutrition and training are a 50-50 proposition during the off-season when the bodybuilders are working toward greater general muscle mass and particularly toward bringing up a lagging muscle group until it is on a par with the rest of their physique. Prior to a competition, nutrition can rise in importance

until it is 75–80% of the process. Over the final week, before you step onstage for a contest prejudging, nutrition is almost the entire ball of wax.

It's easiest to start my discussion of basic bodybuilding nutrition by giving you a list of "dos" and "don'ts" to follow.

DO
• Eat a small amount of protein at each meal. The best sources of protein are animal, specifically: poultry, fish, eggs, nonfat milk products. Good secondary sources of bodybuilding protein are beef, pork, full-fat milk products. Good tertiary sources include rice, corn, lentils, seeds (particularly sprouted seeds), and nuts. You should consume only small amounts of protein at each meal, because your body can digest and use only 20–25 grams of protein at a time. Eating huge protein meals wastes the amounts above these figures, and in some cases the excess can actually slow down the protein digestion process and cause you to digest less than 20 grams per meal.
• Eat a wide variety of fresh fruits, vegetables, and salads. Whenever possible, eat your vegetables raw rather than cooked. When you do eat them cooked, steam rather than boil them because in steaming more nutrients are retained.
• Consume a little vegetable fat each day from grains, seeds, and nuts. Contrary to what even many experienced bodybuilders believe, you need some fat in your diet to keep your body—particularly your skin and nerves—in good health.
• Eat at least three meals each day but aim to consume up to six relatively small meals per day. Your body can digest and utilize smaller snacks more efficiently and easily than large feasts.
• Drink plenty of water (up to 10 glasses per day), particularly distilled water. Water is one of the best body-cleansing agents that nature has provided.

• Include in your diet at least one multiple vitamin-mineral tablet per day. It would be even better to take one or two multipacks of vitamins, minerals, and trace elements each day with your meals. Vitamins and minerals are best utilized by your body when consumed with foods.

• In general, eat as great a variety of foods as possible. Each food has a unique array of vitamins, minerals, proteins, and enzymes, with more of each or less of each than other foods contain. So, understandably, you have the best chance of eating a balanced diet when you consume the widest possible variety of fresh foods. European and North American diets have been studied in detail, and in most of them the same 8–10 daily foods are repeated ad nauseum.

DON'T

• Don't consume junk foods, which I define as foods that are made with sugar or white flour, are highly processed, or are fried.

• Don't consume excessive amounts of animal fats. Eat more low-fat meats (fish and skinless poultry), and be sure to trim all visible fat from beef and pork prior to cooking. Consume fewer dairy products, including full-fat milk.

• Don't use extra salt on your foods. Avoid foods that are highly seasoned. Avoid diet sodas, which have a high sodium content. (Sodium has a great affinity for water; it attracts more than 50 times its weight in water, which is then held within the body for no useful reason and which can increase blood pressure.)

• Don't consume excessive amounts of alcohol; avoid soft drinks that contain sugar.

WEIGHT-GAIN DIET

A surprising number of young women want to increase their body weights. Champion bodybuilders have the best line on this process—heavy training and a high-protein diet. Merely eating larger amounts of protein, however, is not the answer nutritionally. The key is to eat in such a way that your body can efficiently digest and make ready for assimilation into muscle tissue a greater amount of protein each day.

As I have already mentioned in this chapter, your body can digest only 20–25 grams of protein at each meal, under normal circumstances. Men have larger stomachs, and they can digest a few more grams of protein, perhaps 25–30 grams at each meal.

Eating a large meal with 100–150 grams of protein content can actually *reduce* the amount of protein digested at that feeding, because large meals make your digestive system less efficient by clogging it up with food. You will actually digest more protein in a meal containing 20 grams of that food element than you would in one containing 120 grams, and this fact is central to the plan I will outline for digesting a maximum amount of protein each day.

If your stomach can digest only 20–25 grams of protein at each feeding, you will digest 60–75 total grams a day if you eat a normal three meals per day. But if you eat six times—with 2–3 hours between meals—you will *double* the amount of protein your stomach digests each day.

In the weight-gaining diet followed by most experienced bodybuilders, you should eat 5–6 times a day, consuming smaller meals than if you ate only three a day. You more or less snack all day, making sure that your snacks are made up of nutritious foods, not junk foods. Many bodybuilders eat solid food at their three normal mealtimes and consume protein drinks (see the section of this chapter on food supplements for a recipe for a protein drink) between meals, an excellent plan as long as they keep their solid-food meals relatively small.

Following is a sample menu for one day of eating six meals per day in order to gain muscular body weight (assuming a 10:00 P.M. bedtime). Supplements are explained in detail later in the chapter.

Meal 1 (8:00 A.M.)—cheese omelet, glass of milk, supplements

Meal 2 (11:00 A.M.)—protein drink

Meal 3 (2:00 P.M.)—broiled chicken breast, rice, milk, supplements

Meal 4 (5:00 P.M.)—protein drink

Meal 5 (8:00 P.M.)—broiled fish, baked potato, green vegetables, milk, supplements

Meal 6 (10:00 P.M.)—protein drink or boiled eggs whites

Milk is popular as food used for gaining weight, and raw (unpasteurized) milk is more usable in the human digestive system. Many individuals cannot digest milk, however, because their stomachs produce too little of the digestive enzyme that breaks down the sugar in milk. This problem is more common in men than in women, more often observed among African-Americans and Orientals than among Caucasians, and occurs more frequently among older individuals.

If you have this problem, which is called *lactose intolerance*, your stomach will feel bloated with gas soon after you have drunk milk. You might also feel drowsy and lethargic. You can still eat hard cheeses, however, because the lactose (milk sugar) is removed from milk when cheese is produced.

Many bodybuilders use digestive enzyme tablets as a means of digesting more protein at each meal. There are many different types of digestive enzymes available at health food stores. These digestive preparations do help you to digest a little more protein, so they are worth trying if your budget can stand the strain. The most commonly available digestive enzymes are papain and bromelain.

You might find that increased consumption of B-complex vitamins aids you in gaining muscular body weight, because the various B vitamins increase tissue synthesis and improve your appetite. You won't need to worry about taking too much B complex, however, because these are water-soluble vitamins and excesses are eliminated in the urine. It is *conceivable* that you could take in toxic levels of some B vitamins, but practically speaking it is impossible to do.

WEIGHT-LOSS DIET

When most people think about dieting, they immediately turn their thoughts to losing weight. But, as we have already seen, the general topic of diet is a much more complex issue in bodybuilding.

Through proper diet and weight training (plus 30 minutes of aerobic exercise per day, if possible), you can very easily lose body fat and normalize your weight. It is simply a matter of creating a caloric deficit, or of using up a few more calories each day than you consume in your diet. (Do *not*, however, try to measure fat losses on a scale if you are concurrently adding muscle mass to your frame at a fast clip.)

For each accumulated deficit of 3,500 calories, you will lose one pound of stored body fat. So, to lose a pound of fat per week, you need only create a deficit of 500 calories each day; for a two-pound weekly loss, you must create a caloric deficit of 1,000 calories per day, which is relatively easy to do when you are working out regularly, particularly with aerobics included in your training plan.

The weight workout you do each day will allow you to expend 250–300 calories each hour, over and above what your body burns up in normal metabolic processes. Another half hour of aerobics will allow you to expend 150–200 calories, so an hour of bodybuilding and 30 minutes of stationary cycling or mountain biking can give you up to 500 calories to add to your caloric deficit, which in itself would cause you to lose a pound of body fat every week.

In reality, both weight workouts and aerobics tend to stimulate your basal metabolic rate

(BMR), driving it up to a higher-than-normal level for 30–60 minutes *after* you have completed either type of training session. Therefore, the actual caloric-deficit count in a training situation is somewhat higher than the actual number of calories required to complete a set amount of physical activity.

As easy as it is to create a caloric deficit through weight aerobics training, it is much easier to create a large caloric deficit by dieting once you are up to an hour of weight work each day. The easiest way to trim calories out of your diet—above and beyond the obvious step of curtailing your junk-food intake—is to reduce your consumption of fats.

One gram of fat equals nine calories when metabolized in your body for energy, while a gram of either protein or carbohydrate yields only four calories. So, if fats are more than twice as concentrated a source of calories as protein or carbs, it seems logical that reducing fat intake and replacing the fats with protein and carbohydrate foods will reduce total caloric consumption. Indeed, this *does* work, and it is the body-fat-reduction method used by a majority of champion bodybuilders.

The most obvious sources of fats in most diets are beef, pork, full-fat milk products, egg yolks, corn, grain, seeds, and nuts. So, substituting fish or chicken (without its fatty skin) for red meats in your diet will markedly cut your caloric intake. Fish, incidentally, is lower in calories than poultry, and poultry white meat is somewhat lower than dark meat.

Following is a sample daily menu for pain-free weight loss through low-fat dieting:

Breakfast —high-bran whole-grain cereal with nonfat milk, fruit, coffee or tea (use non-nutritive sweetener), supplements
Lunch —broiled fish, rice, salad (with vinegar and/or lemon juice as a dressing), iced tea

Dinner —broiled poultry, baked potato (no butter or sour cream), salad, coffee, supplements
Snacks —raw vegetables, fruit, cold chicken or turkey

Be very careful when dieting to strictly limit the number of calories you drink each day. You can drink 1,000 calories' worth of orange juice in 2–3 minutes, but it would take a half hour or more to eat 1,000 calories' worth of oranges. Why not enjoy the fruit, especially when you would naturally consume less than 1,000 calories if you ate whole fruit rather than drinking the extracted juice?

You will feel a little low in energy when on a diet. You actually must feel this way in order to lose body fat. But if you really feel wasted, eat a piece or two of fresh fruit. Forcing yourself to eat so little food that you go into a large energy debt is an open invitation to binge eating. In the long run you will be far better off if you lose body fat slowly and naturally.

FOOD SUPPLEMENTS

Champion bodybuilders are very fastidious in their use of food supplements—concentrated proteins, amino acids, vitamins, minerals, and enzymes. I have often seen a champion swallow 20–30 capsules and tablets at a meal, and it's not uncommon for one to spend $300–$400 per month on supplements.

As you grow more experienced you, too, will experiment with a wide spectrum of vitamins and minerals. For now, however, it is best to take one or two of the vitamin-mineral multipacks mentioned earlier in this chapter. If you wish to take extra vitamins and minerals, the best to experiment with initially are vitamin C, the B-complex vitamins, potassium, and calcium.

At this point the area in which you can best use food supplements is in adding protein to your diet with the protein drinks I have already

Getting serious in the gym

mentioned. There are many types and brands of protein powders available, and the best ones are made from milk and eggs. We know that fish, milk, and eggs contain the proteins of the highest biological quality for humans. So be certain to read the labels on all available brands of protein powder before buying one. If you go by what they advertise for their products, food supplement distributors have you right where they want you.

Be sure to use the protein—as well as supplemental vitamins, minerals, and enzymes—as a *supplement* to your diet, not as a *substitute* for food. Elite bodybuilders do use food supplements, but only in moderation. I have seen a few misguided novice bodybuilders, however, almost living off food supplements, a very expensive and totally unnecessary practice.

You will get much more nutritional value from your protein drinks if you take them between meals rather than with meals. Indeed, protein drinks are particularly valuable as a quick and convenient replacement for a meal that you might have ordinarily missed.

Here is a good protein-drink recipe that you can whip up in a bodybuilder's best friend, her blender:

10 ounces of nonfat raw milk
2 tablespoons of protein powder
fruit to taste

Soft fruits (such as bananas, peaches, strawberries, and blueberries) are best used in blender drinks for flavoring. One piece—or 4–5 berries—is usually plenty, but suit yourself as to how much you use, because fruit is always a good nutritional investment. You can also add shaved ice to make the drink colder and more like a milkshake, if that's what you like.

Break-in Procedures and Muscle Soreness

Muscles that are stressed more than normal during a workout will become sore a day or two following the training session. This is particularly true of first weight workouts, or weight sessions that come just after you have changed over to a new training program for a particular body part. To avoid excessive soreness, you should break in gradually to any new or unfamiliar routine. Avoiding this soreness as much as possible and eliminating it quickly will put you

on the road to super body-shaping gains much more quickly than if you just allowed marked muscle soreness to affect subsequent workouts.

In the beginning routine in Chapter 4, you will discover that multiple sets (usually 3) of each exercise are recommended. To perform the entire suggested training schedule the first time you walk into a gym, however, would make you so sore that you probably would entertain thoughts of staying in bed for the next few days. Breaking in slowly is the answer to this problem.

For a proper break-in to a beginning program, you should go through the routine doing only one set of each movement, regardless of how many are suggested. Then the second time you are in the gym, go through the program and do two sets on each movement for which two or more sets are noted. Finally, on the third time you go into the gym to work out, perform the entire suggested routine.

It's also a good idea to avoid adding weight in any of the exercises until you have reached the point at which your muscles are no longer sore. This might take up to two weeks for some individuals or only a week for others. The length of time you are sore is related to how hard you tend to push yourself when you break in to the new program.

If you are changing over to a new training schedule from one that you have been following for several weeks, it is best to follow a modified version of the above break-in procedure. I would suggest that in your first attack on the new program you do only two sets of each movement for which two or more sets are noted. For the second workout, you can probably move up to the full training schedule, but use about 10% less weight than you can actually expect to lift on each movement. Then on the third time through, you can do the entire written routine with your best poundages on every exercise.

It's inevitable that you will experience muscle soreness regardless of how carefully you break in to a new program. The best method of relieving deep muscle soreness is frequent hot baths or showers (I personally prefer long bubble baths). Some bodybuilding authorities suggest deep-tissue massage as a means of alleviating muscle soreness, but I have found that this causes more additional pain than the procedure is worth. Others recommend repeating the routine that made you sore only a day after you first did it, again a procedure that I believe causes more harm than good.

Overall, the best cure for muscle soreness is *prevention*. Break in slowly and gradually, and you will save yourself plenty of grief in the days following each workout..

Warm-Ups

Weight training is such strenuous exercise that it would be easy to injure yourself if you failed to warm up properly before a heavy session with the iron. Such a complete preworkout warm-up should consist of light aerobic activity, plenty of calisthenic exercises, stretching of each major muscle group, and then, prior to attacking the heavier weights, at least 1–2 light/high-rep sets on a basic exercise for a particular body part.

Research has shown that stretching a cold muscle can injure it, so you should ride a stationary bike, jump rope, jog around the gym, or occupy yourself with some type of aerobic training for about 10 minutes at the start of your warm-up. This should serve to get your juices flowing, including the start of a light sweat. If you would like to do 15 or even 20 minutes of aerobics prior to your weight workout, feel free to do so, because it can help rather than hurt you to keep doing the aerobic part of your warm-up for an extended period of time.

I do not recommend stretching until after you have done calisthenics. Try to include basic calisthenic movements (e.g., push-ups, sit-ups, side bends, jumping jacks) for all of your major muscle groups, and keep moving from one new type of calisthenic exercise to the next for a minimum of 5 full minutes.

Only then should you attempt to stretch each major muscle and joint in a flexibility session lasting 5–10 additional minutes. Ballistic stretching is harder on your body than slow, gentle, static stretches that are held for 30–60 seconds each. With a little time and observation of other trainees in the public gym where you work out, you can easily assemble a list of 6–10 basic stretches (see also Chapter 9).

After you have finished aerobics, calisthenics, and flexibility work, you should begin to attack the weights—but light ones before you begin to max out. Choose a basic movement with which to start each body-part routine, e.g., bench presses for chest, squats for legs, barbell bent-over rows for back. Do one 20-rep set at about 50% of your projected initial building weight (that weight with which you finally have to begin *working* to finish the suggested number of reps for each set). Then add weight until you are at about 75% of your building poundage, and do a 15-rep set with that implement. Only then are you warmed up sufficiently to attack your true building weights in perfect safety.

Once you are completely warmed up, it is essential to stay warmed up throughout your workout by going for a new set at least every 2–3 minutes. Most weight-training injuries occur when you stand around too long between sets—perhaps talking—and begin to cool off; then you use a too-heavy weight with poor biomechanics and something pops. It's a much better practice to save your conversations for outside the gym or until you have finished your main training session.

You can virtually eliminate injuries in a gym if you follow these 12 commonsense safety rules at all times:

1. Use spotters to stand by and rescue you if

you fail to complete a rep on a heavy exercise.

2. Never train alone.

3. Use catch racks on bench-press benches and squat stands.

4. Always use collars on barbells.

5. Do not hold your breath while lifting a weight.

6. Practice good gym housekeeping, picking up all loose weights and placing them in proper storage racks and areas.

7. Train under competent supervision.

8. Never work out in an overcrowded gym.

9. Warm up thoroughly before every weight workout.

10. Use proper biomechanical (body) positions when doing all exercises.

11. Use a weightlifting belt when doing heavy squats, back exercises, and overhead lifts.

12. Acquire as much knowledge about weight training and bodybuilding as possible through books, magazines, and the champions' seminars.

Record Keeping

It is essential to keep some type of notes on your progress from workout to workout, week to week, month to month, and year to year. Mental notes are chancy when compared with the written notes included in a training diary. With written notes, you can compare your strength and endurance levels weeks, months, and even years back. Usually progress cannot actually be *seen* week to week—often not even month to month—so training diaries are an essential means of demonstrating proof of your progress, which keeps your workout enthusiasm high.

Any bound or loose-leaf notebook can serve as a training diary. Enter the date of each workout first, and then include the entire list of exercises, sets, reps, and poundages done in each workout below that. Here is one of the best ways to record your workouts and the way I recommend that you use:

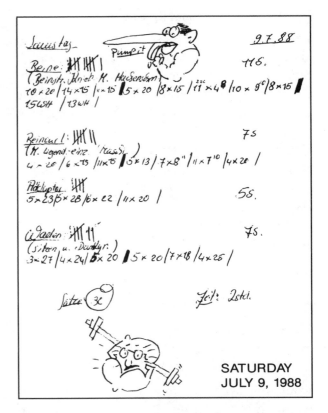

Figure 2-4 (above and opposite). Anja's Personal Training Diary for One Week (Saturday, July 9, 1988- Sunday, July 17, 1988)

1. Bench Presses: 80 × 15, 90 × 12, 100 × 10, 110 × 8

2. Dumbbell Incline Presses: 35s × 8 × 8 × 7

3. Pec-Deck Flyes: 50 × 15, 60 × 12, 70 × 9

4. Cross-Bench Dumbbell Pullovers: 35 × 15 × 15 × 15

In the bench press example, "80 × 15" means that you did 15 reps with 80 pounds for your first set. You also did 12 reps with 90, 10 with 100, and 8 with 110 pounds. On your dumbbell incline presses, you did two sets of 8 and one set of 7 reps with a pair of 35-pound dumbbells (35s). The rest of the example should be self-explanatory.

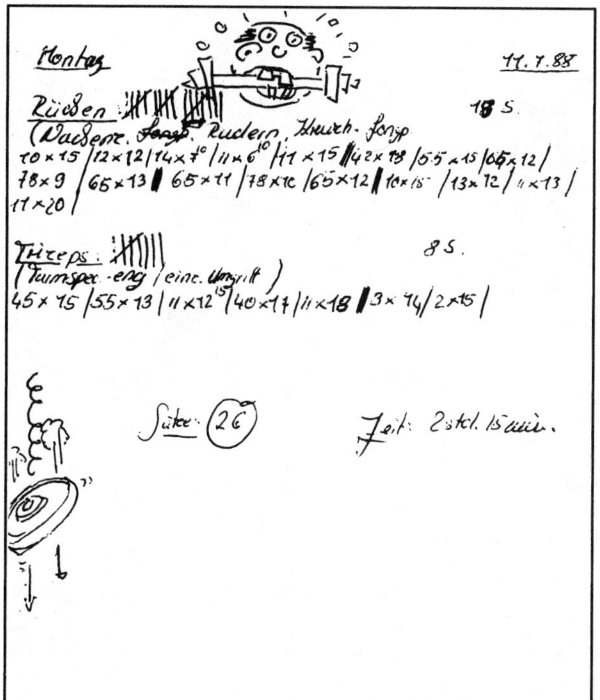

Montag   11.7.88

Rücken   18 S

(Ruders. ... Rudern, Zwisch.-Lange)
70×15 | 12×12 | 14×7 | 11×6¹⁰ | 11×15 | 12×13 | 55×15 | 65×12 |
18×9 | 65×13 | 65×11 | 18×10 | 65×12 | 10×15 | 13×12 | 4×13 |
11×20 |

Trizeps   8 S.

(Turmspez.-eng / eine. Umgrift)
45×15 | 55×13 | 11×12¹⁵ | 40×17 | 11×18 | 3×14 / 2×15 |

Sätze (26)   Zeit: 2 Std. 15 min.

**MONDAY
JULY 11, 1988**

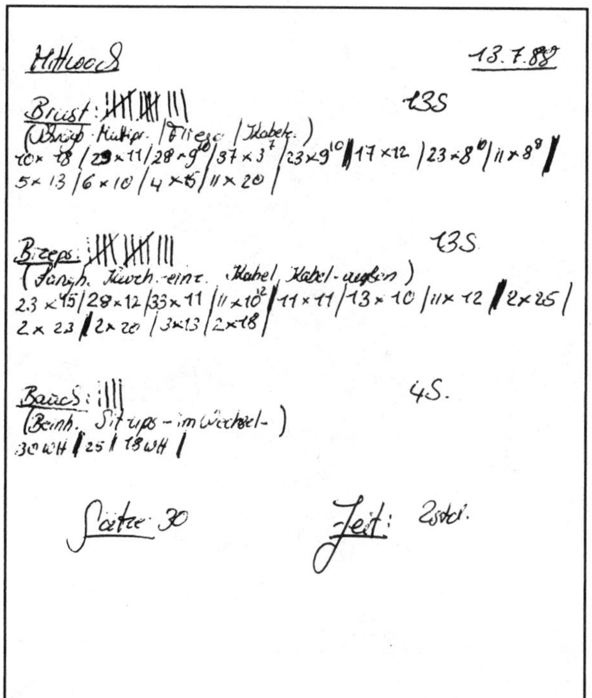

Mittwoch   13.7.88

Brust   23 S

(Brück. Multipr. / Fliege / Kabel)
70×18 | 29×11 | 28×9¹⁰ | 37×3⁷ | 23×9¹⁰ | 17×12 | 23×8⁰ | 11×8⁸ |
5×13 | 6×10 | 4×15 | 11×20 |

Bizeps   23 S

(Langh. Zwisch-eine. Kabel. Kabel-außen)
23×15 | 28×12 | 33×11 | 11×10² | 11×11 | 13×10 | 11×12 | 2×25 |
2×23 | 2×20 | 3×13 | 2×18 |

Bauch   4 S.

(Beinh. Sit ups - im Wechsel-)
30 WH | 25 | 18 WH |

Sätze 30   Zeit: 2 Std.

**WEDNESDAY
JULY 13, 1988**

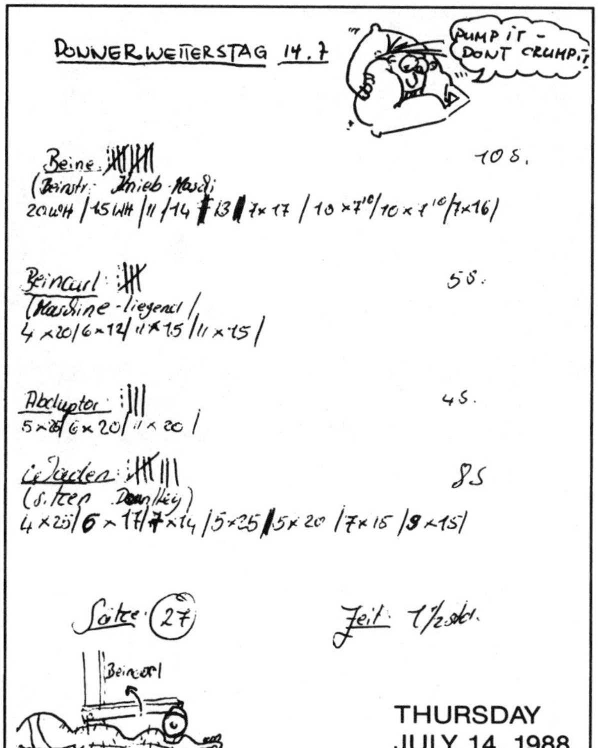

DONNERWETTERSTAG 14.7

Beine   10 S.

(Beinstr. Schieb Maschi)
20 WH | 45 WH | 11 / 14 | 13 | 7×17 | 10×7¹⁰ | 10×1¹⁰ | 7×16 |

Beincurl   5 S.

(Maschine - liegend /)
4×20 | 6×12 | 11×15 | 11×15 |

Abductor   4 S.
5×8 | 6×20 | 11×20 |

ie Jacken   8 S
(Sitzen Dampfeg)
4×20 | 6×17 | 7×14 | 5×25 | 5×20 | 7×15 | 8×15 |

Sätze (27)   Zeit: 1½ Std.

Beincurl

**THURSDAY
JULY 14, 1988**

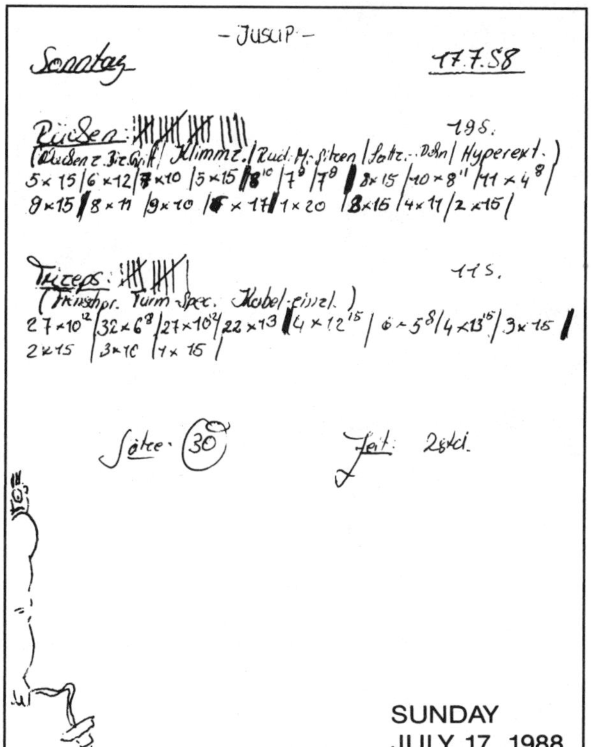

– Jusup –

Sonntag   17.7.88

Rücken   19 S.

(Ruders 2 Br.Griff / Klimmz. / Rud M. sitzen | Latz. | DBn | Hyperext.)
5×15 | 6×12 | 7×10 | 5×15 | 8¹⁰ | 7⁷ | 7⁸ | 8×15 | 10×8¹¹ | 11×4⁸ |
8×15 | 8×11 | 9×10 | 6×17 | 1×20 | 8×15 | 4×17 / 2×15 |

Trizeps   11 S.

(Trizepspr. Turm Spez. Kabel: einzl.)
27×10¹² | 32×6⁸ | 27×10⁷ | 22×13 | 4×12¹⁵ | 6×5⁸ | 4×13¹⁵ | 3×15 |
2×15 | 3×10 | 1×15 |

Sätze (30)   Zeit: 2 Std.

**SUNDAY
JULY 17, 1988**

Being in great shape doesn't make you any less feminine.

The more advanced you become as a body-builder, the more nutritional notes you should include. Actually, you might consider including nutritional notes as soon as you begin making workout notes in your training diary. Again, list the date and time you consumed a particular food or supplement, the type of food supplement, and approximate amounts of each food or supplement. If you want to get fancy, you can total up your calories and grams of protein, fat, and carbs each day.

It is also a good idea to include progress photos from time to time—say at intervals of two or three months—in your diary. These should be shot in basic poses, so they can easily be compared down the road. Every few weeks you can also include your body weight and a list of your measurements, but these do not reveal the quality of your development as clearly as the progress photos do.

Self-Evaluation

The single most important task you have as a potential competitive bodybuilder is not to build muscle mass in general but to balance your physical proportions by doing specialized training to bring a lagging area up to the level of the rest of your body. This can be done only if you evaluate your physique from time to time or have someone else—who is dependable—do it.

Serious bodybuilders usually become their own best critics, as you will find with a bit of experience. The more time you spend in the sport reviewing photos of the elite athletes in it, the better will be your ability to evaluate yourself. It is essential to be hard on yourself rather than easy. Otherwise you will be complacent with an out-of-balance body.

A competent gym owner or competition judge makes a good alternative critic. Avoid asking for criticism from the type of person in the gym who is so impressed with you that he or she can pound you on the back with congratulations for your "awesome" development when he or she happens to be hitting a part of your physique that is particularly below par. If a critic is telling you what your ego wants to hear, get rid of him or her and find out who tells you something that disturbs your ego a bit.

Optimum Physical Condition

Emphasis in this book is on changing the appearance of your body so that with time it approaches the ideal. I wish to emphasize, however, that following a bodybuilding lifestyle will also get you into terrific physical condition for any type of sports participation that might strike your fancy.

If you combine weight workouts with aerobics, consistent stretching, and a solid, healthful diet, you will become a super athlete in a short time. Most pro athletes in sports you watch on television got the way they are by combining these three ingredients with skill sessions in their sport. You can do it, too, so go for it!

3
Aerobics and Cross-Training

The aerobics revolution that swept the world beginning in the early 1980s was comparable in magnitude to the Industrial Revolution that moved humanity from the age of handmade goods and equipment to our current era in which machines do virtually everything for us. At one point it seemed that women were almost universally sedentary, while a short five or six years later virtually every woman had had at least one aerobic dance class and had felt the burn.

The term *aerobics* is drawn from the Greek words meaning "with oxygen." The word was actually coined and popularized during the early 1970s by Kenneth H. Cooper, M.D., who wrote a series of bestselling books on aerobic training. A devoted runner himself, Cooper was naturally biased toward that activity as the best means of collecting aerobics "points," which assured improved endurance, cardiorespiratory health, and aerobic conditioning.

Noted actress Jane Fonda lit the fuse for today's aerobics explosion with her megabestselling book, *Jane Fonda's Workout Book*, published in 1981. The bible of aerobics, this book sold millions of copies, spawned thousands of aero-

bics studios and centers, and drew countless millions of women into a health-and-fitness lifestyle. *Jane Fonda's Workout Book* popularized aerobic dance/exercise classes in which women follow, to music, the movements of a class instructor. This is still the most popular form of aerobic exercise among women.

Currently, cross-training, in which a variety of aerobic activities are combined into a single training philosophy, is the rage. We are aiming for a much more enlightened and effective form of cross-training in this book, so you will not only become lean and physically fit, but, at the same time, will also sculpt your body into almost any form you like. With Anja-style cross-training, you can become a superwoman physically if you are sufficiently motivated to do so, something the conventional concept of cross-training won't give you an opportunity to achieve.

We definitely include a variety of aerobic activities in our cross-training program, but we also include a comprehensive weight-training program that allows you to rapidly resculpt your entire body. Our stretching routine will make your muscles and joints more supple and even further enhance the graceful appearance of your body. Add in the nutritional plan I recommend, and you have at your disposal a potent program to dramatically improve your health, fitness levels, and especially your physical appearance in the shortest possible length of time.

In this short chapter, I'll discuss the ins and outs of various forms of aerobic exercise. Stretching comes into the picture in Chapter 9 and nutrition in Chapter 11. Most of the rest of the book is devoted to an in-depth discussion and practical application of weight training. On your marks? Get set. Go!

The Aerobic Effect

Scientists can tell us precisely what it takes to achieve an aerobic effect and what you need to do to improve your aerobic conditioning at least a bit during each training session: You must elevate your pulse rate to between 70 and 80% of its maximum and keep it there for at least 12 minutes.

Within reason, the longer you keep your pulse rate within this target zone, the more of an aerobic effect you provide to your cardiorespiratory system. It is possible, however, to push things too far. Doing excessive amounts of aerobics can lead to such conditions as tendinitis, chronically sore joints, and reduced resistance to infectious diseases. As a result, most aerobics enthusiasts seldom spend more than an hour at a time in working on their favorite mode of aerobic exercise.

Competitive bodybuilders, whom I consider to be the ultimate cross-trainers, do the maximum possible amount of aerobic training daily when a contest approaches, because aerobic training—unlike the weight workouts they do—burns body fat to fuel muscle contractions. That leads to the super-lean type of physical condition in which I was in the photos taken onstage during my competitive bodybuilding career.

The best way to cram a lot of aerobic activity into a day is to do several different aerobic sessions lasting between 30 and 60 minutes each, with several hours of rest between them. For aerobics purposes, you can consider a weight workout to be rest, because it isn't placing the type of stress on the musculoskeletal system that leads to injuries from excessive amounts of aerobic exercise. I think it's also important to vary the type of aerobic training done each session if you can—running one session, stationary cycling the next, and perhaps a classic aerobic dance class the following session. This spreads the stress around to a broader base of different muscles and connective tissues, reducing the possibility of incurring an over-use injury.

There are formulae for determining your target pulse rate during an aerobics session, but I've personally found it difficult to impossible to measure my pulse rate accurately when I'm in the middle of some type of physical activity. Therefore, I think you'll find it more convenient to simply master a general rule of thumb for how to determine whether you are within your target pulse-rate zone.

You'll be in the target zone if you are exercising steadily and intensely enough to be breathing relatively heavily, but not so heavily that you couldn't carry on some type of conversation. As an example, when I'm on a stationary bike, it's not unusual for me to carry on a telephone conversation with my mother, sister, or one of my friends. By now they're used to hearing me gasp for breath occasionally, and I'm used to keeping my intensity level sufficiently under control that I can still keep talking.

My Favorite Aerobic Activity

Believe me, I've done every form of aerobic activity possible, but it has been only over the past

Mountain biking is my favorite aerobic activity.

I ride my mountain bike 3–4 times a week for 30–60 minutes at a time.

couple of years that I've come up with one I'll enjoy and stick with for life. I discovered my favorite form of aerobic activity the first time I climbed on a mountain bike and took off cross-country on a stiff ride.

Mountain bikes are constructed and geared so you can take them almost anywhere, over virtually any type of terrain in any weather. I've yet to ride up the side of a building in a hurricane, but I am not willing to accept that it's impossible to accomplish with a mountain bike until I prove so to myself. These versatile bikes are the greatest thing since sliced bread!

There are a lot of open fields, parks, hills, and

forests near where I live, and I've tried to explore every part of them on my mountain bike. It's so enjoyable to ride my bike that I almost fail to notice that I'm breathing heavily and growing progressively more fatigued. I'm sure it's the amount of variety in terms of both surroundings and physical challenges that distracts me from the fact that I'm actually out there exercising. I can't get this type of feeling in any other way, regardless of how hard I try.

Mountain bikes and riding equipment aren't that expensive, and many bicycle shops will rent you equipment for your first ride or two, so you can orient yourself and decide whether you want to stick with mountain biking. You'll want to, so be prepared to pull out your credit card and purchase your bike, helmet, and knee and elbow pads.

Walking
. . . .

The least expensive and least complicated form of aerobic exercise is fast walking, or what is sometimes called power walking. This involves merely getting dressed for the weather outside, putting on sturdy shoes (you can even purchase footwear specifically designed for this activity at athletic equipment stores), and walking fast and hard enough to get your breathing in gear.

If you have trouble accelerating your pulse and respiration rates, just pick a long, steep hill and start slogging up it. It won't be long until you are breathing heavily enough to achieve an aerobic effect.

You'll also find it both beneficial and enjoyable to go on long, less-intense, relaxing walks, particularly if you take along the man in your life or a couple of your kids. My son is a little young yet (under a year) to go walking with me, but I'm looking forward to going out with him in a couple of years. At the rate he's growing, he'll probably be walking my legs off in three or four years!

Running
. . . .

Since I was in my midteens, I've relied on cross-country running to stimulate an aerobic effect. You'll discover that running is one of the world's most popular and widely used forms of aerobic training. It's also one type of aerobic exercise that results in a plethora of injuries if you happen to approach it incorrectly.

In my experience, the women who have injury problems from running are the ones who be-come so compulsive with the activity that they do it every day of the week, month in and month out. If you can discipline yourself to run every second or third day—filling in the days in between with other forms of aerobic training—you should have very few injury problems.

It's also very important to warm up properly before taking a run. This involves going through a full stretching program, as outlined in Chapter 9. This may sound excessive to some women, but believe me, you'll thank me for insisting that you warm up so thoroughly prior to a run whenever you're around a group of runners who are discussing their injuries. You'd think that the only thing compulsive runners run for is a chance to discuss their injuries. Holy M*A*S*H* unit!

If you haven't been very physically active, it's also important to break in slowly and gradually to the activity in order to prevent typical over-use injuries from occurring. This will make the activity a bit mechanical and less free form than it will become later when you're in shape to run for almost unlimited distances. At some point you'll have to wear a watch, keep an eye on it, and probably keep written notes of how many minutes you ran and which days you chose running as your main aerobic activity. At the very least, keep reliable mental notes on these things.

Even an out-of-shape woman can jog for 8–10 minutes reasonably comfortably the first time out. Once you've done this, don't push it. Wait a day or two and run for 10–12 minutes the next time. Gradually increase the length of each run until you're on the road or going cross-country for an average of about 30 minutes each session. This will give you almost 20 minutes in the aerobic target zone each run, which will provide you with a considerable aerobic effect, particularly when combined on off days with mountain biking, walking, swimming, and/or aerobic dance classes.

Since you are being mechanical anyway in terms of writing down a record of each run's duration, be sure that you shake up your schedule a little. Don't just go up 1–2 minutes each time out. Go up 2, down 3, up 4, down 2, up 3, and so forth, and just keep upping your average each week in the amount of running you do.

Aerobic Dance Classes

Exercise classes still form the backbone of most women's aerobics programs. They can be a lot of fun if you have a good instructor and are able to stay within your limits during an entire one-hour class. If you're having trouble with a class, switch instructors as many times as it takes to find one who gives the type of class that most benefits you and that you most enjoy. Aerobics centers tend to have many different instructors, giving you the option of trying out several.

I spend less time on aerobic dance sessions than I used to, simply because I'm spending more time on my mountain bike and have to come up with biking time somewhere. But on some weeks when the weather is particularly nasty outside, I'll spend a lot more time than usual in a dance studio and less on my bike. The more you can vary the type and amount of aerobic activities in which you indulge, the better off you'll be in the long run.

Cross-Training

About the only limitation you'll encounter when you are cross-training is time availability, because in my experience the human body is capable of withstanding almost any amount of exercise, as long as it's varied in nature. If this wasn't true, you wouldn't see elite triathletes spending 6–8 hours per day practicing their three activities and thriving on it.

Weight training should form the backbone of your cross-training program. Perhaps my cross-training program when I'm at peak intensity can serve as a model for you. I train with weights using a three-on/one-off program. This involves doing three different routines:

Day 1 —chest, triceps, biceps
Day 2 —legs, calves
Day 3 —back, shoulders, abdominals

Within the foregoing split routine, I do two different programs for each of the days represented. So the first time I go through a four-day cycle, I do one type of routine on each day, and the second time through I do a different type of routine. In other words, every eight days, I do six distinct workouts, two each for every body part.

My mind and body require this type of variety in my weight workouts. Mentally, I stay more interested in pumping iron when I'm doing something different all of the time. Physically, I'm less apt to incur a weight-training-oriented over-use injury when I vary the type of training program I'm doing for each muscle group.

My precise personal weight routines—including every exercise, set, and rep performed—are listed in Chapter 13. Use them as a guideline only, because you'll ultimately want to come up with some that are similar to, yet different from, my own routines.

Within each eight-day weight-training cycle, I also have eight days on which I can do aerobics and two weight-rest days on which my program of aerobics can be particularly heavy. Prior to every aerobic and weight workout, I have to do a warm-up, too. Each of these warm-ups includes an abbreviated, but nonetheless comprehensive, stretching program. So I'm getting plenty of stretching, regardless of the mode of physical activity I choose to do at any particular time.

At peak intensity, I'll try to do two hours of aerobics each day in addition to the weight and stretching sessions. That means I'm going to be sweaty three or more hours per day, but I can

Aerobic dance is a great way to have fun and burn excess body fat at the same time.

always take a shower when I'm finished and end up refreshed.

As with my weight workouts, my aerobics sessions feature plenty of variety. I'll do one type of cycling each day—either mountain biking or pedaling a stationary bike. I'll also do one type of run—either on the flat or up stadium bleachers. And I'll also do about an hour in an aerobic dance class each day.

How do I schedule all of this in? I'll do my stiffest aerobics session of the day rather early in the morning, usually even before I eat anything. Doing an aerobics session on an empty stomach actually burns more fat than usual, because there's less glycogen (blood sugar stored in your muscles) available to fuel the anaerobic part of each session, and you will burn fat for fuel very early in the session.

In the middle of the day I do my weight-training session. The intensity of this particular workout varies, but when I was preparing for body-building competitions it was extremely intense, with each session lasting about an hour and a half. Nowadays I'm less interested in building— or even in maintaining—a high degree of muscle mass, so my weight workouts are shorter (usually lasting only about an hour) and quite a bit less intense.

After two or three hours of rest, I'll do a more moderate aerobics session. This is usually a good time to take an aerobic dance class, since a lot of these classes are scheduled for the late afternoon or early evening. If I need to get in a third aerobics session, I'll do it within an hour or two of going to bed each night.

When I do a lot of high-intensity weight work—as I prepare for a competitive bodybuilding appearance, for instance—and concurrently have to limit my calorie intake in order to reduce body-fat stores to the absolute minimum, the weight work and diet are extremely hard on my body. Usually I'll come down with some type of infectious illness (whatever happens to be going around at the time—a cold, flu, whatever) after I've peaked for a bodybuilding show. This is one big reason why I'm currently out of competition. My giving birth recently also has something to do with it, but I definitely dislike having to heap so much abuse on my body.

On the other hand, high volumes of aerobic work in conjunction with a normal diet and lower-intensity weight workouts tend to make me as healthy as a horse. My personal energy levels go up rapidly, I feel great all of the time, I sleep like a log, and I generally couldn't have a better sense of well-being.

Please don't draw the conclusion from the foregoing discussion that I have anything against weight training. It's just that I have a bit of a bias against pushing my weight workouts well past the normal thresholds of human endurance. Done with moderate intensity, weight workouts are a highly beneficial component of every cross-training program. There's no other form of physical activity that changes your physical appearance more quickly than bodybuilding.

A Final Note on Aerobics

An average woman—even one who is relatively athletic—tends to carry too much body fat for optimum aesthetic appeal. One reason for this is that a woman's body is used to burning glycogen to fuel muscle contractions. One of the greatest benefits of aerobic activity is that it teaches your body to burn stored fat to provide the calories for muscle contraction, which in the long run makes you more of a lean, mean fighting machine than is possible under any other circumstances.

4
Basic Exercises and Routines

· ·

At this point, I firmly believe that you have sufficient knowledge of weight training to be able to take safe and productive workouts without a personal coach hovering over you like a mother hen and then demanding her $50 fee at the end of your session. Most of this chapter is devoted to precise descriptions (with equally precise photo illustrations) of a basic pool of 26 weight-training movements for the various parts of your body. The last few pages of the chapter contain a series of three suggested training routines that incorporate the exercises you will have just learned.

It's vitally important that you learn from the start how to correctly perform each weight-training exercise presented in this chapter. These exercises will form the foundation of every workout you perform for the rest of your life, and you don't want to develop poor exercise habits that will be difficult to change down the road. If you learn correct exercise form from the beginning, you'll never have to relearn a basic movement when you're a more experienced bodybuilder.

I have a set procedure for teaching new students how to perform an exercise correctly, a procedure that has been tested with literally hundreds of novices over the years. Here is how you should do it:

• Carefully read all the directions for the exercise while referring to the accompanying illustrations.
• Repeat the above steps until the instructions are perfectly clear to you.
• Stand in front of a mirror without a weight or weights in your hands and run your body through the movement until you have the physical feel of it down pat.
• Repeat the above step but use light weights.
• Gradually increase the weights you are using in the new movement while constantly monitoring your form in the mirror for potential flaws.
• If you have a cooperative experienced bodybuilder available, ask him or her to critique your form, and then make any corrections that the more experienced trainee suggests.

Carefully following these sequential steps will lead to total mastery of free-weight movements. In comparison, machine exercises are much easier to learn, because once you are in the machine, it tracks the resistance along a correct arc for you. With a machine, you couldn't move a weight through an incorrect arc if you tried!

I believe that a serious weight trainee should never cease trying to learn more about her favorite physical activity. This rule applies not only to exercise performance but also to training techniques and dietary practices. While I will teach you in this chapter—as well as in chapters 6 and 8—how to perform a total of about 75 exercises in their most basic form, most weight movements do have performance nuances that take time to learn. Gaining experience in the gym and comparing notes with other bodybuilders will help you learn the subtleties.

Many of the performance nuances can be picked up by regularly reading weight-training and bodybuilding magazines such as *Flex*, *Sport Revue*, and *Muscle & Fitness*. Others can be mastered by attending training seminars run by champion bodybuilders and asking the right questions. ("Is there a way I can get more out of my dumbbell side laterals so my deltoid muscles more closely resemble yours, Anja?") A few more can be learned on our own in the gym by simply playing around with new grip widths, body attitudes, and so forth.

Exercises in this chapter begin with those that benefit the largest muscle groups of the body and gradually move downward to the smaller parts of the body. So while there may seem to be nothing systematic about the order in which I present exercises, there is a method to my apparent madness.

Leg and Gluteal Exercises

SQUATS

Areas Emphasized—Doing squats is probably the number one exercise for stimulating the most muscles in a human body. The main muscles emphasized are the quadriceps (at the fronts of

Squats—start and finish

your thighs), the gluteus maximus (glutes), and the erector spinae (spinal erector muscles) of the lower back. Strong secondary emphasis is on the hamstrings, hip flexors, and upper-back muscles. Because squats stress so many muscles under such extreme intensity, they also tend to stimulate the body's metabolism, making it easier for you to achieve a lean and muscular appearance than if you failed to include squats in your leg routines. Personally, if I had to choose a single exercise to perform for the remainder of my bodybuilding life, it would be squats.

Starting Position—Although the photos with this exercise fail to illustrate it, squats normally require the use of a support rack in order to get the weight placed correctly across the shoulders. You

Squats—midpoint

feet at about shoulder width, your toes angled slightly outward.

Movement Performance—Keeping your head up and your back as erect as possible throughout the movement, slowly bend your legs and sink into a full squatting position. It's important as you sink into the squat that your knees travel directly out over your toes and in a forward direction. Without bouncing in the bottom position, reverse the procedure and return to an erect standing posture. Repeat the movement for the suggested number of repetitions. At the end of your set, step forward and replace the bar on the squat rack.

Common Mistakes—Most of the common squatting mistakes involve doing a "powerlifter" rather than a "bodybuilder" squat. A powerlifter does all sorts of things to make it easier for her to lift an extremely heavy weight, and none of the little cheats she uses helps her build the type of leg muscle a bodybuilder is after. The first mistake is to allow the bar to ride very low on your back rather than up across your shoulders, a position that will force your torso into a forward angle that exceeds 45 degrees. Even with the bar high on your shoulders, such an acute torso lean throws too much pressure off the quadriceps and onto the gluteus maximus and spinal erector muscles. The biggest mistake, however, is learning to squat by keeping your knees directly above your feet and just dipping your hips—a simulation of a correct squat. Properly performed, your knees should travel forward over your toes as you lower yourself into the deep squat, and then backward as you rise up until your legs again assume a straight position.

Training Tips—In the second photo illustrating this movement, you'll notice that I have squatted down to a position in which my legs are slightly above parallel with the gym floor. When you first start doing squats, this is probably about as far

should use a rack. Load up the bar with a substantial poundage, be sure the collars are locked on each end of the bar, and step in front of the bar. The barbell is going to be positioned across your shoulders, the bar resting across the trapezius muscles of your upper back, which provide a natural pad to protect your spine from the weight on the bar. Grasp the bar with your hands set about halfway between your shoulders and the plates on each side; this will help you balance the bar in the correct position throughout the movement. Place your feet at about shoulder width directly beneath the bar, bending your legs enough so you can position both the bar and your feet correctly with ease. Straighten your back and keep your back muscles tensed throughout your set. Straighten your legs to lift the bar from the rack, step back one pace, and set your down as you'll want to go until you learn to control the movement efficiently. But you should really squat down all the way, until the backs of your hamstrings touch your calves. If you experience any particular problems balancing yourself as you squat, try elevating your heels by standing with your heels resting on either a pair of thick barbell plates or a 2 × 4-inch (6 × 8-centimeter) board. Most bodybuilders wear a weightlifting belt when they lift the heavier weights to protect their lower backs and abdomens from injury. If you happen to have an old knee injury, you might also want to wrap your knee with elastic gauze bandages, a technique explained in Chapter 5.

ANGLED LEG PRESSES

Areas Emphasized—This movement affects the same major muscle groups as squats, except that most of the pressure on lower- and upper-back muscles is removed. Primary stress is on the quadriceps muscles while doing leg presses, with significant secondary stress on the buttocks and hamstrings. The upper-back and arm muscles come into play to a degree in helping to brace your body in the machine as you execute the movement.

Starting Position—There are three basic types of leg-press machines. Evolutionarily speaking, the first leg-press machines allowed you to lie on your back and push the weight directly upward along rails (this is called a vertical leg-press unit). Later, several equipment manufacturers produced leg-press machines in which you sit erect and push the weight (which is attached to the end of a large lever) directly forward, parallel to the gym floor (this is called a horizontal leg-press unit). The newest and most popular type of machine allows you to lie on your back and push the weight up rails set at a 45-degree angle with the gym floor (this is called an angled leg-press unit). The movements on each machine are similar, but I'll restrict myself to discussing leg presses on an angled machine.

Sit down in the machine, your back resting flat against the backboard and your hips wedged in the corner formed by the machine seat and backboard joint. Bend your legs enough so you can position your feet at about shoulder width in the middle of the weight carriage. For the basic leg press, be sure your feet are set parallel to each other.

Straighten your legs fully and rotate the stop bars at the sides of your hips to release the weight carriage. Then grasp the handles provided to steady your body in position during the movement. Be sure to keep your head back against the padded backrest throughout your set.

Movement Performance—Slowly bend your legs to allow the weight carriage to slide down its rails toward your hips. As you reach a position in which your legs are bent almost fully, be sure that your knees travel out to the sides a bit so they clear each side of your rib cage, rather than coming to rest heavily against your chest. Without bouncing in the bottom position, reverse the movement and slowly push the weight carriage back to the starting point. Repeat the movement for an appropriate number of repetitions. At the end of your set, lock the stop bars back into position and slowly lower the carriage down to rest against the stops. Only then can you safely exit the machine.

Common Mistakes—One of the most common mistakes in performing heavy leg presses is to hold your breath during the movement, an act that builds up terrific pressure in your vascular system and occasionally will result in small—but very unsightly—hemorrhages in the corners of your eyes. Another error is to bounce the weight off your chest by keeping your knees together and allowing the carriage to descend too quickly. You must also be sure that you keep your back flat at all times; some bodybuilders allow their backs to round forward up near the shoulders, something that can result in a painful back injury.

Angled Leg Presses—start and finish

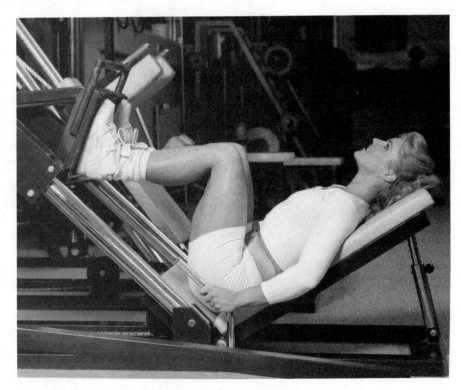

Angled Leg Presses—midpoint

Basic Exercises and Routines | **41**

Training Tips—I have included photos that show in greater detail two alternative foot-position angles used in performing leg presses. When you angle your toes outward as acutely as I have done in the first photo, you will be working your inner thigh muscles more intensely than the rest of the quadriceps complex. If you angle your toes inward, you will be placing greater stress on the outer sections of your quadriceps, which gives you a nice sweep to the outer thigh that is much sought after among competitive bodybuilders.

Angled Leg Presses (variation with toes pointed outward)

Angled Leg Presses (variation with toes pointed inward)

LEG EXTENSIONS

Areas Emphasized—This is a strict isolation movement that places almost its entire stress quotient on the quadriceps muscles at the fronts of your thighs. Minimal stress is also shared by the forearm muscles (which help you grip the seat handles to brace yourself in the machine) and the trapezius muscles (which also help brace you in the machine).

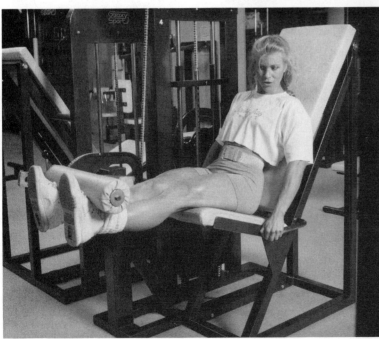

Leg Extensions—start and finish

Leg Extensions—midpoint

Starting Position—Sit down in a leg-extension machine and hook your insteps beneath the roller pads attached to the end of the machine lever arm. Slide yourself backward until the backs of your knees rest firmly against the edge of the seat. Recline against the backrest. Reach down and grasp the seat handles, keeping your arms straight to help brace yourself in the machine.

Movement Performance—Using only quadriceps strength, slowly straighten your legs as fully as possible. Hold this top position for a slow count of two in order to intensify the peak-contraction effect of the movement, and then slowly return to the starting point. Repeat.

Common Mistakes—The most common mistake made in leg extensions is performing the movement with too quick a cadence and no static hold at the top point of the exercise. Many bodybuilders also cut their leg extensions short, not performing the entire possible range of motion. Doing less than a full movement gives you less than full benefit from the exercise.

Training Tips—As with leg presses, you can emphasize different sections of your quadriceps by alternating toe angles. Normally leg extensions are done with the feet flexed and toes angled directly upward when in the top position of the movement. This type of exercise works the entire quadriceps muscle complex more or less equally. By angling your toes inward about a 45-degree angle, you can stress the outer sweep of your quadriceps muscles more. By turning your toes outward at about a 45-degree angle stress is switched more to the inner sections of your quadriceps, particularly to the teardrop-shaped vastus medalist muscle just above your knees.

When you do machine movements for your legs, it is possible to perform the exercise with one leg at a time as well as with both legs simultaneously. Doing one-legged movements has the advantage of making each repetition more intense than if the legs were worked together. This intensity occurs because you don't have to split your mental focus between the two limbs but rather can concentrate all of it on the single working leg.

LYING LEG CURLS
Areas Emphasized—This is an isolation movement for the biceps femoris (hamstring) muscles at the backs of your thighs. If done with toes pointed, it also will stimulate the gastrocnemius muscles of the calves.

Starting Position—Lie facedown on a leg-curl apparatus, hooking your heels beneath the roller pads attached to the lever arm of the machine. Straighten your legs and slide forward until your knees are at the edge of the bench toward the lever arm. Grasp the handles provided on each side of the bench to steady your body in position throughout the movement.

Movement Performance—Use hamstring strength to slowly bend your legs as completely as possible. Hold the top point of the movement for a slow count of two to increase the peak-contraction effect of the exercise, and then slowly lower your legs back to the starting point. Repeat for the desired number of repetitions.

Common Mistakes—Allowing your hips to come up off the bench as you do leg curls can significantly shorten the exercise's range of motion. One of the best ways of avoiding this is to use a leg-extension machine that has the bench part angled upward a bit in the middle, one that resembles the machine shown in the photos accompanying this exercise description. Another way of keeping your hips on the table is to raise your shoulders upward by either resting your elbows on the bench or by simply pushing upward against the machine handles.

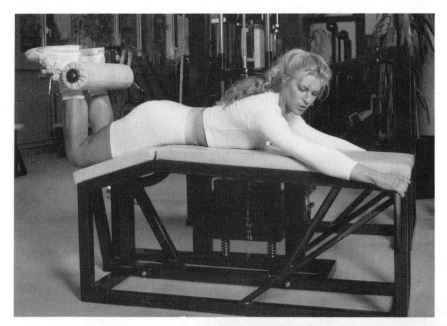

Lying Leg Curls—midpoint

Lying Leg Curls (variation
in arm position)—midpoint

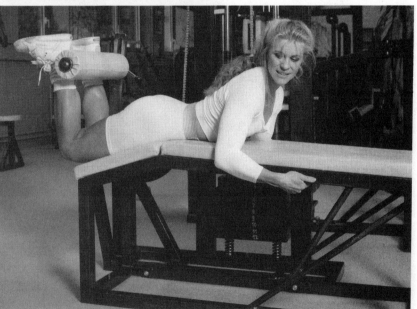

Training Tips—This movement is most effective at isolating the hamstrings from the calves when it is performed with the feet flexed rather than with the toes pointed. Since you can do exercises that are more specifically for the calves, forget about pointing your feet and do everything with feet flexed. As with leg extensions, you can change foot angle to shift stress to different sections of the biceps femoris muscles. Feet straight upward works the entire muscle group, toes angled outward at 45 degrees works the inner part of the muscle complex more, and toes angled inward at about 45 degrees works the outer quadriceps muscles more intensely. As with leg extensions, you can perform leg curls with one leg at a time to increase your mental focus on the working muscles.

Back Exercises

. . . .

LAT MACHINE PULLDOWNS BEHIND THE NECK

Areas Emphasized—Lat pulldowns can be done both in front of and behind your neck. Both variations place intense stress on the latissimus dorsi muscles, biceps, brachialis, and forearm flexors. When you pull the bar to a position behind your head, you stress the upper lats more than the lower sections of the same muscle group.

Starting Position—Attach a lat bar handle that is either straight or angled downward at each end to the end of the cable running through an overhead pulley. Take a grip on the handle with your hands set 4-6 inches (12-16 centimeters) wider than your shoulders on each side. Be sure that your palms face forward. Straighten your arms fully and allow your body weight to pull your body down until you are sitting on the machine seat. Wedge your knees beneath the restraint bar to keep your body braced solidly in one position as you do the movement. Relax your lats and allow the weight to stretch them as fully as possible prior to starting

Lat Machine Pulldowns Behind the Neck—start and finish

the movement. Arch your back and keep it arched throughout the movement.

Movement Performance—Being sure to keep your elbows back as far as is comfortable, use back rather than arm strength to pull the bar directly downward until it touches your trapezius muscles at the base of your neck. Hold this peak-contracted position for a moment and then return slowly to the starting point. Repeat the movement for the stated number of repetitions.

Common Mistakes—Failing to keep your back arched as you do this movement will prevent you from fully contracting your lats with each repetition. Pulling with your arms rather than your upper-back muscles is another common mistake, even among experienced bodybuilders. Jerking the bar downward is also taboo.

Training Tips—Try varying the width of your grip on the lat bar, moving your hands both inward and outward to see how grip-width changes affect your lats as you do the movement. There is also a lat bar handle that will give you a shoulder-width grip, with your hands parallel rather than facing forward; you can use it for pulldowns behind the neck, too.

Lat Machine Pulldowns Behind the Neck—midpoint

Parallel-Grip Front Lat Machine Pulldowns—start and finish

PARALLEL-GRIP FRONT LAT MACHINE PULLDOWNS

Areas Emphasized—As with all variations of lat machine pulldowns, this movement places intense stress on the latissimus dorsi muscles, biceps, brachialis, and forearm flexors. When you pull the bar down to a position in front of your neck, you stress the lower lats more than the upper sections of the same muscle group.

Starting Position—Attach a lat bar that permits a parallel-hands grip to the end of the cable running through an overhead pulley. Grasp the handles with your palms facing inward toward each other. Fully straighten your arms and allow your body weight to pull you down until you can wedge your knees beneath the restraint bar as you sit in the lat machine seat. Fully relax your middle-back muscles in order to stretch your lats prior to starting each repetition. Arch your back and keep it arched throughout your set.

Movement Performance—Use latissimus dorsi strength to pull the bar slowly downward until it touches your upper chest at the base of your

Parallel-Grip Front Lat Machine Pulldowns—midpoint

neck. Be sure to keep your elbows as far back as possible throughout the downward and upward cycles of the exercise. Slowly return to the starting point and repeat the movement as many times as desired for each set.

Common Mistakes—Jerking the weight and doing shorter-than-normal movements are the most common mistakes made in front lat pulldowns. It's also easy to forget to keep your back arched as you do the movement, which robs you of much of the developmental benefit of this movement.

Training Tips—I'm using a rather wide grip in this movement. You can try two additional parallel-grip handles for it, one in which your grip is restricted to shoulder width, the other in which your hands are set very close together. In the second variation, you will find you'll have to arch your back even more than usual in order to get the handle pulled completely down to your upper chest. Front pulldowns can also be done with a variety of widths of overgrip on a straight bar handle or one in which the ends are angled slightly downward.

One-Arm Dumbbell Bent-Over Rows—start and finish

ONE-ARM DUMBBELL BENT-OVER ROWS

Areas Emphasized—While pulldown movements primarily are intended to develop width in the upper back, all types of bent-over rows build thickness into the lats and other upper-back muscles. Secondary emphasis is on the posterior deltoids, biceps, brachialis, and forearm flexor muscles. Since this movement is performed with the upper back supported, there is much less lower-back emphasis than with other types of bent-over rows that are performed without the upper back supported.

Starting Position—Let's start out by describing how to do the exercise with your right arm.

Then you can simply reverse all of the directions to learn how to do it with your left arm as well. Start out by placing a moderately heavy dumbbell on the gym floor parallel to a flat exercise bench and toward one end of the bench. Place your left knee on the bench while keeping your right leg extended and its toes in contact with the gym floor. Place your left palm flat on the bench about 2 feet (60 centimeters) ahead of your left knee. Hold your left arm straight throughout the movement to support your torso in position. Reach down and take a grip on the dumbbell, keeping your hand oriented so the dumbbell handle is parallel to the bench throughout the movement. Fully straighten your right arm and push the dumbbell a few inches forward in

One-Arm Dumbbell Bent-Over Rows—
midpoint

order to completely stretch your right lat prior to executing the movement. Rotate your right shoulder a few inches toward the floor to stretch your lat muscle farther.

Movement Performance—Attempting to use just the strength in your right latissimus dorsi, bend your arm and slowly pull the weight upward and slightly to the rear until it touches the side of your waist, as illustrated. As you pull up the weight, your right shoulder should rotate slightly upward, and you should keep your working elbow in close to your side throughout the upward and downward cycles of the exercise. Hold the peak-contracted position for a moment and then slowly lower your arm back to the starting point. Repeat. Be sure to do the same number of sets and reps for each arm, alternating between the two.

Common Mistakes—Jerking the weight upward and doing short, choppy movements are common mistakes that rob your working muscles of

much of the benefit they should be receiving. Concentrate on a long, slow movement in order to get the most out of your dumbbell rows.

Training Tips—You'll find that your exercise form deteriorates most quickly when you try to use a weight that is too heavy for you at present. Using a moderately heavy poundage with precise form will do you a lot more good in the long run than trying to lift up something you really can't handle.

BARBELL BENT-OVER ROWS
Areas Emphasized—As with dumbbell rows, barbell bent-over rows are excellent for adding thickness to the upper-back muscles, most specifically to the lats and traps. But unlike in dumbbell rows, there is considerable stress also placed on the spinal erectors when a barbell is used in the movement. Strong secondary stress is on the posterior deltoids, biceps, brachialis, and forearm flexor muscles.

Starting Position—Place a barbell on the gym floor at your feet and load it up with a moderately heavy weight. Set your feet about shoulder-width apart and bend over and take a shoulder-width overgrip on the barbell handle. Keeping your knees slightly bent at all times (a technique that removes potentially harmful stress from your lower back), straighten your arms and raise your head and shoulders upward until your torso is parallel to the gym floor. Relax your lats fully and allow the weight to stretch your back muscles maximally prior to initiating each repetition.

Movement Performance—Without moving your legs or torso, slowly bend your arms and pull the weight directly upward from a position hanging at straight-arm's length beneath your shoulders to a second point at the bottom of your rib cage. As you pull the weight upward, be sure to keep your elbows in at your sides as tightly as

Barbell Bent-Over Rows—midpoint

possible. Hold the peak-contracted position for a moment and then slowly lower the weight back to the starting point. Repeat the movement for the desired number of reps.

Common Mistakes—Locking out your knees can cause a lower-back injury, so keep them slightly bent at all times. Be sure to avoid rocking your torso upward and downward as you do the movement, something that most often occurs when you have added too much weight to the bar.

Training Tips—This movement is often performed with wide-diameter Olympic bar plates that come into contact with the floor and terminate the movement short of full arm extension. In such a case, I suggest that you stand on a thick block of

wood or on the flat surface of a sturdy exercise bench, both of which will allow you to lower the weight much farther without the plates contacting the gym floor. In most cases, I'd suggest that you wear a weightlifting belt when doing your heavier sets of barbell rows.

STIFF-LEGGED DEADLIFTS

Areas Emphasized—While this movement is primarily intended for developing the erector spinae muscles of the lower back, it places equally strong stress on the buttocks and leg biceps muscles, making it a great all-around lower-body movement. Secondary stress is on the remaining back muscles and the forearm flexors.

Starting Position—Place a moderately heavy barbell on the gym floor at your feet. Keep your feet together, or set them slightly apart if it's more comfortable for you, and bend over at the waist to take a shoulder-width overgrip on the bar. With your knees bent, slowly stand erect with the weight, so when your legs are straight the bar rests at straight-arm's length directly across your upper legs. Stiffen your legs and keep them—and your arms—straight throughout your set.

Movement Performance—Keeping your back flat and head up, slowly bend forward at the waist as far as is comfortably possible. Without bouncing the weight in the bottom position, reverse the movement and slowly return to an erect posture. Repeat the movement for the required number of reps.

Common Mistakes—You don't need to use an extremely heavy poundage on this movement, just a moderate weight. Going too heavy will ultimately lead to a lower-back injury. Be sure that you don't pull off to one side as you slowly straighten up from the low position; doing so will also place a harmful degree of stress on your lower back.

Stiff-Legged Deadlifts
—start and finish

Stiff-Legged Deadlifts
—midpoint

Training Tips—As with barbell bent-over rows, the diameter of the barbell plates you use could terminate stiff-legged deadlifts short of the full possible range of motion if you do the movement standing flat on the gym floor. Once you have gained confidence in your balance during a set of stiff-legged deadlifts, you should graduate to doing them while standing on either a thick block of wood or on a sturdy, flat exercise bench to insure that you are getting a full range of motion. I don't recommend using a weightlifting belt for stiff-legged deadlifts, because the belt will probably end up pinching the sides of your waist. As long as you perform the movement slowly and deliberately, there is no reason to believe you will injure your lower back.

Chest Exercises
. . . .

BENCH PRESSES

Areas Emphasized—Bench presses are sometimes called upper-body squats, because they involve so many muscle groups—if they are performed correctly. The most intense stress is borne by the pectoral muscles (particularly the lower and outer sections of that muscle complex), deltoids (particularly the anterior and medial sections of the muscle), and triceps. Strong secondary stress is on the lats and those upper-back muscles that impart rotational motion to the scapulae.

Starting Position—It's easiest to learn this movement on a Smith machine, which tracks the barbell correctly for you. Once you have the machine version down pat, you'll find it less difficult to graduate to a free-weight movement. Either variation of bench presses works the same muscle groups. Load up the bar with a moderate weight and lie back on the flat bench set between the machine uprights, positioning your shoulder joints directly beneath the bar. You can either place your feet on the floor or you can bend your legs fully and rest your feet on the bench itself. Reach up and take an overgrip on the bar that places your hands 4–6 inches (10–15 centimeters) wider than your shoulders on each side. Straighten your arms fully and rotate the machine bar so that its hooks come completely free from their attachment points on the machine uprights. That releases the bar, while a turn in the opposite direction relocks it at the end of your set.

Bench Presses—start and finish

Movement Performance—Being sure to keep your elbows back as far as possible throughout the movement, slowly bend your arms and lower the bar down until it lightly touches your chest. Without bouncing the bar off your chest, slowly straighten your arms and return to the starting point. Repeat the movement until you have fully fatigued your chest, shoulder, and arm muscles.

Common Mistakes—Arching your back excessively, particularly if it involves lifting your glutes from the surface of the bench, will make the movement shorter and easier to perform, but in the long run the arching robs the working muscles of much of the resistance they should receive. Bouncing the bar off your chest is also counterproductive, as is cutting any movement short of its full potential range of motion.

Training Tips—When you move to a free bar for this exercise, the only real difference is that you'll have to expend a bit of mental concentration on balancing the bar for the first workout or two. As soon as this becomes automatic, you'll discover that you can get a lot out of regular barbell bench presses as well. Whether you do the movement with a barbell or on the Smith machine, you should experiment with various grip widths on the bar. A relatively narrow grip width (with perhaps only the width of your hand between index fingers) shifts emphasis more to the inner sections of the pectorals (the part we call the "cleavage," between the individual muscles) and to the triceps. Each change of grip width will attack the chest, shoulder, and arm muscles from a somewhat different angle. The accumulation of many attack angles will give you the ultimate degree of chest muscle development.

Bench Presses—midpoint

Incline Presses—start and finish

INCLINE PRESSES

Areas Emphasized—When you move from doing bench presses on a flat surface to benching on an incline, you shift emphasis from the lower outer pectorals to the upper section of the muscle group. You particularly stress the tie-ins between the upper pecs and the anterior deltoids, while concurrently placing significant pressure on the triceps muscles. Secondary stress is on the remainder of the pectoral muscle complex, the medial deltoids, and those muscles of the upper back that impart rotational movement to the scapulae.

Starting Position—Again, it's a little easier to learn to do incline presses on a Smith machine than with a free bar, so I'll explain the machine

movement. Sit on the seat of the incline bench set between the uprights of the machine and lie back on the inclined surface. Place your feet on the floor on either side of the foot end of the bench. Reach up and take an overgrip on the sliding bar so that your hands are set 4–6 inches (10–15 centimeters) wider than your shoulders on each side. Fully straighten your arms and rotate the machine bar so that its hooks come completely free from their attachment points on the machine uprights. That releases the bar for use, while a turn in the opposite direction relocks it at the end of your set. At the beginning of the set, your shoulder joints should be directly beneath the bar.

Movement Performance—Being certain

Incline Presses—midpoint

to keep your elbows as far back as possible throughout the movement, slowly bend your arms and lower the bar until it touches your upper chest at the base of your neck. Without bouncing the bar off your chest, slowly reverse the movement and press the bar back up to a position at straight-arm's length, directly above your shoulder joints. Repeat the movement for the required number of repetitions.

Common Mistakes—With both benches and inclines, many misguided weight trainees will allow their elbows to drift forward, a little cheat that removes stress from the pectorals and places it more on the triceps and upper-back muscles. As with bench presses on a flat bench, you should avoid arching your back upward, particularly while lifting your hips from the bench. This shortens the range of motion but robs your working muscles of much of the stress that they should be receiving. Never bounce the bar off your chest.

Training Tips—While you will find it almost impossible to take a narrow grip on the bar when doing inclines, you should experiment with various grip widths to see how each one affects the upper pectorals. You should also try different angles on incline benches. The most commonly used angle is 45 degrees, but a bench with a 30-degree angle shifts stress more directly onto the upper pecs than does the bench with a higher incline, which places greater emphasis on the deltoids.

DECLINE PRESSES

Areas Emphasized—Decline presses shift stress primarily to the lower outer sections of the pectorals, with proportionately less intensity placed on the anterior deltoids. The triceps still receive plenty of emphasis, but the upper-back muscles are isolated from the movement.

Starting Position—Although the free-weight version is described and illustrated here, this exercise can also be performed on a Smith machine. Place a barbell on the support rack and load it up with a moderate poundage. Lie back on the decline bench so your shoulders are only a couple of inches (5–6 centimeters) from the supports. Reach up and take an overgrip on the bar with your hands set about the same distance apart as for bench presses and inclines. Straighten your arms to remove the weight from the rack and move the barbell forward slightly to a position directly above your shoulder joints.

Movement Performance—Being sure to keep your elbows back throughout the movement, slowly bend your arms and lower the barbell downward until it touches the middle of your chest. Without bouncing the weight off your chest, slowly reverse direction and press the weight back up to the starting point. Repeat.

Common Mistakes—The most common mistake bodybuilders make when doing declines is to cut the movement short by lowering the bar to the lower edge of the rib cage rather than to the middle of the chest. You won't, however, have to worry about arching your back as you have when performing benches and inclines, because it's virtually impossible to arch on a decline bench.

Training Tips—As with benches and inclines, you can also do decline presses on a Smith machine. Whether you do them on a machine or with

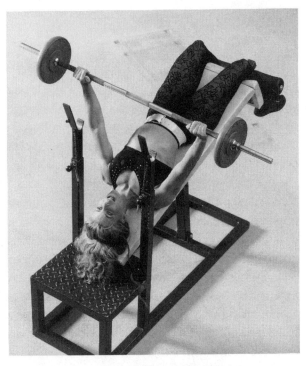

Decline Presses—start and finish

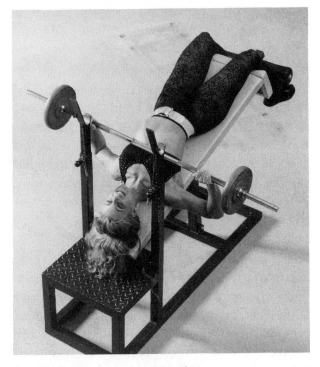

Decline Presses—midpoint

a free bar, experiment with various grip widths. You can also try a variety of degrees of decline on your bench. With decline presses—as well as with both bench presses and inclines—you should be careful to have a spotter standing at the head end of the bench ready to rescue you if you happen to miss a repetition.

FLAT-BENCH DUMBBELL PRESSES

Areas Emphasized—This movement stresses the same muscle groups as do normal bench presses with a barbell or presses on a Smith machine. Primary emphasis is on the lower outer pectorals, anterior medial deltoids, triceps, and

Flat-Bench Dumbbell Presses—start and finish

Flat-Bench Dumbbell Presses—rotating palms toward feet

Flat-Bench Dumbbell Presses—midpoint

those upper-back muscles that impart rotational movement to the scapulae. You will find that with dumbbell versions of flat, incline, and decline presses you get a longer range of motion than with equivalent barbell versions. This is because there is no bar across your body to contact your chest and terminate the movement short of where the weights can be lowered if they are held in each hand. It's much more difficult to get dumbbells into the proper position to press them, however, when compared to using a barbell for the same movements.

Starting Position—Grasp two moderately heavy dumbbells and sit at the end of a flat exercise bench with the weights resting on their ends on your knees (the handles will be vertical when they are in the correct position). Rock backward and lie flat on the bench, simultaneously pulling the dumbbells upward to your shoulders. Press the weights to straight-arm's length directly above your shoulders. Bend your knees and place your feet up on the

bench or place them on the floor on either side of the bench to balance your body in position as you do the movement. Rotate your arms at your shoulder joints so your palms are facing inward toward each other at the start of the movement.

Movement Performance—Being sure to keep your elbows back throughout the movement, slowly bend your arms and lower the dumbbells downward to as low a position below your shoulder joints as is comfortably possible. As you lower the weights, rotate your hands so your palms are facing your feet in the bottom position of the movement. Without bouncing the weights off your chest, slowly reverse direction and press them back to the starting point, rotating your hands again so your palms face each other at the top point of the exercise.

Common Mistakes—Using weights that are too heavy will cause your form to degenerate, because you will have to cut movements short of their potential range of motion. Be sure to avoid arching your hips up off the bench during the movement, because this also will shorten the potential range of motion of the exercise. Never do dumbbell bench presses in a ballistic manner; rather, you *must* be certain to control the weights precisely at all times in order to avoid injury and to stress the working muscles as completely as they should be stressed.

Training Tips—This exercise can be changed by giving the flat exercise bench either a slight incline or a slight decline by placing a block of wood under the legs at the appropriate end of the bench.

PEC DECK FLYES

Areas Emphasized—Pec Deck Flyes isolate stress on the pectoral muscles, particularly the inner and outer sections of the muscle group. Minor secondary stress is placed on the anterior and medial heads of the deltoid muscles. This exercise can be performed on either a Nautilus machine or a freestanding Pec Deck machine.

Starting Position—Adjust the height of the machine seat so that your upper arms will be parallel to the floor during the movement. Some seats can be adjusted with a pin, others by turning the seat, which is attached to a large screw. Sit on the seat and press your upper back against the vertical pad attached to the machine. Force your elbows against the padded surface of the movable pads, hands resting over the top edge of the pads. Allow the movable pads to travel to the rear as far as possible, completely stretching the pectoral muscles.

Movement Performance—Use your pectoral strength to move your elbows forward in semicircular arcs until the movable pads touch each other directly in front of your chest. Slowly return the pads to the starting position and repeat the movement for the desired number of repetitions.

Pec Deck Flye—start and finish

Training Tips—You can vary the height of the seat on both types of apparatus for a somewhat different feel in your pectorals as you do the movement. You can also do the exercise with only one arm at a time, which intensifies the stress on your pectorals by allowing you to concentrate more fully on the muscle action.

Seated Smith-Machine Overhead Presses—start and finish

Seated Smith-Machine Overhead Presses
(to the front)—midpoint

Seated Smith-Machine Overhead Presses
(behind the neck)—midpoint

Shoulder Exercises

SEATED SMITH-MACHINE OVERHEAD PRESSES

Areas Emphasized—All variations of overhead presses place the most intense stress on the anterior deltoids and triceps, with lesser amounts of stress on the medial posterior delts and the upper-chest/upper-back muscles.

Starting Position—Since it is a bit easier to learn this movement on a Smith machine than with a free bar, I'll explain the machine movement to you. Place a flat exercise bench between the machine uprights directly perpendicular to the sliding bar. Sit down beneath the bar so your shoulder joints are directly under the sliding bar when you are sitting erect. Reach up and take an overgrip on the bar, setting your hands about 2–3 inches (6–8 centimeters) wider than your shoulders on each side. Straighten your arms fully and then rotate the bar in your hands to release it (be sure to rotate it in the opposite direction when finished with your set, to relock it on the uprights).

Movement Performance—Being sure to keep your elbows back throughout the movement, slowly bend your arms and lower the bar down to touch lightly on your upper chest at the base of your neck. Without bouncing the bar off your shoulders, reverse the movement and slowly press the weight back up to a position at straight-arm's length. On the next repetition, the bar should be lowered down behind your neck to lightly touch on your trapezius muscles before it is pressed back up to straight-arm's length. Alternate reps to the front and back of your neck until you have completed the required number of counts for your set.

Common Mistakes—The most common mistake made in pressing the weight up from in front of your neck is to incline your torso backward; fight this temptation and keep your torso erect. Never bounce the bar off your upper chest or traps, and don't ever allow your elbows to travel forward ahead of the bar.

STANDING PRESSES BEHIND THE NECK

Areas Emphasized—As with the Smith-machine overhead presses just described, presses behind the neck with a barbell place the most intense stress on the anterior deltoids and triceps, with lesser amounts of stress on the medial posterior delts and the upper-back muscles. When I have been in competitive bodybuilding shape, I've received more compliments for the depth and roundness of my shoulder development than for any other body part, and I feel that presses behind the neck have done the most for that particular muscle complex.

Starting Position—Place a moderately heavy barbell on the gym floor at your feet. Take an overgrip on the bar with your hands set 4–6 inches (12–16 centimeters) wider than your shoulders on each side. Dip your hips and clean the bar up to your shoulders in one smooth motion, pushing it all the way up to straight-arm's length overhead. Your feet should be set about shoulder-width apart, and your knees should be locked throughout the movement. If you were doing presses from the front of your neck, I'd also caution you against inclining your torso backward at the waist to help cheat up the weight, but the very nature of pressing from behind your neck forces you to keep your torso bolt upright as you perform the exercise.

Movement Performance—Being sure to keep your elbows back as you do the movement, slowly lower the weight straight downward until it lightly touches your trapezius muscles at the back of your neck. Without bouncing the barbell off your traps, reverse direction and slowly press the weight back up to the starting point. Repeat the movement for the correct number of repetitions.

Common Mistakes—Kicking with your legs and/or bouncing the bar off your traps to get the movement started are the most common errors made in doing presses behind the neck. Both of these mistakes can be avoided if you are careful to perform the movement slowly and deliberately rather than with a quick, jerky cadence.

Training Tips—In the photo illustrating the finish position of this movement, you'll notice that I'm looking up at the bar. If you have any problem balancing the weight when it's overhead, looking up at it like this will solve it; otherwise, just keep your eyes focused directly forward. Presses behind the neck can be performed either standing or seated on a Smith machine, as well as in a seated position at the end of a flat exercise bench. (The second of these variations is probably the one most commonly used by serious iron pumpers.) I'd also suggest that you experiment with a variety of grip widths. The width illustrated is about as wide as you would ever want it to be, so try moving your hands a few increments inward to see how the narrower grip feels on your shoulders as you do your presses behind the neck.

Standing Presses Behind the Neck—start and finish

Standing Presses Behind the Neck— midpoint

UPRIGHT ROWS

Areas Emphasized—This exercise is the premier movement for developing the crucial deltoid-trapezius tie-ins that give your shoulders a complete look when they become well developed. Upright rows place the most emphasis on the deltoids (all three heads: anterior, medial, and posterior) and trapezius muscles. Second stress is on the biceps, brachialis, and forearm flexor muscle complexes.

Starting Position—I am using an EZ-curl bar for my photos illustrating this exercise, but a straight-handled barbell, a bar handle attached to the cable leading through a floor pulley, or two dumbbells can also be used. Regardless of the apparatus, take a narrow grip (the width of the palm of your hand is about right) in the middle of the bar, palms facing toward your body throughout the movement. Set your feet about shoulder-width apart and stand erect with your arms hanging straight down and your hands with the bar in them resting lightly against your upper thighs.

Movement Performance—Being sure to keep your elbows above the level of your hands throughout the pulling motion, slowly bend your arms and pull the weight directly upward until the backs of your hands touch the underside of your chin. Throughout the upward and downward motion of the exercise, the bar should be no more than about 2 inches (6 centimeters) away from your torso. At the top point of the exercise, squeeze your shoulder blades together and hold the peak-contracted effect for a moment before lowering the weight back to the starting point. Repeat.

Common Mistakes—Almost universally, beginning weight trainees tend to drop the bar from the top point of the movement back to the tops of their thighs. The downward momentum of the weight should be resisted so that the bar comes down a bit more slowly than it went up. There is

Upright Rows—start and finish

Upright Rows—midpoint

just as much potential for development during the negative (downward) cycle of each repetition of upright rows as during the positive cycle. Another common mistake is allowing your torso to move forward and backward as you do the movement; it's best to keep your body entirely motionless, except for your arms and shoulders. You should never jerk the weight at any point along its potential range of motion.

Training Tips—To emphasize the deltoid aspect of upright rows more, you can try using a shoulder-width grip on the bar. You'll find that you can't pull it any higher than about the middle of your chest (see the second exercise photo illustrating upright rows for the approximate top position allowed by a wider grip). For greater trapezius involvement, move your grip inward until it is as narrow as possible, with your hands actually touching each other in the middle of the bar. As mentioned earlier in this exercise description, you can also perform upright rows with two dumbbells (which is sometimes a good way to do it if you have a slight shoulder injury you're trying to protect) or with a straight bar handle attached to the cable running through a floor pulley. I'd suggest trying every variation, picking the two that work best for you, and rotating them in and out of your shoulder routine on a regular schedule.

DUMBBELL SIDE LATERALS

Areas Emphasized—This is an isolation movement that puts the most stress on the medial (side) head of your deltoid muscle complex. The anterior delts also bear a portion of the load, but most of the work is done by the medial section of the muscle. Minor secondary stress is on the trapezius muscles of the upper back.

Starting Position—Grasp two light dumbbells, set your feet about shoulder-width apart, and allow your arms to hang down from your shoulders in such a manner that the weights are pressed together 3–4 inches (9–12 centimeters) in front of your hips, palms facing inward toward each other. Bend your arms slightly and keep them rounded

like this throughout the movement. Bend slightly forward at the waist and maintain that torso attitude throughout the movement.

Movement Performance—Being sure that the dumbbell handles are kept parallel to the gym floor all the way as they are moved upward, slowly raise the weights in semicircular arcs out to your sides and slightly forward until they reach about eye level. At the top point of the movement, you should actually have the front plates of the dumbbells slightly below the level of the back plates (as if the dumbbells were bottles of milk and you were trying to pour the milk out). Hold this peak-contracted point for a moment and then slowly lower the weights back along the same arcs to the starting point. Repeat the movement for the designated number of repetitions.

Common Mistakes—The most common mistake I see inexperienced women make while they are performing dumbbell side laterals is doing the movement with their palms facing forward rather than toward the gym floor. With palms forward, this becomes an anterior deltoid isolation movement, which you don't need to do since every pressing exercise (e.g., bench presses, presses behind the neck, and so on) strongly stresses this same area. Be sure that you avoid swinging the weights upward. They should be moved slowly and only by pulling hard with the medial deltoids to complete the movement.

Training Tips—To achieve greater mental concentration during the movement, perform it with one arm at a time, holding onto a sturdy upright object with your free hand to brace your body during the execution of your lateral raises. In this case, be sure to do the same number of sets and reps with each arm. In subsequent chapters of this book, you'll learn how to do this exercise with cables as well as with dumbbells. There are many brands of exercise machines available in larger gyms on which you can duplicate this movement.

Dumbbell Side Laterals
—start and finish

Dumbbell Side Laterals
—midpoint

Arm Exercises

STANDING BARBELL CURLS

Areas Emphasized—This is the most fundamental of all biceps exercises. Standing barbell curls place direct stress on those potentially shapely muscles on the fronts of your upper arms. Secondary emphasis is on the brachialis muscles, which lie beneath the biceps, and on the forearm flexors.

Starting Position—Place a moderately heavy barbell on the gym floor in front of you and step up to it, setting your feet parallel to each other and slightly less than shoulder-width apart. Bend over and take a shoulder-width undergrip on the bar (so your palms face away from your body at the start of the movement), and then stand erect with your arms running straight down at your sides from your shoulders, the bar resting across your upper thighs. Pin your upper arms to the sides of your rib cage and keep them immobilized like this throughout the movement.

Movement Performance—Being sure to keep your wrists straight (not flexed) throughout each repetition, use biceps strength to slowly curl the weight in a semicircular arc from your legs up to a position just beneath your chin. Reverse the movement and slowly lower the weight back along the same arc until it is again resting on your thighs. Repeat the movement for the suggested number of repetitions.

Common Mistakes—There are several ways in which you can cheat while doing barbell curls. The most common is to bend forward a bit, snapping your torso backward to get the weight started, and then bending your torso backward to help finish a repetition. You can also cut the movement short, but doing so merely robs you of some of the stress your biceps should be receiving. The use of an EZ-curl bar also robs your biceps of some

Standing Barbell Curls—start and finish

growth-inducing stress. This popular piece of equipment locks your hands in a position in which your thumbs are rotated partially inward, and that shifts stress from your biceps to the brachialis. I know you'll frequently see people using an EZ-curl bar, but you'll actually get a better biceps workout using a straight-handled barbell.

Training Tips—If you develop a tendency to move your torso forward and backward to help cheat up the weight, you can break yourself of the habit by doing your barbell curls with your back pressed against the gym wall, your feet set far enough away from the wall that you won't be able to move your torso at all until you've finished your set. You'll find that you can't use as much weight this way, but you'll actually be stimulating your biceps more thoroughly with the lighter poundage.

Try varying the width of your grip on the bar. A

Standing Barbell Curls—midpoint

STANDING DUMBBELL CURLS

Areas Emphasized—As with standing barbell curls, dumbbell curls place intense stress on the biceps muscles, with lesser emphasis on the brachialis and forearm flexor muscle groups.

Starting Position—Grasp two moderately heavy dumbbells, set your feet about shoulder-width apart, and stand erect with your arms hanging down at your sides and your palms facing inward toward each other. Pin your upper arms to the sides of your rib cage and keep them there throughout the movement.

Movement Performance—In one way, dumbbell curls are superior to barbell curls, because you can supinate your hands more completely on the dumbbell movement. The function of the biceps is to both flex (bend) the arm and supinate the hand. I'll explain *supination* for your right hand, and you can easily do the mirror image of it with your left hand. Starting with the moderately heavy dumbbell in your right hand, your palm should be facing inward toward your leg at the beginning point of the movement. Using biceps strength alone, slowly curl the weight forward and upward in a semicircular arc. About a third of the way up, begin to supinate your hand, which means turning your right wrist so your palm is facing upward as you execute the middle portion of the curl. At the top of the movement, you should actually exaggerate the supination by continuing to turn your wrist as far as possible (you can see me doing this in the illustration). Once you have curled the weight all the way up, then reverse the procedure, turning your wrist in the opposite direction as you lower the weight. This opposite movement is called *pronation*. The actual standing dumbbell curl movement is done with both arms simultaneously curling the weights upward and supinating the hands. Then the weights are lowered as the hands are pronated.

wider grip—which was popularized by Arnold Schwarzenegger, incidentally—tends to work the inner head of the biceps more intensely. On the other hand, a narrow grip works the outer biceps lobe harder. If you really want to work specifically on your brachialis muscles, try doing barbell reverse curls in which you use an overgrip on the bar, your hands set about shoulder-width apart. Reverse curls intensely stress both the brachialis and the powerful supinator muscles of your forearms.

Earlier in this exercise description, I recommended doing barbell curls with your wrists held straight. This type of curl to a large degree will isolate the forearm flexor muscles from the movement. If you happen to want to develop your forearm flexors along with your biceps in the same movement, however, you can flex your wrists once the bar has reached the halfway point (at which your forearms are parallel to the gym floor).

Common Mistakes—Failure to supinate the hand is a common problem, one that robs you of much of the developmental value of dumbbell curls. Cheating the weights up by rocking your torso forward and backward is also a no-no.

Training Tips—Standing dumbbell curls can also be done alternately, one weight going up as the other descends, somewhat like a seesaw at a playground. You can make your dumbbell curls more strict by doing them seated at the end of a flat exercise bench. Seated dumbbell curls can also be done alternately.

Standing Dumbbell Curls
—start and finish

Standing Dumbbell Curls—midpoint

PULLEY PUSHDOWNS

Areas Emphasized—This movement isolates stress on the triceps muscles at the backs of your upper arms, particularly placing stress on the outer of the three triceps heads.

Starting Position—Attach a short bar handle to the end of the cable running through an overhead pulley. The best type of handle for this movement is one in which the ends are angled slightly downward, but even one that is perfectly straight will give you good triceps action. Take an overgrip on the handle at a width in which the ends of your thumbs would touch each other if you extended them. Set your feet a comfortable distance apart, about 6 inches (20 centimeters) back from the pulley, and pull the weight down so it rests across your upper thighs while your arms are straight down at your sides. Press your upper arms against the sides of your torso and keep them motionless in this position throughout your set. Lean slightly forward at the waist and maintain that torso inclination until you have finished your set.

Movement Performance—Keeping your wrists straight throughout the exercise and moving only your forearms, allow the weight to move your hands in a semicircular arc from the tops of your legs to a position against your upper chest in which your arms are completely bent. (In many respects, this arc is the reverse of the one you executed when you performed the standing barbell curls.) Reverse the movement and use only triceps strength to push the bar handle back along the same arc until it again touches your upper thighs. Repeat the movement for the desired number of repetitions.

Common Mistakes—The most common mistake is pushing the handle straight down rather than in a semicircular arc. You should also be sure to avoid letting your elbows move outward to your sides as you execute this movement. If you make

Pulley Pushdowns—start and finish

Pulley Pushdowns—midpoint

either of the foregoing mistakes, it is probable that the weight you are using is too heavy and should be reduced.

Training Tips—Over the years I've gotten a lot out of doing this movement with a shoulder-width overgrip on a longer bar handle. It can also be performed with an undergrip, although you'll discover that you can't use as much weight with that grip. Both of these variations will be explained and illustrated in detail in upcoming chapters.

LYING BARBELL TRICEPS EXTENSIONS

Areas Emphasized—These triceps extensions isolate stress almost entirely on the triceps muscles, particularly on the meaty inner and middle heads of the three-lobed muscle group.

Starting Position—Assume a narrow overgrip in the middle of a light barbell (there should be about one hand's width of space between your index fingers). Lie back on a flat exercise bench and position your feet flat on the bench by bending your legs to at least a 90-degree angle. Extend your arms straight up from your shoulders as if assuming the finish position of a narrow-grip bench press. Although I am using an EZ-curl bar in the illustrations accompanying this exercise description, you can just as easily use a straight barbell. The grip width, in either case, is the same.

Movement Performance—Keeping your upper arms and the rest of your body motionless,

Lying Barbell Triceps Extensions—start and finish

slowly bend your elbows and lower the bar to the rear, going downward in a semicircular arc until the bar lightly touches the surface of the bench just above your head. Without bouncing the weight off the bench, use triceps power to slowly move it back along the same arc to the finish point. Repeat the movement for the suggested number of repetitions.

Common Mistakes—The most common mistake made in doing any type of triceps extension is to allow your elbows to travel outward as you lower the weight. They must always remain stationary and pointed directly upward. Another error is to lower and raise the weight directly downward and upward along a vertical plane. The movement should always be semicircular.

Training Tips—Some bodybuilders prefer lowering the bar to either their foreheads or to eye level. That sort of variation is called "skull busters" for the obvious reason—you might actually bust your skull if you lose control of the weight for a moment. You should try various grips, from one as narrow as hands touching each other in the middle of the bar to one about shoulder-width apart. Each grip-width change will give you a little different feel in the triceps as you execute the movement. Barbell triceps extensions can also be performed on incline and decline benches set at various angles, something that will provide you with more variety to spice up your workouts. Regardless of the bench angle, however, it's always the same movement, and it stresses the same area—the triceps.

Lying Barbell Triceps Extensions—midpoint

Twisting Incline Sit-Ups—beginning of movement

Abdominal Exercises

. . . .

TWISTING INCLINE SIT-UPS

Areas Emphasized—All variations of sit-ups place direct stress on the rectus abdominis muscle wall, and particularly on the upper half of the complex. When you do the movement twisting from side to side, you also involve the intercostal muscles and, to some extent, the external obliques.

Starting Position—Make a low angle on a sit-up board (usually this is a ladderlike affair; hooks on the end of the board can be slipped over the rung at the most appropriate height for your

set). Lie on your back on the board, with your feet at the upper end, and hook your toes and insteps under the roller restraint or the thick loop of leather provided at the top end of the bench. Bend your legs to about a 30-degree angle and keep them bent like this throughout the movement. This knee bend takes some of the pressure off your lower back as you do the movement. Place your hands behind your head or neck and keep them there as you do your entire set.

Movement Performance—Slowly curl your torso off the board by raising first your head, then your shoulders, your upper back, and finally your lower back. As you sit up, twist your torso

Twisting Incline Sit-Ups—midpoint

Twisting Incline Sit-Ups (forward sit-up variation)—midpoint

about 45 degrees in relation to your pelvis, going first to the right and alternating right–left on each succeeding repetition. Once you feel pressure come off your abdominal muscles, reverse the procedure and return almost to the starting point. In order to keep continuous tension on the abdominal muscles, it's best to terminate the movement just short of the bench, rather than actually lying back down on the board between reps. Immediately begin your second repetition, this time twisting to the opposite side. Continue this side-to-side twisting sit-up movement until you have completed the desired number of repetitions.

Common Mistakes—The most common error made in doing any type of sit-up is to jerk your entire torso free of the board at once, rather than curling yourself upward. The movement should always be slow and controlled. Never use added weight held behind your head in this exercise, because doing so can actually broaden your waist. If

you want to increase intensity, merely raise the foot end of the bench incrementally as your abdominal muscles grow stronger and better toned.

Training Tips—The farther you twist in each direction, the greater will be the stress on (and ultimate development of) the intercostal muscles at the sides of your waist. I personally like to use a procedure on this movement in which I start out with the first rep directly forward, the second twisting to the left, the third forward, the fourth twisting to the right, the fifth forward, the sixth twisting to the left, and so on until I've finished my set.

INCLINE LEG RAISES

Areas Emphasized—This movement also places major stress on the rectus abdominis muscle wall, but more on the lower half of the muscle complex than on the upper half, which sit-ups do.

There is still a little intercostal involvement, but much less than in any type of twisting abdominal exercise.

Starting Position—Adjust the abdominal board to an appropriate angle for your set. Lie back on the board with your head at the top end. Grasp either the sides of the board or the restraint provided at the top of it to immobilize your upper body as you perform the movement. Bend your legs about 30 degrees and keep them bent at this angle throughout your set in order to remove undesirable stress from your lower back.

Movement Performance—Use abdominal strength to slowly raise your feet in a semicircular arc from the starting point to a position directly above your hips. Reverse direction and return almost to the starting position, terminating the downward arc of your legs with your heels just clear of the board. Repeat the movement with continuous tension on your midsection muscles for the recommended number of repetitions.

Common Mistakes—Never bounce your heels off the board, because that would negate the continuous tension effect of the movement. Avoid twisting from side to side, as you did with sit-ups. Never allow momentum to take over the movement; it should always be performed with a slow, controlled cadence.

Training Tips—To add intensity to incline leg raises, simply raise the head end of the board in increments as your midsection muscles grow stronger. I've seen some women add weight to this movement by holding a dumbbell between their feet, but I recommend that you avoid this practice. It will undoubtedly broaden your waistline over a period of time by overdeveloping your external oblique muscles.

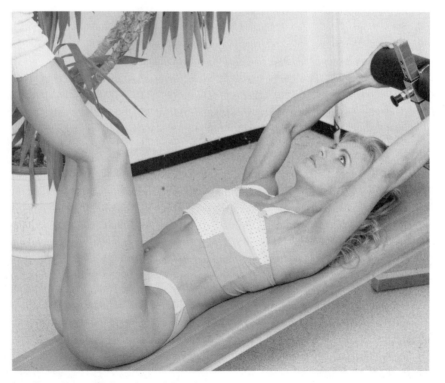

Incline Leg Raises—midpoint

Calf Exercises

. . . .

STANDING CALF MACHINE TOE RAISES

Areas Emphasized—This is the most basic movement for developing the gastrocnemius muscle of your calf, which looks like an upside-down heart when well developed and viewed from the rear.

Starting Position—Step up to the standing calf machine and bend your legs sufficiently to allow your shoulders to be positioned comfortably beneath the pads attached to the lever arms of the machine at about shoulder level. With your legs still bent, position your toes and the balls of your feet on the calf block in such a way that your heels are hanging completely off the block. You should set your feet about shoulder-width apart and point your toes forward, so your feet end up parallel to each other. Straighten your body to assume the weight attached to the machine lever arms, and then allow that weight to force your heels as far below the level of your toes as is comfortably possible.

Movement Performance—Moving only your feet and ankles, use calf strength to rise up as high as possible on your toes. Hold this peak-contracted position for a moment and then slowly lower yourself back to the starting point. Be sure that you don't bounce in the bottom position of the movement. Repeat the exercise for the suggested number of reps.

Common Mistakes—You'll frequently see women jerk the weight upward, often in a two-stage effort that involves heaving the weight up about halfway, propelled by a bounce out of the bottom position. Then they kick their knees to get the weight up the rest of the way. The movement should never be jerky but always smooth and controlled. Never bend your knees until you have completed your set and wish to exit the machine.

Standing Calf Machine Toe Raises—start and finish

Standing Calf Machine Toe Raises— midpoint

Training Tips—A common practice in doing various calf exercises is to vary foot angles from one set to the next. The most common angles are toes pointed outward at about 45 degrees, toes pointed straight forward, and toes angled inward at about 45 degrees. You can also achieve different effects on the working muscles by changing the width of your foot placement on the calf block. Try moving your feet inward, perhaps even so far that they touch in the middle of the block. Or move them outward to a point somewhat wider than the breadth of your shoulders.

SEATED CALF MACHINE TOE RAISES

Areas Emphasized—When you do calf raises with your knees bent at a 90-degree angle, the gastrocnemius is largely isolated from the exercise and most of the stress is placed on the broad, flat soleus muscle, which lies beneath the gastrocnemius. The soleus muscle is what actually gives your calf width when it is viewed from the front or back, so it's vital that you develop it to the limit.

Starting Position—Sit down on the seat of a seated calf machine and place your toes and the balls of your feet on the crossbar provided for them. Then pull the padded surfaces back toward your torso and rest them on top of your knees (these are usually adjustable in height by means of a pin, which is set in the column attached to the pads).

Seated Calf Machine Toe Raises—start and finish

Seated Calf Machine Toe Raises—midpoint

Push up with your toes so that you can push the stop bar forward to release the weight. Allow the weight attached to the lever arm of the machine to push your heels as far as is comfortably possible below the level of your toes and the balls of your feet. As you can see, my feet are set about shoulder-width apart and parallel to each other in the basic movement photos.

Movement Performance—Slowly rise up on your toes as high as possible, holding the peak-contracted position for a moment before slowly returning to the starting position. Without bouncing in the bottom position, initiate another rep. Repeat the movement until you have done the required number of repetitions.

Common Mistakes—Avoid bouncing in the bottom position. Try to keep from jerking at any point along the full range of motion in this exercise. Keep everything smooth and under full control.

Training Tips—In the close-up photos of this movement, you can easily see how I angle my toes either inward or outward for different effects on the muscles of my lower legs. You should experiment with different toe positions to find the ones that work best for you. Generally you will find that the soleus muscles respond best to somewhat lower reps than you would use to train your gastrocnemius muscles. In my own case, I like reps in the range of 15–25 for the gastrocs and reps of 10–15 for the soleus muscles.

Seated Calf Machine Toe Raises (variation with toes pointed outward)—midpoint

Seated Calf Machine Toe Raises (variation with toes pointed inward)—midpoint

Suggested Beginning-Level Routines

· ·

Now that you've mastered 26 basic exercises for all parts of your body, it's time to combine them into training routines that you can use immediately to begin improving your body's appearance, your general health, and your physical strength. I have formulated three routines for you, each of which should be performed three nonconsecutive days per week (e.g., Mondays, Wednesdays, and Fridays). Start out with Routine #1 in Figure 4-1 and follow it for six weeks, and then switch to Routine #2 for another six weeks, and finally move on to Routine #3 for an additional six weeks. After 18 weeks of steady training on these three graduated-intensity programs, you will be safely through the beginning level of weight training and ready to move on to the even more highly intense intermediate-level training schedules presented in Chapter 6.

If necessary, review all of the beginning-level information and training tips presented in Chapter 2 before actually starting to pump iron. Repetition can be boring, but it's the key to full mastery of those diverse topics discussed in that chapter. I don't think you can read it through too many times. Each time you review the information in Chapter 2, you'll notice something new that didn't register on your conscious mind during a previous reading.

Okay, are you dressed for your workout and ready to go? Remember that starting weights are expressed as a percentage of your body weight (c/o Bwt.). Let's get into the gym and start pumping iron!

Figure 4-1. Beginning-Level Workout Routines

Routine 1

Exercise	Sets	Reps	% Bwt.
Angled Leg Presses	3	10–15	50%
Lat Machine Pulldowns Behind Neck	3	8–12	25%
Stiff-Legged Deadlifts	3	10–15	30%
Bench Presses	3	6–10	20%
Upright Rows	3	8–12	20%
Standing Barbell Curls	3	8–12	20%
Pulley Pushdowns	3	8–12	15%
Twisting Incline Sit-Ups	2	20–25	—
Standing Calf Machine Toe Raises	3	15–20	50%

Routine 2

Exercise	Sets	Reps
Squats	4	10–15
Lying Leg Curls	3	10–15
One-Arm Dumbbell Bent-Over Rows	4	8–12
Parallel-Grip Front Lat Machine Pulldowns	3	8–12
Stiff-Legged Deadlifts	2	10–15
Incline Presses	4	6–10

Exercise	Sets	Reps
Flat-Bench Dumbbell Presses	3	8–12
Standing Presses Behind Neck	4	6–10
Dumbbell Side Laterals	3	8–12
Standing Dumbbell Curls	4	8–12
Lying Barbell Triceps Extensions	4	8–12
Incline Leg Raises	3	20–25
Seated Calf Machine Toe Raises	4	12–15

Routine 3

Exercise	Sets	Reps
Squats	5	10–15
Leg Extensions	3	10–15
Lying Leg Curls	4	10–15
Barbell Bent-Over Rows	4	8–12
Lat Machine Pulldowns Behind Neck	4	8–12
Stiff-Legged Deadlifts	3	10–15
Machine Incline Presses	4	6–10
Barbell Decline Presses	4	8–12
Machine Overhead Presses (Front and Back)	4	6–10
Dumbbell Side Laterals	3	8–12
Upright Rows	3	8–12
Standing Barbell Curls	3	8–12
Standing Alternate Dumbbell Curls	2	8–12
Pulley Pushdowns	3	8–12
Lying Barbell Triceps Extensions	2	8–12
Twisting Incline Sit-Ups	2–3	20–30
Incline Leg Raises	2–3	20–30
Standing Calf Machine Toe Raises	4	15–20
Seated Calf Machine Toe Raises	3	10–15

5
Intermediate-Level Training Tips

· ·

If you have been mastering and using the information in each chapter sequentially, you should already notice improvements in your appearance and physical condition. The first thing you'll be aware of is a strength increase, which becomes evident during the first one or two weeks of training. While men tend to gain their strength relatively evenly in both upper and lower bodies, women grow stronger much more quickly in their legs.

Over your first 4–6 weeks of steady training, you will probably go up 20–30 pounds on squats and leg presses and 5–10 pounds on leg extensions and leg curls. Upper-body strength improves more slowly, but you will at least gain several new reps each month on torso and arm movements, if you don't actually go up in weight on these exercises.

Most novice bodybuilders take up the activity believing that only the strength component of their physical condition will improve. By now, however, you may have personally discovered that both flexibility and cardiorespiratory endurance also improve. Granted, flexibility and endurance improve more slowly than strength, but they *do* go up. For faster results, add stretching and aerobics to your training schedule.

The more quickly you go through a weight workout (i.e., the less you rest between sets), the more quickly cardiorespiratory fitness improves. Combining strength-training sessions with aerobic workouts will result in truly outstanding heart and lung fitness.

As long as you are careful to use a complete range of motion on all weight-training movements, you will gradually improve full-body flexibility. By combining strength-training workouts with stretching sessions (as outlined in Chapter 9), you can develop flexibility that will probably impress a circus acrobat after a year or two.

During a period of 6–12 months of combined weight training, aerobics, and stretching, you can develop an ultimate degree of physical fitness, with all three components—strength, cardiorespiratory fitness, and flexibility—nearly at maximum levels. Once you achieve this type of physical condition, you will find that it is relatively easy to maintain it at high level. It is much like a jet airliner, which requires much more fuel per minute of flight to climb to an altitude of 35,000 feet than it does to continue cruising for hours at that flight level.

This series of photos illustrates my yearly progress from novice in 1982 to runner-up Ms. Olympia in 1988.

1982

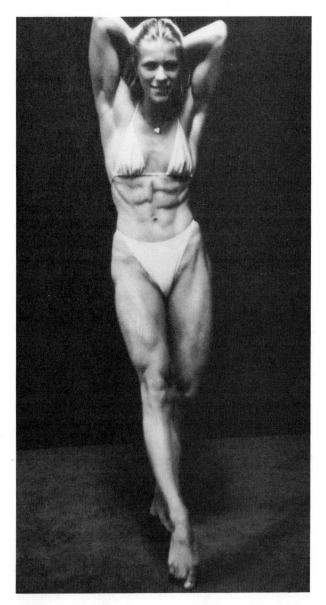

1983

1984

1985

1986

1988

Training Partners

One classic debate among experienced weight trainees concerns whether it is best to work out with a training partner or by oneself. Each alternative has ardent proponents, who have valid reasons for following their chosen philosophy. I personally prefer to use a partner in the gym, but I have trained for extended periods of time on my own when one has been unavailable, so I thoroughly understand each argument.

Women who prefer having a training partner say that the partner helps them stay motivated to train hard all of the time. Invariably, a healthy competitive spirit develops, with each partner trying to outdo the other in terms of the weight used and reps performed on each movement in their routine.

Interestingly, male-female partnerships are more common these days than same-sex partnerships. On an average, men are significantly stronger than women pound for pound, while women have better endurance and higher pain thresholds than men. As a result, a male partner might stimulate you to train heavier, while you might push him to do more reps each set and go more quickly from one set to the next.

Sometimes having a training partner causes a woman to train more consistently. You are much less likely to miss a scheduled training session when you know that workout partner is waiting patiently for you at the gym. And you are equally less likely to arrive at the gym later than you should for a session of pumping iron.

On the flip side of the coin, each training partner will be forced to give up some of his or her general training philosophy in a compromise between workout styles that may be naturally divergent. Sometimes an inexperienced trainee will totally follow a more experienced woman's program in an effort to learn the secrets of successful bodybuilding training. But sooner or later playing second fiddle becomes boring or unproductive for the junior partner, and she either goes solo or starts to look around for a better partner.

Another weakness of training partnerships is that they tend to do away with spontaneity from one workout to the next. Some of the greatest bodybuilders competing today have learned that they get more out of their workouts if they do a different type of routine every time they train each body part. This technique is called *muscle confusion*, and it is discussed in greater detail in Chapter 7. For now, you need to understand that this is a very productive advanced training principle when it is used correctly, but it can't be used easily if you have a training partner going around the gym in your wake.

An ultimate bodybuilder develops an instinct for precisely what her body requires in terms of exercise each day, and she can then tailor that day's workout to these requirements. Training becomes almost an existential experience, which can only occur when an experienced woman trains on her own.

If you decide to give a training partner a trial, look for someone of nearly equal strength levels (so you don't have to change the weight on the bar every set), one who works out at the same time of day as you do, and one who trains the same number of days each week. Once you locate a candidate, sit down and discuss where your training philosophies may overlap and diverge. Compromise a bit and then give it a try!

Training to Failure

In serious iron pumping, training intensity is exactly what you make of it. The higher the intensity of each workout, the greater the degree of muscle hypertrophy resulting from it.

Train in a public gym for a few days and you'll see many women just going through the motions. They are lackadaisical as they use relatively light training weights, and they receive little benefit from their workouts. Some women actually train like this on purpose, totally petrified that they will push too hard and end up with—ugh!—real muscles.

As you already know at this point, well-toned skeletal muscles are a desirable trait and one that is somewhat difficult to attain. They add feminine curves to your body, improve sports performance and physical condition, and add quality to life in general. From my viewpoint, I can't understand why any woman wouldn't want to achieve a high degree of muscle hypertrophy. I certainly hope you agree with me on this score.

In order to achieve maximum hypertrophy, you need to understand the concept of *training to failure* each set. Later I will discuss the various methods of pushing some sets *past* the normal failure point. The closer to failure you push a set—and the farther past failure you can train—the greater the amount of hypertrophy you will achieve from your workouts. There is a linear, one-to-one relationship between training intensity and bodybuilding results.

Training to failure involves pushing a set to the point at which your muscles have become momentarily too fatigued to complete another full repetition in strict form. You'll still, for instance, be able to curl a barbell upward for part of a repetition in good form—or complete a full rep by cheating with leg kick and back bend—but you won't be able to do another full, good rep without resting for a few seconds to allow your fatigued biceps muscles to recover some of their contractile ability.

The first thing you will notice about pushing a set to the point of momentary muscle failure is that it hurts! The farther you push a set, the more it will hurt, but the more you will get out of it. This pain is experienced both immediately (during a set) and later (in the form of muscle soreness 2–3 days after your workout for a particular body part).

I must emphasize that the immediate form of pain is not dangerous in any way. It is merely an intense burning sensation in the working muscles caused by a rapid, heavy buildup of fatigue toxins. While a muscle is contracting intensely, blood flow into and out of it is hampered, and fatigue by-products cannot be flushed out of the muscle. As soon as you terminate a set and relax, the working muscles' normal circulation is restored, fatigue toxins are rapidly flushed away and eliminated, and the pain quickly abates.

One of the oldest and truest maxims in bodybuilding is: *no pain, no gain*. As long as you can distinguish the difference between injury pain and fatigue pain, you should look forward to and welcome the onset of pain in your muscles. Ultimately, you will grow better able mentally to withstand this pain, which allows you to burst past the pain barrier that halts lesser women and make greatly accelerated gains in strength, body mass, and muscle tone.

Training Past Failure

If pushing a set to failure gives you accelerated results from your workouts, pushing *past* failure yields even greater and faster gains. There are five methods of past-failure training—cheating reps, forced reps, burns, descending sets, and negative repetitions. Let's take each training principle in turn and describe how you can use it yourself in one of your upcoming gym sessions.

The cheating method involves first pushing a set to the failure point in strict form and then using extraneous body movement to drive yourself to complete 2–3 additional reps beyond failure. Let's say you have been doing standing barbell presses with 60 pounds as a means of improving your shoulder and triceps muscles. After six full reps, you fail to push the seventh one higher than the top of your head. All this means is that your fatigued deltoid and arm muscles can no longer do a rep with 60 pounds, but you can undoubtedly complete one with 55, a second with 50, and perhaps a third with 45 pounds. So how do you progressively remove weight from the bar within 2–3 seconds on successive past-failure reps?

The easiest way to accomplish this task is to cheat just enough to ram the bar past the sticking point, from which you can complete a new repetition on your own before lowering the bar back to shoulder level while resisting the weight's downward momentum. You will almost instinctively learn how to cheat on various basic exercises. For shoulder presses, to illustrate, you need to simply kick a bit with your knees to get the bar started and incline your torso backward a few degrees to complete the movement.

It should be obvious that you will need to cheat a little harder on each successive rep, but let's go through the reason why anyway. Once your shoulder and arm muscles have reached the failure point, they are fatiguing very rapidly with every extra rep. To compensate for the delts and tris losing strength and contractile ability, you merely cheat a tad bit more on each new repetition.

One truism in bodybuilding is that inexperienced trainees cheat to make a set easier to complete, while veteran women cheat to make it harder. To make a set harder to complete, always do 6–8 reps to failure in strict form first and then cheat just enough on each past-failure rep to get past the movement's sticking point.

More than 2–3 cheating reps—or 2–3 forced reps, for that matter—put you into a state of rapidly diminishing returns. Your muscles grow overly fatigued very quickly until they can't contract powerfully enough to get further benefit from a set past the second or third past-failure repetition.

The main advantage of cheating reps is that they do not require a training partner to spot and assist you. The main disadvantage is that cheating is an imprecise means of effectively removing iron from the bar. Sometimes you don't do enough of a cheat to blast the bar past its sticking point. Other times you cheat too much and the bar flies up to the completion point, robbing your targeted muscles of most of the stress they should receive.

In forced reps a bar is lightened much more precisely but a training partner is required, sometimes even two. Let's use as an example incline presses for the upper chest, anterior deltoids, and triceps. You load up an Olympic bar with 115 pounds, station your partner on the flat platform at the head end of the bench, take a correct grip on the bar, and then have your spotter help you remove the weight from the rack up to a starting position, your arms straight and the bar directly above your shoulder joints. Do a set to failure in strict style. As soon as you fail, your partner pulls up on the middle of the bar just enough to remove 5–10 pounds from the bar, the absolute minimum amount that will allow you to force out another rep. On a second forced repetition, your buddy pulls up even harder, and on a possible third rep, he or she pulls up still more on the bar.

Obviously, forced reps are more precise than cheating counts, because a third party can easily gauge how hard to tug up on the bar. As with cheating reps, more than 2–3 forced repetitions are gilding the lily.

Both cheating and forced reps are extremely high-intensity training techniques. It would be foolhardy to jump into full-scale use of either principle in each gym session, because you would experience intense muscle soreness in the days following such an all-out workout. Start out with one cheating or forced-reps set on a single basic movement for each body part as you come to it in the rotation of your split routine. After a week's break-in, add another past-failure set, and increase high-intensity sets by one each week per body part, until you reach peak intensity.

It would be inaccurate to say that forced reps and cheating work for everyone. A significant number of women bodybuilders get all of the muscle stimulation they require from simply going to failure on several or all sets of a movement. Pushing past the failure point inevitably sends this type of bodybuilder into a state of overtraining in which she makes no gains.

Burns are another means of pushing a set past failure and do not require a spotter standing by. Burns are a great technique for use in a home gym, where a competent training partner is often unavailable.

Burns are so named because they are rapid, short-range movements that cause the muscles to feel like someone is ironing them. As in a set taken to failure, this deep burning sensation rapidly abates as soon as you complete a set, when full and unimpeded blood circulation returns to the resting muscles.

With the women I coach, I find it easiest to teach the burns principle using sets of standing calf raises on a machine. This is because it's easy to bounce upward and downward over a three- to four-inch range of motion (ROM) on standing calf raises, with the machine controlling the movement. So let's use this exercise to illustrate the burns technique.

After your warm-up, load up the calf machine with a weight heavy enough to stop you after the 10th to 15th full positive and negative cycle of a repetition. Dip your knees in order to position the machine yokes across your shoulders, position the balls of your feet 10–12 inches apart on the edge of the calf block, and finally straighten your torso and legs to bear the weight, making certain that you keep your body straight until

you complete your set. Relax your calf muscles so that the weight attached to the yokes across your shoulders pushes your heels as far below the level of your toes and the balls of your feet as is comfortably possible.

Start your set with slow movements over the longest range of motion you can achieve. Let's say you begin to lose a half inch of ROM each rep at the 10th, until you reach the point of repetition 15 at which you can't get your heels any higher than the level of your toes and the balls of your feet. We'll consider this as having pushed your set to the point of failure.

After the 15th rep, relax your calves suddenly so you rebound out of the bottom position of your movement, pushing maximally hard with your calves in order to drive upward until your heels are approximately at the level of your toes. Immediately bounce back downward and upward again. Continue the set until you can no longer stand the pain, allow the weight to return to its supports by bending your knees, and step away from the machine. Alternately stretch each lower leg for 15- to 20-second bouts, until the burning sensation goes away. Then fire yourself up for another set of calf raises with burns at the end of it.

I've just described how to do burns in the bottom position of a calf-training movement. Burns can be performed in either the middle or upper range just as profitably. On pulley push-downs for your triceps, for example, you can do 8–10 quick burns over a 6-inch range of motion in the middle of the movement. On leg extensions for your quadriceps, you can perform burns over the upper 4–6 inches of ROM, lowering down from the top point of your exercise and immediately raising the weight back up to the straight-legged position.

When I don't have a training partner for a workout, I'll do burns on the last set or two of nearly all basic exercises performed in my routine. I particularly believe you profit from doing burns in the upper ROM of each bodybuilding exercise. This is because you are contracting a maximum number of muscle fibers when a working skeletal muscle is fully contracted. This technique is called *peak contraction*, and it's fully discussed in Chapter 7. For now, believe me when I say that you place more intense stimulation on a muscle when weight is still on it in the position at which the muscle is maximally shortened, or contracted.

To review, all of your burns must be performed after you have done a set to failure with full positive and negative cycles of an exercise. The burns should be quick, short, bouncy movements. You should do something in the range of 10–15 burns each set you push past the point of momentary muscle failure.

As with cheating and forced reps, burns are a highly intense style of training, much more intense than normal to-failure sets. To avoid debilitating muscle soreness, gradually begin using this technique over a period of several weeks. Start with one set of burns on a single basic exercise for each body part and then add a new set of burns each succeeding week until you are doing enough to saturation-bomb every muscle group.

A few bodybuilders will experiment with cheating reps, forced reps, burns, descending sets, and negative repetitions only to discover that these techniques are too intense. Following them will cause such a trainee to overtrain, with the negative results already pointed out. In severe cases of overtraining, you can even begin regressing from workout to workout, week to week, until you take a brief layoff and drop the aforementioned high-intensity techniques from your training philosophy once you are back in the gym.

Overtraining is one of the most important training problems for serious women weight trainees to avoid. It will be discussed in detail later in this chapter, so pay attention to what I say in that vitally important section of this book.

Descending sets are another high-intensity training principle you can utilize in your workouts to smash past the normal failure point. Descending sets were popularized by the famous Austrian-born American bodybuilder and actor Arnold Schwarzenegger. He referred to this technique, back in the 1970s when he was using it in every workout, as *stripping sets*, a designation still occasionally heard in public gyms and eating establishments where bodybuilders congregate. Call the principle whatever feels natural to you, keeping in mind that it is most commonly referred to as descending sets these days.

While you can sometimes perform descending sets on your own, they usually require one or two spotters. I'll now describe the use of two training partners to help you with a descending set of barbell preacher curls, which are done to build up the lower section of your biceps, down near the elbow. Load up a barbell with small plates (the sequence on each side must be identical), leaving the collars off the bar. Be sure you have thoroughly warmed up your arm muscles, so it becomes impossible to injure your biceps. For the sake of illustration, let's say you have loaded up the bar with 65 pounds, the outer few plates on each side being five pounders.

Drape yourself over the gym preacher bench and have one partner hand you the bar at straight-arm's length; take a medium grip on the barbell handle. Slowly curl the weight upward and downward in strict form over a full ROM until you fail on the seventh or eighth rep. With one partner stationed at each end of the bar, they can alertly and simultaneously remove a predetermined number of plates (say 5–10 pounds) from each end of the bar once you've failed and the bar is again at the starting point with your arms locked straight. Continue your set for 3–5 additional counts with the lightened barbell until you fail again. Your partners can then strip another 5–10 pounds off each end of the bar, allowing you to grind out 3–5 final, excruciatingly intense repetitions.

I have witnessed several elite-level women bodybuilders doing more than the described two-weight reductions in a descending set. But in my own experience, the muscles become excessively weakened by fatigue after two strips, making a third, fourth, or fifth poundage drop superfluous.

On machine movements you can get by with doing descending sets with a single partner, who kneels by the weight stack and swiftly moves the pin each time you fail a rep. On lying leg curls for your hamstrings, for example, a partner can almost instantly lighten the weight if she is alert and quick with the pin.

You can even do stripping sets with no training partner at all if you have available a rack of fixed pairs of dumbbells in 2½- or 5-pound increments. Warm up your shoulder-girdle muscles and then start at the heavy end of the weight stack. Grasp the heaviest pair of dumbbells with which you can accomplish at least 6–8 reps of standing dumbbell presses, cleaning them to your shoulders. You are now ready to do overhead presses in descending-sets fashion without the aid of a spotter.

Do 6–8 repetitions to momentary failure, immediately rack the dumbbells, and instantly pick up the next lightest pair of weights; clean them to your shoulders, and do as many strict reps as possible. Continue working down the rack like this until you either reach the lightest available pair of dumbbells or come to the point at which you can no longer complete at least 4–5 reps, regardless of how hard you struggle.

You have just completed a solo set of descending-sets reps, and your shoulder and arm muscles will be so pumped up that they'll look like balloons, very hard and crenulated balloons. Initially, you probably won't need to perform more than one all-out stripping set of each exercise.

But after a few workouts, you may wish to jump your training intensity upward by adding a second or even a third descending set to each basic exercise in your training schedule.

In my own case, I use descending sets a bit conservatively in comparison with many elite bodybuilders. Let's use lat machine pulldowns to illustrate how I integrate stripping sets into a back workout. Assume that I'll complete four sets of pulldowns before moving on to a new back movement.

On the first three sets of pulldowns, I will take each one as close to the failure point as possible, given that day's energy levels and my available mental drive. The fourth set is also taken to failure but extended with descending sets. My training partner knows when I'm at the failure point, and she pulls down on the lat bar with enough pressure to give me 2–3 highly intense forced reps. She quickly moves from a position behind me to a point beside the weight stack and instantly moes the selector pin to lighten the weight by 10–15 percent. I repeat the process of going to failure with the lightened weight, with her again giving me 2–3 forced reps. One last drop in poundage with forced reps and descending sets will burn out my back and arm muscles, and I will have done everything possible to bomb those muscles to the limit of human endurance.

With pulling exercises, it's essential to use straps to reinforce your grip on the bar. Otherwise you'll probably lose your grip on the lat bar before you've driven yourself to the max on your set of pulldowns. I'll explain and show you with sequential photos how to use these straps a bit later in this chapter.

Every new intensity technique—including descending sets—takes you one more rung up the ladder of training intensity. Show a little respect for new training principles and slowly work each one into your system. If you slowly augment your use of a new intensity technique, you will avoid painfully sore muscles two or three days after a harder-than-usual gym workout.

Negative reps can also be exploited to help you stress a muscle to the utmost in a workout. Each repetition is divided into two cycles—the positive (upward) and negative (downward) movements. Twenty-odd years ago German exercise physiologists experimented with the positive and negative cycles on various exercises, eventually concluding that the negative cycle of a repetition can accelerate muscle hypertrophy *if* a heavy weight is placed on the muscles resisting the eccentric (negative) cycle of each rep.

Bodybuilders quickly embraced this new technique and by now nearly all serious trainees place some type of emphasis on every negative repetition. In the purest form of negatives, a training partner lifts a very heavy weight up for you, whereupon you slowly lower it while mightily resisting its downward momentum. Obviously, it's difficult to find other people in the gym who are willing to give up some of their own workouts to help you with pure negatives.

A much easier method—called negative emphasis—can be used in most machine movements. It doesn't require the use of a training partner. As with the burns principle, let's use a calf movement to illustrate negative emphasis in action during an actual training session. Let's use calf presses on a leg-press machine.

Load up a 45-degree-angled leg-press machine slide, sit in the machine, and place only your toes and the balls of your feet on the bottom edge of the slide. I normally do calf presses with my feet about shoulder-width apart, feet parallel to each other.

Straighten your legs and hold them straight throughout your set. Relax your calf muscles so your toes travel a few inches toward your face. This places a beneficial prestretch on your calf muscles. Never neglect stretching your calves on weight exercises as well as between sets. Return to the completely stretched point at the end of each full rep.

Once you are set up correctly, slowly extend your feet to the limit and then return to the starting point. Continue to do the movement with both legs until you experience a moderate burning sensation in your gastrocnemius muscles. Immediately start the second phase of this technique by pushing up with both feet and lowering with only one, being careful to resist the downward force of the weight as strongly as you can with the one foot that is lowering it. Be careful to alternate working legs with each succeeding repetition until you can't stand the pain or are unable to push the weight out to full-foot extension.

Going up on two and down on one places very heavy stress on the muscles over the negative cycle of each movement, and this is what negative emphasis entails. As long as you do machine exercises only, you will profit greatly from using this technique. You'd look pretty goofy and perhaps might seriously injure yourself on free-weight bench presses if you tried this technique and took one arm off the barbell handle. You'd probably injure yourself as the heavy end of the bar crashed down on your chest or neck. Of course, doing benches on a machine (e.g., Nautilus, Universal Gym machines, or any of several more found in commercial gyms) is an appropriate practice.

If you want to emphasize the negative on a free-weight movement, the easiest way is to lower the weight more slowly than usual. I recommend that beginning bodybuilders get into the habit of taking 2–3 seconds to raise the weight and 3–4 seconds to lower it. To emphasize the negative, you should still take 2–3 seconds to raise it but extend the lowering cycle until it takes up to 6–8 seconds to complete the movement.

Supersets

Supersets comprise about three additional rungs up the ladder of training intensity that you are actively climbing. You are already familiar with the two most common means of increasing training-resistance intensity—gradually increasing the number of repetitions you do with a set weight in an exercise and progressively adding new plates to the barbell, dumbbells, or machine used in a particular movement. When you learned how to increase training resistance in Chapter 2, you mastered the art of combining each of the foregoing methods over an extended period of time to stimulate increases in muscle mass and strength.

When playing with weights and reps on an exercise, you can also increase resistance intensity by keeping poundages and repetitions constant for several sets of an exercise while systematically decreasing the length of rest intervals between sets.

Relatively inexperienced weight trainees usually play only with weight-rep schemes, while competitive bodybuilders use all three methods, emphasizing shortened rest intervals when peaking for a competition. This technique of gradually reducing rest intervals between sets is called quality training, and it is discussed in greater detail in Chapter 7.

One way weight-training enthusiasts decrease the average length of rest intervals between sets is to combine two exercises one right after the other, with minimal rest between them (certainly no longer than 3–5 seconds) and a normal length of rest interval between exercise compounds. Such two-movement compounds are called supersets.

The least intense form of supersets combines two exercises for antagonistic muscle groups such as biceps-triceps, forearm flexors-extensors, chest-back, or quadriceps-hamstrings. I al- ways recommend that a novice to supersets start with biceps-triceps compounds, because they use up less energy than other groupings and place less stress on the cardiorespiratory system. Then as aerobic and local muscle endurance improves, the novice can move up to chest-back supersets and a little later to supersets for the quads and hamstrings.

Let's use a typical biceps-triceps combo to illustrate how you should do supersets. So that you won't waste time moving between exercises, start by setting all of your equipment for alternate dumbbell curls right next to an overhead pulley on which you will do pushdowns. Pick up the dumbbells and do a set of 8–10 reps, going to within about 90% of failure. Immediately set down the dumbbells, step over to the pulley, grasp its handle, and do 8–10 reps of pushdowns with about the same degree of intensity as you did the set of curls. This completes one superset for two antagonistic muscle groups. Rest 60–90 seconds and then repeat the superset. Rest again, and conclude this section of your upper-arm workout with a third dumbbell curls-pulley pushdowns superset.

A significantly more intense superset combines two exercises for the same muscle group. Following are examples of this type of superset for each primary muscle group that you will train:

Legs = Angled Leg Presses + Leg Extensions

Lats = Front Pulldowns + Stiff-Arm Pulldowns

Pectorals = Dumbbell Incline Presses + Incline Flyes

Deltoids = Dumbbell Side Laterals + Machine Rear Laterals

Calves = Seated Calf Machine Toe Raises + Standing Calf Toe Machine Raises

Biceps = Seated Dumbbell Curls + Pulley Preacher Curls

Triceps = Lying Barbell Triceps Extensions + Close-Grip Bench Presses

With some experimentation, you will discover many other superset combinations for each body part. There are hundreds of them, so don't get lost safari hunting for your full bag of supersets.

A final, very intense type of superset is called pre-exhaustion (pre-ex) supersets. I will discuss this more intense technique shortly, after you understand the difference between basic and isolation exercises as well as their various uses in a serious bodybuilder's workouts. This is necessary because pre-ex supersets compound a basic movement and an isolation exercise for the same torso muscle group.

Basic vs. Isolation Exercises

Experienced and novice bodybuilders alike are often ignorant of the differences between the various functions of basic and isolation exercises. Those who do take the time to explore the differences between these types of movements, however, will not only get a lot more out of their workouts but will also become effective competitive bodybuilders much sooner.

Basic exercises are those that work large muscle groups in conjunction with other large and/or small body parts. Typical examples of basic exercises are barbell bench presses and seated pulley rows. Benches primarily work the pectorals, but your deltoids, triceps, and even some upper-back muscles also come into play when blasting a heavy weight up off your chest to straight-arm's length. While pulley rows primarily stress the lats, also affected are your traps, erectors, biceps, brachialis, and forearm flexor muscles.

In contrast, isolation movements stress a single muscle group—or sometimes even part of a muscle—in relative isolation from the rest of your muscle complexes. For the chest muscles, a pec-deck flye movement isolates the pectorals, with only a minimum assist from the anterior deltoids. The lats can be isolated by doing barbell bent-arm pullovers or pullovers on a Nautilus machine, both of which stress the upper-back muscles with minimal help from the chest muscles.

You will find a comprehensive list of the best basic and isolation exercises for each muscle group in Figure 5-1 on the following page. Check it out as you read the rest of this section, because it will make things a lot clearer for you.

A good example of an isolation movement that hits just one section of a muscle group is incline dumbbell flyes, in which mainly the upper pectorals are stressed. Only minimal assistance is given by the lower and middle pecs and the anterior delts when you perform this exercise.

Intelligent bodybuilders will concentrate mainly on basic exercises during an off-season building cycle, because these movements develop the most muscle mass. Prior to a competition, however, they will shift the focus increasingly toward isolation movements, which add detail to each muscle group and deep separations between the major muscles.

Only a handful of veteran competitive bodybuilders will perform either all basic or all isolation movements in their routines. Usually they will utilize a mix of the two types of exercises, with emphasis on one or the other. In my own case, I do about 65% basic exercises and 35% isolation movements in the off-season. When peaking for a competition, I reverse this ratio, doing 35% basic exercises and 65% isolation movements.

Bodybuilders with only a few weeks or months of steady training behind them should base their entire workout on basic exercises. As they gain experience and greater physical devel-

Figure 5-1. The Best Basic and Isolation Exercises for Each Muscle Group

Body Part	Basic Exercises	Isolation Exercises
Quadriceps	Squats, Leg Presses (all versions), Front Squats, Lunges	Leg Extensions, Leg Adductions, Leg Abductions, Front-Leg Kicks
Hamstrings, Glutes	Squats, Leg Presses, Lunges, Stiff-Legged Deadlifts, Good Mornings, Hyperextensions	Lying/Seated/Standing Leg Curls, Rear-Leg Kicks
Middle Back (Lats)	Chins, Pulldowns, Pulley/Barbell/Dumbbell/T-Bar Rows	Bent-Arm/Stiff-Arm Pullovers, Stiff-Arm Pulldowns
Upper Back (Traps)	Barbell/Cable/Dumbbell Upright Rows	Barbell/Dumbbell/Machine Shrugs
Lower Back (Spinal Erectors)	Deadlifts, Stiff-Legged Deadlifts, Power Cleans	Hyperextensions, Machine Lower-Back Movements
Chest (Pectorals)	Incline/Flat-Bench/Decline Barbell/Dumbbell/Machine Presses, Parallel Bar Dips	Incline/Flat-Bench/Decline Dumbbell/Cable/Machine Flyes, Cable Crossovers
Shoulders (Deltoids)	Barbell/Dumbbell/Machine Overhead Presses, Barbell/Dumbbell/Cable Upright Rows	Dumbbell/Cable/Machine Front/Side/Bent-Over Laterals
Biceps	Chins, Pulldowns, Standing Barbell Curls, Standing Dumbbell Curls	Dumbbell/Machine/Cable Concentration Curls
Triceps	All Bench/Overhead Presses, Parallel Bar Dips (torso erect)	Standing/Seated/Incline/Flat-Bench/Decline Barbell/Cable/Machine Triceps Extensions
Forearms	Barbell/Cable Reverse Curls, Reverse Preacher Curls, Hammer Curls, Zottman Curls	Barbell/Dumbbell Wrist Curls (preferably with flat bench supporting forearms), Standing Behind-Back Wrist Curls
Calves	Jumping Squats, Free-Weighted Calf Raises	Standing/Seated Calf-Machine Raises, One-Legged Calf Raises, Calf Presses, Hack-Machine Calf Raises
Abdominals	Sit-Ups, Leg Raises, Hanging Leg Raises	Crunches (all variations, including machine), Barbell/Dumbbell Side Bends

opment, they can begin to incorporate more isolation movements into their routines. The first isolation exercises that will usually be included are various types of dumbbell lateral raises for the deltoids, concentration curls for the biceps, pulley pushdowns for tris, and leg extensions and leg curls for the upper legs.

Over a period of a year or two, bodybuilders gain sufficient experience to be able to include isolation exercises in approximately half of their routines. A 50-50 ratio of basic/isolation movements is perfect for most advanced bodybuilders. Contest aspirants like me can play with various ratios of basic/isolation exercises until they work out a system that uniquely suits them.

The key to deciding what ratio is best for you is to evaluate which physical quality you most need to improve—muscle mass or intramuscular detail. Ultimately most serious weight trainees will adopt my approximate ratios of 65/35 in the off-season and 35/65 when they are in a peaking cycle prior to a competition.

Knowledge of which isolation and basic exercises are best for you comes in handy when you have a lagging torso muscle group, be it pectorals, deltoids, or latissimus dorsi. On such laggards you can use a high-intensity training technique called pre-exhaustion supersets in which both isolation and basic movement for a particular torso muscle group are combined.

When a torso muscle complex lags, it's usually because the arm muscles tire too early for you to get the most out of a basic exercise for the targeted muscle. For example, the smaller triceps muscles fatigue and fail long before you have pushed your larger pectorals to the limit with bench presses or your delts to the wall with standing barbell presses. And your similarly smaller biceps tire and fail before you've gotten sufficient lat stimulation from barbell rows, chins, or lat machine pulldowns.

The secret to solving this problem lies in first doing an isolation exercise for the torso group, a movement that pre-exhausts your torso muscle complex. Then you immediately superset that isolation movement with a basic exercise for the same area. It's essential that you rest no more than 3–5 seconds between supersets, however, because a pre-exhausted muscle recuperates very quickly; and if too much time elapses while you're hunting up equipment for the second movement, you spoil most of the pre-ex effect.

To most efficiently use pre-exhaustion, remember to put out equipment for both exercises beforehand so that you can drop one piece of resistance training equipment and *immediately* pick up the other piece. Allowing a pre-exed muscle only 10 seconds of rest allows it to recover up to 50% of its original energy reserves and strength.

Typical examples of pre-exhaustion supersets for each torso muscle group are as follows:

Chest = Flat-Bench Flyes + Bench Presses

Delts = Dumbbell Side Laterals + Standing Barbell Presses

Lats = Barbell Bent-Arm Pullovers + Lat Machine Pulldowns

Now that you understand how pre-exhaustion works, you should be able to come up with several other pre-ex supersets for each torso muscle group. It will doubtless seem like I'm beating a dead horse, but break in slowly to pre-ex, or you will rue the day I wrote this section.

Pre-exhaustion can also be used on your quadriceps muscles. Many bodybuilders fail to complete an extra, vitally important rep or two of squats because their lower backs—not their quads—fail to bear up under the stress placed on the lower body. In such a case, you can superset leg extensions (an isolation exercise for quads) with squats (a basic movement). Or you can perform stiff-legged deadlifts and leg curls as a biceps femoris pre-ex superset.

With a little time to experiment and a degree

of ingenuity, you will be able to expand on these methods of utilizing various basic and isolation movements for each muscle complex. When you've mastered their use, you'll be well on your way to winning contest gold.

Split Routines

All beginners to pumping iron start out working their whole bodies in one session either twice or three times per week. But as you get more advanced, the volume of your workouts becomes so great that you can't train your entire physique in one session. You might go great guns for the first 30–40 minutes—stressing the first body parts in your program very intensely, only to run out of gas for the second half of your session and ending up just going through the motions.

Adopting a split routine in which you divide your body into two equal groups of muscle complexes and working out more than three times per week is the answer to a thorny question: How can I train *all* of my muscle groups equally intensely?

In the most basic split routine, you indeed divide your muscle complexes into two relatively equal groups. Then you train the first grouping of body parts on Mondays and Thursdays, the second grouping on Tuesdays and Fridays. This way your overly long full-body workouts are cut in half, and you can bomb every muscle group— even the little ones—with maximum training intensity using some of the techniques already discussed in this chapter.

One huge benefit from following a four-day split routine is that you program in more recovery time for each muscle complex. Instead of doing everything three times per week on non-consecutive days, you drop back to doing every body part only twice a week. This may seem like splitting hairs, but I can assure you that you will notice a pickup in the pace at which you are making bodybuilding gains when you decrease

the frequency of muscle group routines and shorten your workouts, devoting maximum physical and mental energy to every set you perform for each muscle group in your overall training schedule. I can confidently predict accelerated gains because I've personally coached scores of women over the years who experienced faster gains when they adopted a four-day split routine.

There are numerous ways in which you can divide your body parts into approximately equal groups. You will find a selection of suggested four-day split routines in Figure 5-2. Pick one you like, and then go to it!

Figure 5-2. Suggested Alternative Four-Day Split Routine Body-Part Groupings

Alternative 1

Mon./Thurs.	Tues./Fri.
Abdominals	Upper Legs
Chest	Back
Shoulders	Biceps
Triceps	Forearms
Calves (hard)	Calves (easy)

Alternative 2

Mon./Thurs.	Tues./Fri.
Abs (hard)	Abs (easy)
Chest	Upper Legs
Back	Upper Arms
Shoulders	Forearms
Calves (hard)	Calves (easy)

Alternative 3

Mon./Thurs.	Tues./Fri.
Abs	Calves (easy)
Upper Legs	Back
Chest	Shoulders
Biceps	Triceps
Calves (hard)	Calves (easy)

To allow for more recovery time than a four-day split routine gives—recovery time that will actually accelerate rather than decelerate your rate of progress—you can easily modify the four-day split to a two-on/two-off program. Looking at Figure 5-2, you will see that each of the three alternatives has a Monday/Thursday component and a Tuesday/Friday module. Simply pick the alternative you think you will like and do that alternative's Monday/Thursday split on Day 1 and the Tuesday/Friday section on Day 2. Rest on Days 3 and 4, and repeat the program beginning on Day 5.

The two-on/two-off split gives you two full-body workouts every eight days versus two full-body routines in seven days with the four-day-per-week split. This probably doesn't sound like much—taking a single extra day of rest for each two full-body cycles—but it will make all the difference in the world in your progress. As you grow more experienced as a bodybuilder, you will find that less frequent workouts give you better gains (all else being equal) because the harder you train the longer you will need to rest your body between the times you train each muscle group. The further you advance in the sport, the harder you will train as a natural consequence of progressing as a serious trainer.

Another way to split up your routine so you still make two full-body cycles every eight days is the three-on/one-off program so popular among serious bodybuilders during both off-season building cycles and precontest peaking phases. With this type of split routine, you need to divide your body parts up into three relatively equal groupings. This is traditionally done on a basis of total energy expended in each workout, rather than on number of body parts, but it works out pretty much the same if you also do it according to muscle groups. Alternative ways of splitting up your physique for a three-on/one-off program are presented in Figure 5-3.

After choosing the alternative that you feel is best for you through either basic instinct, actually experimenting with each variation, or some advice I will present on muscle priority in a moment, take the first section (conveniently labeled Day 1) and do it on the first training day. Then progress to the second section on Day 2 and the remaining grouping on Day 3. Rest one full day and then begin the cycle anew on Day 5.

If you find that your progress is tapering off a bit once you have progressed from a two-on/two-off program to this highly popular three-on/one-off split, simply modify the second type of program to a three-on/two-off split. Again, the day of extra rest will actually speed up your rate of developmental improvement. Then after a few months of three-on/two-off workouts, you can probably move up in training frequency to a three-on/one-off program, which is the one I follow.

Figure 5-3. Suggested Alternative Body-Part Splits for a Three-On/One-Off Routine

Alternative 1

Day 1	Day 2	Day 3
Chest	Back	Legs
Biceps	Shoulders	Calves
Abs (hard)	Forearms	Abs (easy)

Day 1	**Day 2**	**Day 3**
Chest	Shoulders	Legs
Back	Upper Arms	Forearms
Abs (easy)	Calves	Abs (hard)

Alternative 3

Day 1	**Day 2**	**Day 3**
Chest	Upper Back	Quads
Shoulders	Biceps	Hamstrings
Triceps	Forearms	Lower Back
Abs (hard)	Calves	Abs (easy)

Alternative 4

Day 1	**Day 2**	**Day 3**
Quads	Back	Chest
Biceps	Hamstrings	Shoulders
Calves	Triceps	Forearms
Abs (easy)	Abs (hard)	—

Refer to Figure 5-3 to see the first type of three-on/one-off program. There is a very good reason why I follow it. It's called muscle priority training, the next topic covered in this chapter.

Muscle Priority Training

Every bodybuilder has body parts that respond relatively quickly because of a combination of favorable genetics, an intuitive "feel" for training that muscle group, and an ease of setting up a direct link between your mind and that muscle as you are training it intensely in a workout. Within the grouping of areas that respond most quickly, some body parts respond a little more or less quickly than others. Again, it usually amounts to subtle differences in genetics, feel, and mind-muscle links.

At the other end of the continuum are muscle groups that respond sluggishly—if at all, it sometimes seems—body parts that can be labeled only as laggards. Every bodybuilder from rank novice up to a multiple Ms. Olympia winner has weak points. But the really successful athletes in our sport are the ones who are able to bring their weak areas up—despite unfavorable genetics, less than optimum feel for the exercises that develop that area, and a mental approach that is under par when they are working that group.

The most fundamental tool you have for bringing up weak areas to the level at which they match the rest of your physique is—you've guessed it—muscle priority training. At its most basic level, muscle priority involves training a slow-to-respond muscle group early in your training session each workout day, when you have an optimum amount of physical and mental energy to expend in saturation-bombing it. The converse of this rule is also true—you should work naturally responsive muscle complexes later in your routine, when you have started to run out of gas.

The principle of muscle priority training can hold true also when you are trying to settle on a particular type of split routine. Then it would be a good idea to schedule weaker areas that require the most intense type of training on the first workout day, less responsive areas next, and (if you are using a three-on/one-off program) the least responsive muscle groups on the final day of the split. Of course, within each individual workout day, you still should follow muscle priority by programming your least responsive area ahead of a somewhat more easily developed muscle area. This is sort of assigning priority within priority.

After a year or two of consistent, hard training—sometimes even sooner—you will have discovered which are your easiest and hardest muscle groups to train, from the most responsive of the responsive down to the least responsive of the unresponsive. If you get to the two-year point and are unable to evaluate yourself by observing your physique in the mirror in a variety of standard poses, get some help.

The owner of the gym where you train will almost always be able to give you a good evaluation. He or she will have gained experience in evaluating members over the years and will have observed your training and physical progress. If the gym owner hasn't already made a conscious appraisal of the strengths and weaknesses of your physique, he or she will have done so subconsciously. It might just take a quick question to prompt an expert answer.

Another excellent source is an older and more experienced bodybuilder—male or female, it really doesn't matter that much—who will probably have more expertise in evaluation than the gym owner. Some women seem hesitant to ask me anything in the gym where I train, perhaps fearing that I might not have the time to help. I think I speak for all elite bodybuilders when I say that I have a great desire to give something back to a sport that has treated me very well. Just use good sense and ask after my workout is over, rather than jumping in front of the mirror in the middle of a set and blurting out your request. The higher you go as a serious bodybuilder, the greater will be your appreciation of the degree of sustained mental focus necessary to get the most out of each training session.

My strong points over the years have been leg, calf, delt, abdominal, and arm development, and my weak areas—or at least the ones to which I have to give maximum priority when formulating my training programs—have been chest and back. By dint of consistent use of the muscle priority principle and specialized high-intensity work on these weak points, I have ultimately brought them into balance with the rest of my physique.

Now look again at the four alternative split routines in Figure 5-3. I mentioned that I follow the first listed program. On Day 1, I immediately train chest (a slower responding area) with biceps (very easy) following it, and I finish off with a stiff abdominal workout. That's what I mean about setting priorities within priorities. I'm very fresh after a full day of rest and can train chest with an ultimate degree of intensity and still have enough fuel in my tank to at least do justice to biceps and abdominals.

On Day 2, I begin with my other slow-developing area, back, which is trained with maximum mental and physical ferocity. My momentum carries me through a solid shoulder workout and even through some direct training for my forearms, both strong points. For a second time, I set priorities within priorities.

On Day 3, my energy reserves are less than on the previous two training days, but I've saved my strongest two muscle groups for that day. Since I don't have to concentrate quite as intensely to get in a sufficiently high-powered workout on legs and calves, this isn't that much of a problem. Of course, physical energy is flagging just as much as mental focus, but still I have plenty to adequately attack my lower body, and even to get in a token midsection workout. Day 3, then, is an example of a reverse priority in that I save my faster responding muscle groups until last in my split routine.

It doesn't take a genius to figure out that I would also profit from following Alternative 2, because chest and back are bombed on Day 1, my more easily developed shoulders, upper arms, and calves on Day 2, and my very easily developed legs, forearms, and abdominals on Day 3. In fact, I have used this type of three-on/one-off split extensively in the past. But through experience—your greatest teacher, if you are intelligent enough to trust it—I have learned that Alternative 2 doesn't work quite as well as Alternative 1, so I consistently use the first split routine.

Alternative 3 in Figure 5-3 gives major priority to the pushing muscles of the upper body—chest, shoulders, and triceps; and it assumes that legs and lower back need the least attention. Alternative 4 is for a bodybuilder who has weak quadriceps and biceps, but very strong chest and shoulder development.

At the beginning of this section, we established that you have your own unique responsive and unresponsive muscle groups, so I probably haven't suggested a three-on/one-off split that is just right for you. Feel free to come up with one that is tailored to those strengths and weaknesses you see in your own physique, but keep in mind that these can and do change from time to time.

Before we move on to another topic, let's treat a worst-case scenario in priority training. A few bodybuilders have one muscle group that grows almost by magic, while another group fails to respond to the hardest and most consistent workouts. I've seen a couple of bodybuilders whose

upper bodies were excellent, but their legs were extremely weak despite herculean efforts to create total physique harmony. What can they possibly do to correct such lopsided development?

In such a case, I would suggest totally ignoring the stronger areas for a few months to concentrate all of your time and energy on the lagging body part(s). You aren't going to lose your ability to bring up your upper body if you fail to train it for the next six months. But you *will* be able to improve your legs if you go three-on/one-off on just those lower-body parts: Day 1 for quadriceps, Day 2 for hamstrings, and Day 3 for calves. Then once your lower body has caught up, no more that 8–10 weeks of balanced training will return your upper body to its original level. The net effect is drastically improved proportional balance.

Some bodybuilders may have to repeat the steps outlined above two, three, or more times in order to achieve total physical harmony. And even then, that harmony may never be quite total. It will, however, be closer to complete physique proportional balance than is possible using any other method of training. You can totally rely on muscle priority training.

When to Change Programs

In Chapter 4, I outlined three basic training programs, or routines, each of which should be followed for six weeks at a time before you switch to the next highest level of routine. Many bodybuilders go on for years following each new training program for six weeks, making good gains ad infinitum, provided they continue to increase intraworkout intensity on a regular basis. But other alternatives exist, and you should consider them.

Personality has something to do with how long you can profitably follow one routine. If you are the type of woman who enjoys a set routine in her life in general—and one who likes to see progress in carefully measured steps—you might want to follow a particular training program for 6–12 months before moving on to a different one.

It is not unprecedented to stick to a program for years at a time. Arnold Schwarzenegger, winner of 13 international bodybuilding titles (among them seven Mr. Olympia titles), had such a philosophy. He noted: "The early years of a bodybuilder's experience in the gym should be devoted to learning what works best for his unique body. Once this has been determined, stick with what works for you. I used the same biceps training program for each of the years I competed in the Mr. Olympia, beginning with a second-place finish in 1969, first-place finishes from 1970 to 1975, plus a comeback in 1980 for my seventh Mr. Olympia win."

Arnold had a very systematic bent to his personality. He had his main goals in life in mind long before he began to achieve each one in turn. Nothing swayed him from his path once it was set—in bodybuilding, in his acting career, and in his various highly successful business enterprises. I might point out that any woman with a similar personality and approach to life would do well to take a lesson from history's greatest male bodybuilder.

At the opposite end of the scale are individuals who are easily bored. Force one of these men or women to follow a set training program for more than a few days at a time, and you'd have mutiny on your hands. Many great female bodybuilders use a system in which they change to a new program every time they enter the gym to train a particular body part. This system, which works quite well for them, is called muscle-confusion workouts, and I will discuss it in depth in Chapter 7.

For the majority of bodybuilders, the answer lies somewhere between these two extremes when it comes to deciding when to jump into a new program. I'd suggest evaluating how you feel following the first three suggested routines for six weeks at a time. If they seem to bore you, then try changing them more frequently, say every four weeks, or even as often as every week. If you feel a great deal of confidence in sticking to the same program for longer than six weeks, then stay with it for as long as it is productive for you.

Once past the most basic levels of serious iron pumping, you have to make most of the decisions for yourself. I can suggest alternatives and inform you about which alternative has the greatest chance of working for you. But I simply can't project myself into your body, monitor the biofeedback it is giving you at all times, and make the final decision for you.

Overtraining

Overtraining is bodybuilding's biggest bugaboo. Just when your training is going great and you're making almost sensational gains, you suddenly screech to a halt. You begin to feel as if you would rather wrestle King Kong than go into the gym to pump iron. You cease making gains altogether. Perhaps you even begin to lose some of the hard-earned muscle mass, tone, and strength you've built up during the past few months.

Top bodybuilders walk a tightrope between training as hard as possible every day and actually overtraining. Sometimes you push a little too hard and end up overtrained. Then it's time to go back to the drawing board if you intend to regain the speed of muscle growth you experienced only a few short weeks ago.

Any of the following 14 symptoms is a sure sign that you are overtraining:

1. Mental and/or physical lethargy that doesn't abate partway through a workout
2. Chronic fatigue

3. Wanting to avoid the gym

4. Loss of strength and/or endurance with the weights

5. Nagging minor injuries

6. Hitting a plateau of strength and muscle development

7. Loss of appetite

8. Deterioration of motor coordination

9. Loss of mental concentration

10. Onset of a cold, flu, or other infection

11. Insomnia or an inability to wake up readily in the morning

12. Nervousness, jumpiness

13. Elevated morning pulse rate

14. Elevated morning blood pressure

Riding a stationary bike for 15 minutes at a time is a good way to incorporate aerobics into your workout.

You might not have heard that monitoring your morning pulse rate and blood pressure can tell you whether or not you are overtraining, but cross-country skiers and other extremely dedicated endurance athletes have long used this technique to tell whether they are overtraining and should back off a bit in their workouts. Blood pressure cuffs are available in most drugstores these days. You can teach yourself how to use one very quickly and then keep a running record of your morning blood pressure over a period of weeks and months. The same goes for taking your pulse rate before you climb out of bed each morning. A spike in either or both of these values is a certain indication that you are slipping over the edge from optimum training into an overtrained state.

What causes overtraining? Highly intense weight workouts are not the culprit. You most frequently overtrain when you consistently work out too long each day and exhaust your body's recovery ability. Unless you permit your body—your skeletal muscles in particular—to recover fully between weight workouts, you simply won't make gains in muscle quality and tone, regardless of how hard, heavy, and consistently you pump iron.

It's easiest to understand the recovery cycle if you visualize it as being like your bank balance. In order to maintain a positive balance in your checking account, you have to deposit more money over a period of time than you withdraw by writing checks against your account balance. Obviously if you write checks for more money than you have on deposit, you will overdraw your account, and the bank begins to take an unhealthy interest in you and your account. Right?

You can also overdraw your energy account. You make deposits in your energy account by getting adequate rest and following a healthful, well-balanced diet. You make energy withdrawals by training, by failing to rest sufficiently throughout the day (out shopping for hours in that new mall in your neighborhood, for example), and by failing to follow a healthful, well-balanced diet.

What can you do when you have overtrained? First, you should take a one-to-two-week complete layoff from training in the gym. Don't even be tempted to go in there to talk with your friends, because sooner or later you'll jump on a Lifecycle, and a few minutes later you'll actually be pumping iron. *Stay completely out of the gym for two weeks!*

Such a layoff from bodybuilding workouts allows your body sufficient time and rest to fully recover its energy reserves and make itself ready to begin making gains in muscle mass once you get back into a systematic weight workout program.

As soon as you begin to feel as if you can't stay away from the gym any longer, you have fully recovered physically and can stand to train again. But when you do get back into the gym, be sure to follow a shorter and more intense training program. I suggest cutting back on the volume (length) of your workout by about 20% and increasing its intensity by the same 20%. You are working out just as hard but doing the workout in a shorter amount of time, which makes the session much more highly intense in nature.

When you are doing marathon workouts, it's impossible to train with maximum intensity. Even if you consciously think you are pushing hard, your subconscious mind is holding you back. It says, "Don't go for the 10th rep because it will make you so fatigued that you won't have any energy left to get through the last half hour of your training session."

When you are pushing as hard as possible in a workout, however, you simply can't do 20–30 sets per body part. Pushing to—or sometimes past—failure on every post–warm-up-set is so tiring that you probably won't be able to do more than 10–12 sets for larger and more complex muscle groups and no more than 6–8 sets for smaller body parts.

Here's my number one rule for avoiding overtraining: Always do fewer total sets than you think you need for each muscle group, and cut your workouts back to no more than 4–5 sessions per week.

There are also mental causes of overtraining. Following the same training schedule like a robot month after month numbs your mind, which can lead to overtraining your body. The best way to avoid this problem is to use muscle-confusion training by working each muscle group completely differently each time you step into the gym to attack it. Think of muscle confusion as following a nonroutine routine. With thought and ingenuity, you should be able to do the same chest or shoulder program no more often than once per year, with all of the arm and delt workouts in between being wildly different from those that have preceded them.

My second rule is: When you are using muscle confusion, think of it as anything but an actual routine—your body and mind will never grow bored with it, and you'll keep making good gains from your workouts. But at the same time, don't use this type of program as an excuse to slack off; you should be training harder than ever, because you're constantly encountering new training stimuli.

Poor nutrition often leads to overtraining. This is particularly true when it comes to eating junk foods too frequently. While some bodybuilders—and serious ones at that—don't grow pudgy on junk foods, these empty-calorie foods undermine the body's ability to recover between workouts. This leads to my third rule for avoiding overtraining: Always follow a well-balanced, nutritious diet liberally supplemented with amino acids, protein concentrates, vitamins, and minerals (particularly the electrolyte minerals calcium, magnesium, and potassium). Of course, you can make a good case for sodium

being an electrolyte mineral, but I have never seen a sodium deficiency in a bodybuilder yet, since normal food at home and in restaurants is usually highly salted, which makes it overly high in sodium content.

Staying up every night talking with your friends, working on a school project, or—as was the case here—writing a book, is also a sure route to failure in recovering from workouts. So is being nervous all of the time. You have to get enough sleep and rest, and you have to plug up all nervous-energy leaks, or you'll end up overtrained just because you can't control your emotions. You may have guessed my fourth rule: Maintain a tranquil mind at all times, and be sure to get at least eight hours of sound sleep each night.

Every woman overtrains at least once in her bodybuilding career. If you can learn from this experience when it happens to you and avoid overtraining in the future, you will make optimum progress in the sport. You'll build the physique you've always dreamed about, and you'll win some big titles along the way. You have my promise on that.

Coping with Injuries

Injuries are the bane of any bodybuilder's existence. While a bodybuilder works like a dog to improve her physique, the injury demon sets up roadblocks to competitive success. Whenever you incur an injury, it will take two or three times as long to reach peak training intensity again as the duration of the injury itself. It should be obvious that injury prevention should rank high on your list of bodybuilding goals.

I've been lucky enough to suffer only a couple of minor injuries, so I've been able to keep improving my physique and gaining general muscle mass at a steady—albeit nonspectacular—rate of speed. As a result, I was able to become a pro bodybuilder at the age of 20 and have placed as high as second in the Ms. Olympia competition.

INJURY PREVENTION

There are two things that you must do without fail if you wish to avoid incurring progress-stalling injuries:

1. Always warm up thoroughly prior to every heavy training session, and be sure to stay warm during your workout by maintaining a relatively fast pace.

2. Always use perfect form in all of your exercises, particularly in the heavy basic movements but also in the lighter isolation exercises.

WARMING UP

A muscle, joint, or other connective tissue that is cold can be easily injured if a heavy weight is used with less than optimum biomechanical form. Therefore, you should spend at least 10–15 minutes systematically warming up your entire body—particularly those areas that you'll be stressing hardest in that workout—prior to approaching the really heavy poundages.

I gave you explicit instructions about how to warm up prior to a heavy training session in Chapters 2 and 3. To review, a properly executed warm-up accomplishes the following processes:

- Increases respiration rate
- Increases heart rate
- Starts perspiration flowing
- Loosens up joints, muscles, and connective tissues
- Particularly loosens up joints, muscles, and connective tissues in the area you intend to attack with weight movements
- Especially loosens up formerly injured areas
- Refines motor coordination
- Mentally prepares a bodybuilder for the heavy workout about to come

A proper warm-up should always begin with some type of aerobic work—fast walking, jumping jacks (in place), rope skipping, and/or stationary cycling. I personally prefer to cycle for about 5–10 minutes, starting out with a slow pace and then gradually increasing the pedal velocity as I become more and more warmed up. At the end of 10 minutes on a stationary cycle, I'm perspiring freely and well on my way toward being fully warmed up.

The next objective is extensive stretching of each major muscle group, particularly those that will bear the brunt of heavy training in that particular session with weights. It must be noted that you should *never* stretch a cold muscle. Scientific experiments have conclusively demonstrated that doing so can cause microscopic tears in the muscle tissue itself and in its connective tissues. Added up over several years' time, these tiny injuries eventually become big ones that will limit your workouts and result in lasting pain.

If you don't know much about stretching, I suggest that you purchase a book called *Stretching* (catchy title, eh?) by Bob Anderson. This book was originally self-published, but it sold so many copies that a large New York City publisher was able to talk Anderson into going to the masses through its production department and distribution system. The book has had a tremendous effect on thousands of men and women who have purchased and read it. If you can find a copy, buy it! The cost is nominal for the value you will receive from it.

Alternatively, many local public gyms have charts posted on their walls listing a variety of stretching movements that you can do to increase the flexibility of various areas of your body. I don't want to give this information away too soon, but all of Chapter 9 in this book is given over to a discussion of stretching philosophy, a list of about 20 common stretches for all areas of your body, and suggested stretching programs that you can make a daily part of your life.

I have digressed a bit and gotten away from the warm-up routine in which you should engage in order to head weight training off at the pass. The third part of your warm-up should consist of a variety of calisthenic exercises such as push-ups, sit-ups, abbreviated aerobic dance movements, and the like, which will begin to place resistance on your skeletal muscles. This is important, because in the final section of your warm-up you actually use light weights in the performance of movements you have chosen for your routine.

Now let's get on with the weights. I personally finish off my warm-up by choosing a basic exercise for the body part I plan to train immediately. With a weight of about 50% of maximum, I do 15–20 relatively quick repetitions with that weight as part of my warm-up. Then with 75% of maximum, I do 10–12 moderately easy reps as the last warm-up set. From there, I do 100% of the max for that particular day for 8–10 repetitions. Then I drop the weight by about 10% immediately, do another set, drop it another 10% and do my final building set with the heavy-poundage basic movement.

CORRECT FORM

I can tell you quite a bit about exercise form. There is a correct biomechanical position that should be assumed and that should be maintained during each exercise. Correct descriptions of all popular bodybuilding exercises can be found in various muscle-magazine articles and in books devoted to the sport. Adapt the correct position(s) and move only those joints and limbs that should be mobile during the exercise.

It is essential to move the weight over the complete range of motion described for it, and it should be moved relatively slowly to prevent momentum from taking over part of the lifting process. Never jerk, bounce, or heave a weight in the bottom position of an exercise, because this can cause microscopic tears in the muscles and connective tissues. Often the long accumulation of such small traumas is what gives an experienced bodybuilder chronically sore joints.

Everywhere I travel around the world to give training seminars, I see bodybuilders bouncing heavy weights off their chests while doing bench presses. How much do you want to bet that these athletes will be complaining of shoulder and elbow pain 10 years down the road?

Make all of the movements slow, smooth, and full, moving only those parts of the body that are supposed to move, and you'll probably never have a joint problem of any consequence. Avoid ego poundages on basic exercises.

INJURY TREATMENT

Occasionally it will be impossible to avoid a serious bodybuilding injury such as a dislocated joint, seriously torn muscle, or a broken bone. In such a case, you should immediately consult a sports medicine physician or an orthopedist whom you trust. Serious bodybuilding injuries should *never* be home- or self-treated, because doing so can often make them more serious and hold back your workouts for an even longer period of time than if you had immediately consulted a good physician.

Less serious injuries can be treated at home. Minor joint pain, minor muscle pulls, minor back injuries, and so forth fall into this category. If you treat these problems forthrightly and correctly, you should be back training at peak intensity within three or four weeks after incurring the original injury.

The main problem with minor joint and muscle injuries is the swelling that inevitably accompanies them. Swelling, one of the body's natural defense mechanisms when an injury occurs, helps immobilize the injured area. But as long as an area is swollen, it won't heal. The actual healing process begins only when the swelling has abated.

To keep swelling under control—and thus speed healing—athletic trainers use a method called RICE, an acronym in which each letter stands for a key process in treating the injury:

R = Rest
I = Ice
C = Compression
E = Elevation

Obviously, every injured area should be *rested* until it is healed, so the first active measure you should take is to *apply ice to the injury site*. The easiest way to do this is to wrap ice cubes and/or chips in a damp towel and then mold the towel closely around the injured area. (It may be necessary to lightly crush the ice so that a tight fit is achieved in which no air pockets are present between the skin and the towel with the ice in it.)

The most common pattern of icing is to place the towel on the injured area for 15 minutes out of every hour, with no icing during the intervening 45 minutes. Keep this pattern up every waking hour for the first 24–36 hours following the time of the injury. Some of the more macho men alternate 15 minutes on ice with 15 minutes off ice, 15 on, 15 off, and so forth for as long as they can stand it. This does help keep swelling under control, but it can be rather painful. Most sane men and all women with whom I've been in contact prefer the 15-on/45-off cycle.

When the towel is first put on your skin, it will hurt. (Have you ever plunged your hand into ice-cold water and tried to see how long you could keep it there?) But your skin will very quickly become numb as a result of the cold, and the joint will gradually become cool until it's almost the same temperature as the ice. I think if you

polled injured bodybuilders and other athletes, they'd tell you that the icing component is their least favorite part of the RICE method of injury treatment.

As an aside on injury-site icing, you should also consider icing chronically sore joints for 15–20 minutes immediately after a workout. This will prevent accumulations of histamines, which can cause continued joint soreness even when there is no other organic problem with the joint. This method is used extensively among major-league baseball players and pro-football quarterbacks to minimize arm and shoulder pain during the days between games.

If you're icing an area consistently, try this method: Fill paper cups with water, placing a tongue depressor in each one to serve as a handle, and freeze them. Hang onto the handle and rub the ice vigorously over the affected joint. All of the top guys I've known who use this method on a regular basis on sore joints swear by it. There's absolutely no reason why women can't profit from their experience.

Compression is the third component of the RICE injury-treatment method. This simply involves tightly wrapping the injured area with an elastic bandage between icings. The compression provided with a tight elastic bandage does much to reduce the swelling. But keep in mind that the bandage should be loosened for a couple of minutes every 15–20 minutes, or you'll end up with some very strange blood-circulation patterns. This is the same type of idea as loosening a tourniquet in applying first aid.

Elevation is the final component of the RICE injury-treatment method. It simply involves placing the injured ankle, knee, elbow, or whatever on a pillow and keeping it above the level of the rest of your body. Liquid runs downhill, so it's difficult for the area to become swollen if it's in a position higher than the main source (the torso) of blood and other body fluids.

If you religiously follow RICE for a couple of

days, you'll find that swelling should be minimal. In many cases, the injured area won't swell up at all, and that means it's ready to be rehabilitated. As soon as possible you'll be back at the gym and training the area with both hard and heavy workouts.

INJURY REHABILITATION

You should begin each postinjury workout session by warming up the injured area, either by using a hot-water bottle (if it's covered with a damp towel, it will conduct heat into the injury site much more efficiently than if it is uncovered and dry) or by sitting in a Jacuzzi or a whirlpool. A good 10–15 minutes of heat should both warm the area and relax it.

Once the area is warmed up thoroughly, begin to lightly stretch the injured section, using the widest variety of flexibility exercises at your command. Use pain as your barometer. Whenever you begin to feel pain in a stretch, back off a bit, and don't return to that amplitude of stretch until a day or two later, when the muscle will be even more thoroughly healed and will probably be able to handle the stretch more comfortably.

After 3–4 days of warming up first and then thoroughly stretching the injured area, you can begin to use very light poundages and high repetitions (try something in the range of 25–30 repetitions per set) on basic exercises that affect the area in question. Again, use pain as your guide, and back off immediately if any single repetition causes any pain at the injury site. Then play another waiting game; a couple of days later, you can try the same weight again, with chances being good that it won't cause a single twinge.

Gradually build up the amount of weight used in each exercise affecting the formerly injured area, and within two or three weeks (4–5 weeks at the outside), you should be right where you were before the incident.

Pay strict attention to all of the injury prevention rules outlined earlier in this section—particularly to the one about being sure you don't waste time between sets, spending five minutes or more discussing the price of gold in Botswana. You should be trying instead to go for every new set after about 60 seconds and certainly no more than 90 seconds of rest—and you'll probably never incur similar injury again. You'll be well on your way toward developing a classically proportioned, artistically symmetrical body with the exact degree of muscle mass and muscular definition that you personally desire.

Sticking Points

No matter how religiously you train and how much you put your heart and soul into your workouts, you will inevitably encounter what we call a sticking point—a cessation of progress.

For bodybuilders, sticking points are tough to take. Up to this point everything has been going right, and suddenly there is no progress. Even if you redouble your efforts, you still don't see any gains; you might even notice a regression in your physical development, which can greatly diminish your self-confidence. Lesser women would immediately throw in the towel and forever swear off pumping iron and following a bodybuilding lifestyle.

Nothing quite that drastic is called for, and there is good news. First, absolutely every woman who has ever become serious about sculpting her body with weights and certain dietary practices has also encountered a sticking point at which she suddenly failed to make additional progress. Many have actually confronted two or more sticking points.

Second, sticking points are made to be broken, and there is a valid strategy for doing just that. Generally you reach a sticking point because you tend to get into a rut in both your training and nutritional programs. You may have a great routine that has worked well for you for two or three years, but suddenly it goes as flat as a tire on a new Porsche. And your diet may have been perfectly suited to your lifestyle—and has improved your cosmetic appearance—but it, too, no longer does the trick.

So it's time for a switch, and a big one. Instead of merely changing diet and training, you're going to have to learn to begin using your *mind* to build the muscles you're still after. This whole idea of the mental approach to serious weight training and bodybuilding is covered in depth in Chapter 12, but I'll hit the high points here. If you get a little more curious about mental attitudes, you can jump ahead and read and digest Chapter 12.

As with a lot of things worth having in life, sculpting a superior body isn't an easy process. You already know that it is very difficult to sculpt the exact type of body form that you have visualized for yourself and gradually are achieving through a strict combination of bodybuilding training, stretching, aerobics, and a tight diet. In order to drive the post-teenyboppers mad with the way you look in a bathing suit, you have been forced to spend a great deal of time on training (certainly more than you would ever have imagined when you first got into this type of lifestyle). It's taken an awesome expenditure of physical effort, plenty of self-discipline at the dinner table, and—but let's not belabor the point—it's also cost quite a bit of money to get to be the way you now are.

The beauty of following a bodybuilding lifestyle, however, is that you can choose to maintain any level of development you have so far reached, and maintenance of existing bodies is very much on the easy side. I'm not going to denigrate your efforts if you decide to drop out at this level, train lighter and more sporadically, and maintain an exceptional (compared to the average woman at the beach or club pool) body that you have already created.

No, my remarks in this section are directed to those elite women who aren't yet satisfied with what they have achieved, and who look down the road a few more miles and see the women they could be, lounging casually—and looking ravishing—at the side of a swimming pool or frolicking in the surf in their choice of ocean.

MENTAL TRICKS

Right now, let's take a good, long, hard look at your degree of motivation to continue. You have to want to be one of the elite women of the world, and you have to want to put in the time and work necessary to achieve that idealized image. Do you really want it? Unless you can answer with a wholehearted YES, then let's forget about the advanced sections of this book. Take your favorite mixed drink down to the edge of the pool and dazzle some of the out-of-towners who probably have never seen anyone as ravishing as you are, with pure sexuality oozing from every pore. As long as a real superwoman doesn't come along, you'll be in heaven.

If you're headed for superwomanhood, for whatever individual reasons you have (and they are all perfectly valid and great with me as long as they are what *you* want to excel for), start out every morning before you get out of bed and again every night as soon as the light is out to use a psychological technique called visualization. Use it twice per day, and it will work wonders in keeping you motivated and on track toward achieving the perfect you.

Start out lying on your back with your arms down at your sides, palms flat against the mattress. You can place a low pillow beneath your knees but not under your head or neck. Spend the first five minutes relaxing yourself body part by body part. By this I mean you should start with your left foot and consciously will it to relax, until it actually makes a weight that indents the mattress. Do the same for your other foot and ankle. Then work on each calf in turn, each thigh, each buttock, your lower back, your midsection muscles, your upper back, your chest musculature, one hand, the other hand, one forearm, the other forearm, and finally your neck. At this point, you will find that you are breathing slowly and rhythmically, and you are much more relaxed than you have been in years. If you just decided to lie there thinking of nothing, you probably would merely fall asleep within a few minutes. But we're going to put this fully relaxed posture to use.

With your eyes lightly closed, use the backs of your eyelids as movie screens against which you are going to project a series of images. Start out by projecting an image of yourself nude, but in much better physical condition than you currently are. Look at how much more tightly your waistline is nipped in and how it rounds sensuously outward and downward in the most feminine of curves. Continuing downward, notice that your thighs are completely devoid of extraneous body fat, and they also show a new curve on both the outer and inner sides that can only be described as sexy. The bottom part of your visualized body is formed by gracefully curved calves, the kind of lower legs that dancers always seem to have and which you have secretly wanted for perhaps your entire life. It's a nice picture, isn't it? Go ahead and savor it for a minute, enjoying the way you will soon appear if you follow the visualization processes I'm teaching you—combined, of course, with continued weight-stretching-aerobics training and a solid, healthful bodybuilding diet.

Allow your gaze to wander upward. Not only is your waistline narrower than it's ever been, but there are actually details of muscle lying just between the surface of an almost paper-thin skin. Just by twisting or bending to one side, these muscles leap into sight so prominently that Stevie Wonder would probably sense them.

From your waistline upward, your torso begins to curve subtly outward and upward on each side, and you have subtle wings of muscle branching up under your arms. Your chest muscles are strong and thickly developed, so they push your breasts outward and even upward, giving them an appeal that you'd previously never imagined possible.

If you turned around and could look in a mirror that showed your entire body from the rear, you would be impressed with the powerful roundness of your buttocks, which rise out of the biceps femoris at the backs of your legs in one bold sweep on each side, with no folds of skin where they might normally be expected to rest. You are somewhat startled by the breadth of your shoulders, which are powerfully corded with muscle and distinctly wider than your hips. Surveying your tiny waistline and flaring hips, you note that you have an ideal hourglass figure that you hadn't noticed before.

Even your arms are solidly built, and whenever you move one of them to accomplish a task, the cords of muscle jump into bold relief. Even your forearms display a power that women have seldom had, but which should have been their birthright from the time of Adam and Eve.

Somehow your neck has grown to keep pace with the rest of the muscular girth of your completely incredible body. Your neck is a tower of sinewy power that supports your head proudly, and you soon begin to improvise hairstyles that would make it possible to show off your neck without your hair interfering in any way.

It's an incredible picture, isn't it? Take a few minutes to live with it, enjoy it, savor it, and realize that it can, indeed, become the real you if you continue to follow a bodybuilding lifestyle.

The more you practice visualization this way and the more real you can make it seem, the closer you will come to achieving the visualized image you have chosen for yourself. Of course you still have a lot of work to do, but it becomes much easier to stay on a strict training and dietary regimen if you have this type of road map to guide you along your journey. And believe me, if you want this, *you can have it!*

THE TRAINING COMPONENT

If you were able to get spiritually into the mental end of progress-barrier bashing in the previous section, it should be no problem at all to change the training program that you've been following. And then you can begin to get some real results in the gym. It's merely a matter of making a few minor changes and then mentally dedicating yourself to start making some realistic physical progress.

From a physical standpoint, sticking points are easily dispensed with. Usually they are caused by getting into too much of a rut in your workouts. Everyone does it. A routine seems to be doing everything you could ever want from it, so you keep doing it over and over, week after week, and maybe even month after month, until Mother Nature says, "Whoa, there. I can't let you get away with this any longer."

A bodybuilder in a rut is a bored bodybuilder, both mentally and physically. Even if the mind doesn't seem to need some new type of stimulus, the body certainly does. So the key is to start following a nonroutine routine in which you do a completely different routine for each body part every time you step into the gym. I will give you a running start at it right now, which should serve to pull you out of the physical doldrums and back into a space where the muscle gains are really coming for you.

Work out a split routine in which you *do* train the same muscle groups the same day each week. But from there on out, the routines you use will look like something right out of *Star Wars*. Let's take the chest as an example. In Figure 5-4 are five different chest workouts that you can plug into the chest holes in your split, just to give you an idea of how it works to follow a nonroutine routine. (Note: In supersets, go right from one exercise to the next, with only a very brief pause.)

Figure 5-4. Suggested Alternative Chest Workouts

Alternative 1

Exercise	Sets	Reps
Barbell Incline Presses	6	15–5[1]
Low-Incline Dumbbell Flyes	4	8–12
Pec-Deck Flyes	4	10–15
Cross-Bench Dumbbell Pullovers	4	10–15

Alternative 2

Exercise	Sets	Reps
Barbell Bench Presses	10	15–5–15[2]
Cable Crossovers	5	10–15
Decline Cable Flyes	5	10–15

Alternative 3

Exercise	Sets	Reps
Incline Dumbbell Flyes, supersetted with . . .	5	8–10
Low-Incline Barbell Presses	5	8–10

Exercise	Sets	Reps
Flat-Bench Dumbbell Flyes, supersetted with . . .	5	8–10
Bench Presses (knees curled over hips)	5	8–10
Parallel Bar Dips, supersetted with . . .	3	max
Cross-Bench Dumbbell Pullovers	3	12–15

Alternative 4

Exercise	Sets	Reps
Bench Presses	15	20–4–20[3]

Alternative 5

Exercise	Sets	Reps
Wide-Grip Benches to Neck	4	10–12
Low-Decline Cable Crossovers	4	12–15
Flat-Bench Dumbbell Flyes (knees curled over hips)	4	10–12
Wide-Grip Parallel Bar Dips	4	10–12
Kneeling Cable Crossovers, supersetted with . . .	4	10–12
Cross-Bench Dumbbell Pullovers	4	10–12

[1]You should pyramid weights-reps on the exercise marked with an asterisk, increasing the poundage and decreasing the reps each succeeding set.

[2]Full pyramid: work up in weight until maxed, and then work right back down again.

[3]Pyramid up in weight to a max, then right back down to the start.

Workout Enthusiasm

. . . .

Another means of smashing past sticking points is to constantly maintain a high level of enthusiasm for your daily workouts. Sure, we all love pumping iron—we wouldn't be this far into this book if we didn't—but it's impossible to be physically and mentally up for every training session, be it with weights, aerobics of various kinds, or stretching exercise. I can, however, give you a couple of tips to jazz yourself up for a workout on those occasional days when you feel like you'd rather wrestle King Kong than push a little iron.

I personally follow a three-point plan for raising lower-than-normal workout enthusiasm lev-els—consistent reviewing of personal goals, going over photos of great women bodybuilders against whom I know I'll soon have to compete, and saturating my system with a little caffeine to help me get a running start once I'm in the gym.

In Chapter 2, I discussed the importance of maintaining a detailed training diary. Part of my own workout log comprises those goals I want to reach each month, plus longer-range goals set at one- or two-year intervals. It's very easy to lose sight of your goals if you fail to constantly review them, and I prevent this by sitting down with my diary right after lunch every scheduled workout day.

The timing for this is crucial, because I have always preferred to work out in the early after-noon, about 1–1½ hours after consuming a high-carbohydrate meal, which will help me last through a gym session with maximum physical energy available. Since I don't like to read while eating (doing so interferes with good digestion, which begins by thoroughly chewing each bite of food), I review my diary as soon as I have rinsed off the dishes I've used for my midday meal.

First and foremost, I spend several minutes reading and rereading the goals I have set for myself and recorded in my training log. Am I on target? If so, great! If not, what has been holding me back? Lackadaisical workouts? Poor diet? Lack of adequate recovery time in the forms of rest between workouts and sleep? By identifying the culprit, I can plan to eliminate it as soon as possible.

A comprehensive training diary also comes in handy as an indicator of how fast you are progressing with your training poundages. As you already understand, there is a direct relationship between how much weight you can use for 5–8 reps in good form and the size and tone of the muscles that actually lift the barbell, dumbbell or resistance machine. But it can be a downer if you expect to find increases in poundage in the training weights you use from day to day, or even week to week.

Resistance increases are much more evident if you compare exercises you did 2–3 months—or even a year—ago with what you are currently doing. It can really give your workout enthusiasm a boost when you see that you were doing incline presses on a Smith machine with 90 pounds for six reps four months ago, and you now can handle 105 pounds for eight counts in the same movement.

Improvements in the proportionately larger and stronger leg and back muscles can be even more dramatic. While you might not be able to identify increases in workout weights from week to week, they are obvious from one year to the next. Think of it—you are actually making vis-

ibly verifiable progress! Wouldn't that make anyone excited about getting into the gym to pump iron?

A second method of peaking out training enthusiasm is to review photos of great female athletes, models, and bodybuilders prior to a gym session. If you are still training for improved body proportions and better muscle tone at this point, you can gain enthusiasm for your workouts by flipping through copies of *Shape*, *Self*, *Elle*, *Cosmopolitan*, and other women's magazines. Just viewing and analyzing the models in advertisements can hype you up to the point where you won't be able to resist getting into the gym or onto your stationary bike, stairclimber, treadmill, or mountain bike.

Collecting muscle magazines is a virtual compulsion among competitive bodybuilders. Men and women alike collect back issues of *Flex* and *Sportrevue*, and I am no exception to the rule. I not only have every copy I've purchased since I began serious training during my midteens but many even older issues, which I've purchased in used book shops or through classified ads in various bodybuilding and weight-training publications.

Back numbers of muscle mags are a treasure trove of information on alternative ways to train, eat, and prepare mentally for upcoming competitions. There are several good bodybuilding books on the market—including one truly great one, which you are holding in your hands—but the knowledge and wisdom of a book is frozen in time the day it is published. So where do you go for the latest, most up-to-date bodybuilding information?

Muscle magazines can be viewed as monthly updates to this and other comprehensive bodybuilding manuals. As a result, I subscribe to all of the best ones and carefully store and preserve each new issue of *Flex* like its pages were printed in gold ink. Outstanding fitness magazines like *Flex*, *Sportrevue*, and *Muscle & Fitness* have editorial staffs in constant contact with champion bodybuilders who have evolved new means of training, eating, and psyching up, all of which are immediately published and made available to the public.

I not only reinforce my knowledge of the bodybuilding lifestyle in older issues of *Flex* and other muscle magazines, but I also flip through these periodicals to view photos of potential competitors for an upcoming Ms. Olympia. I gain further inspiration by seeing who has been victorious at each new competition, and I review trends in judging. Are they going for huge muscle mass this year (bad for me) or for a combination of shape, balanced proportions, and sharp muscularity (all good for me)?

Many competitors even reveal their future competitive plans, plus the ways in which they intend to reach their goals. Nothing snaps me to attention faster than seeing a great new photo of one of my closest competitors and reading about how she plans to obliterate Anja Langer at the next Olympia. This makes my blood boil, and nothing can keep me away from the weights then!

For many bodybuilders, a third means of boosting low levels of enthusiasm for training is to drink a cup of coffee before they leave for the gym. The caffeine gives them a first-stage boost to their moon rocket. Coffee is quite acidic, however, and some bodybuilders find that it upsets their stomachs sufficiently to retard their progress through a heavy gym workout. In such cases, drinking coffee must be avoided.

I personally have a cappuccino machine in the kitchen of my home, which allows me to brew a cup or two to drink while I'm going through last year's body mags to review photos and articles about those women I plan to meet onstage soon in an IFBB (International Federation of Bodybuilders) pro competition, such as the Ms. Olympia. If I've first viewed photos of my main competitors while sipping a cup of cappuccino, I can

dash out to my car and set new speed records between my house and the gym. I am so enthusiastic that I simply can't wait to start pumping heavy iron!

Heavy vs. Light Training

There are divergent schools of thought when it comes to choosing which barbell, dumbbell, or machine poundage to use in each workout. Let's explore the extremes at each end of the continuum between heavy/low-rep training and light/high-rep workouts. Then I'll give you a method of combining both types of training modes.

The classic training method has been to go as heavy as possible on every exercise in your routine, usually sacrificing what could be considered optimum form in the process. Since muscles grow larger and larger when subjected to progressively heavier weights, this does make some sense. A good recent example of a female competitive bodybuilder who followed this method is Vera Bendel, who has placed in the top three at a couple of pro competitions. To some extent, I believe, Bev Francis (a consistent third- and second-place finisher at the Olympia) also uses this method, since her original weight-training background was for athletic improvement and then competitive powerlifting.

The most extreme form of the heavy-iron group would include athletes who believe that only 2–4 all-out sets on each muscle group will develop an optimum physique. The only woman I can recall who has used this extreme system effectively was Deborah Diana, an overall U.S. Champion in the early 1980s.

Critics of extremely heavy training are legion, and I am one of them. Women who work out in this manner tend to be massively developed but blocky in appearance. The accumulation of thousands of heavy sets of squats and deadlifts eventually broadens their waistlines and damages full-body symmetry.

Muscle mass just for the sake of mass is not an intelligent approach to bodybuilding anyway. After all, how much muscle mass is enough? Unless it is combined with balanced proportions, nice symmetry, and plenty of intramuscular detail, the judges will score this type of competitor quite low. Many can't cope with such placings, and they either gravitate toward powerlifting or exit the iron game completely.

No less of an authority than seven-time Mr. Olympia winner Arnold Schwarzenegger has stated that "heavy-duty" training bodybuilders are unable to achieve contest-level muscular detail. I agree wholeheartedly with Arnold. While general separation between muscle groups is possible when you are following a heavy-duty routine, striations throughout each individual muscle cannot be achieved without following a wide variety of exercises for each body part, using moderately heavy weights for higher reps (12–15 per set) and concentrating intently on the working muscles as you slowly perform each repetition.

Many young bodybuilders fail to take into consideration the risk of long-term, chronic joint injuries, which are very common among the heavy-training group. Women's bodybuilding is not that old a sport—the first true competitions took place in 1979—but there are already many women who trained extremely heavy and are now experiencing racked-up lower backs, chronically sore knees, shoulders, and elbows, and many other injuries related directly to training with excessively heavy weights. Among men, these injuries are pandemic.

There is also the question of femininity. Is a woman with arms bigger than most men's feminine? To most people, probably not. There is a fine dividing line between enough feminine muscle and too much, and it's very easy to go across this line and lose femininity if you train with prodigious weights.

In counterpoint to the heavy-iron-only women are the "pump artists," who seem to spend half of their available time in the gym pumping out light set after light set of 15–20 reps in each exercise. Just as the heavy-duty freaks do, pumpers *do* develop some degree of muscle mass but a greater degree of intramuscular details than the heavy bombers.

The answer to optimum bodybuilding training lies somewhere in the middle of the spectrum between the heavy-iron women and the light-training pump artists. This method is called holistic training. I personally train holistically and recommend the method to all bodybuilders—champions and lower-level trainees alike—who wish to make fast, aesthetic gains from their workouts.

Skeletal muscles are made up of long strands of cells attached end to end. Each of these cells responds by growing larger from the overload you place on it. Heavy/low-rep training enlarges one section of a muscle cell, while light/high-rep training enlarges another section. Medium/middle-rep training enlarges even a different component of each muscle cell.

Wouldn't it make a difference if you did workouts that expand all three sections of the muscle cell, those brought out by heavy, medium, and light training? It most certainly would make a difference, and training holistically like this builds the best possible quality of muscular development.

The most commonly used form of holistic training is the pyramid—(or more commonly, the half-pyramid)—system of working out. In pyramid training, a bodybuilder starts out with a light weight on a selected exercise and performs a relatively high number of reps the first set (as an example, let's say that she does 20 counts). With each succeeding set, the poundage is increased and the reps correspondingly decreased until a maximum poundage for 3–5 reps has been accomplished. Then the system reverses itself, with weight subtracted from the bar and reps increased correspondingly, until she is back where she started.

Holistically speaking, she will have performed high-rep sets with lighter poundages, mid-rep sets with medium weights, and low-rep sets with near-maximum poundages. The full pyramid is effective, but a bit excessive in the number of sets performed of a basic movement, so half-pyramids are much more commonly utilized, frequently with one high-rep pump set done once the maximum set has been completed satisfactorily.

Let me give you an example of a half-pyramid in action. In this case, it is the exact squatting workout I did last week. The weights will seem to be a little funny to American readers, because I use a metric set and have had to convert kilograms to pounds for the sake of those still using the old system of measurements. Anyway, here is the series of squats I did:

Set Number	Weight (lb.)	Reps
1	132	20
2	176	15
3	198	12
4	220	10
5	242	8
6	262	6
7	286	5
8	308	3–4
9	220	18

Many forms of holistic training are available to you. Let's take an upper-back session as an example. In this case the poundages and reps are arbitrary, but very close to what many bodybuilders would use.

Exercise	Sets	Weights	Reps
Front Lat Machine Pulldowns	5	120–170	12–5*
Seated Low-Pulley Rows	5	110–130	8–10
Standing One-Arm Low-Pulley Rows	3–4	50–60	15–20

In this example, the asterisk is used to denote an exercise that has its weights and reps pyramided. It should be obvious to you that this is the heavy movement of the sample back program. Seated low-pulley rows have each set performed with a medium weight, with reps in the range of 8–10 per set, making it the medium exercise of the back-training schedule. Finally, 3–4 sets of 15–20 reps with an even more moderate poundage make the standing one-arm low-pulley rows the light movement of the routine. Heavy, medium, light—a perfect example of holistic training within one body part.

Many successful bodybuilders—myself included—make holistic changes in our workouts from session to session rather than from one exercise to another. The pyramid example of one of my squat workouts would be done on the heavy day. A medium squatting day might consist of a couple of warm-up sets followed by 6–8 sets of 8–12 reps with a consistent weight, say 220 pounds (100 kilos to my way of thinking). A light squatting day might be really kinky. I'd load the bar with 176 pounds and squat with it for 10 full minutes, allowing not even the briefest pause at the top of a repetition to rest my screaming leg muscles.

This type of holistic squatting routine *is* painful, but it does work wonders. I am constantly being complimented for the excellence of my quadriceps and gluteus maximus development. Holistic training on squats and other lower-body movements have been instrumental in allowing me to achieve such high-level leg development.

Individualized Routines

Earlier in this chapter, I discussed the subject of changing from one training program to a new routine. Mainly the discussion revolved around how many weeks or months should elapse before it would be appropriate to make such a change. As is the case with most bodybuilding variables, your decision to make a change is a highly individual matter.

Throughout this book you have been introduced to a number of suggested routines. This is a necessary evil, because beginning and intermediate bodybuilders know so little about how their bodies respond to individual training variables that it is impossible for them to formulate routines that will precisely satisfy their own unique physical needs.

As time passes and you become more attuned to your own physique and what it is telling you it needs, you will become better able to formulate your own training programs. Once you reach a certain skill level, you should always do what your body tells you rather than following a new program suggested by me or by some other high-level bodybuilder. There's no way I can project myself into your body and gain a sense of what it needs. Besides, you are already in there and have been constantly monitoring the biofeedback signals your body is constantly sending you.

You already have a good idea of how you should divide up your various body parts for the split routine you intend to follow. From reading this book and countless body-part training articles published in weight-training magazines, you no doubt have a pretty clear idea of how to construct a routine for each muscle group.

If you're like most enthusiastic young women, you've probably already experimented with some of your own homegrown training schedules. Some of them gave you a good pump and others didn't. So you retained the good routines—or even just parts of routines—and jettisoned the worthless ones. This is a natural way of learning how to bodybuild, because everyone likes to experiment with new training and dietary variables they've read or heard about, all in an effort to discover what works best for their unique, individual body.

At training seminars, I often liken the bodybuilding process to a scientific experiment. Your body is one big laboratory, and within that lab you try various experiments. Some show no results at all. Others show minimum results but also show promise of leading to something even bigger. A rare experiment here and there will be a smashing success, a breakthrough that gives meaning to a broad spectrum of existing—but heretofore unfocused—data. Your job as a bodybuilder is to experiment constantly with new variables in your body lab in an effort to evolve the ideal training and nutritional programs for your unique physique.

There are general rules in bodybuilding that apply to everyone. But usually even the most universal rules of training and nutrition must be modified slightly to conform to your individual physique's special needs.

I can give you several suggestions for formulating your own routines, but even they will probably have to be modified a bit to fit your own needs. Try these rules when drawing up your next training schedule:

- Follow the muscle priority training principle, as outlined earlier in this chapter.
- In general, schedule large muscle groups that require the greatest amount of energy expenditure first in a routine, with smaller groups later.
- Use abdominal work either as a good warm-up activity prior to your main routine or as a means of tapering down at the end of a session.
- Never schedule calf training prior to squats, because doing calves first will make your legs so shaky that it will be difficult to squat efficiently.
- Always program torso work before upper-arm exercises.
- Always save forearm workouts until last in your routine. It's difficult to grasp a bar once you have a good pump in your forearm muscles.

With time and with practice in making up your own routines, you will soon be confident enough in your abilities to make up new programs for less experienced women in the gym.

Joint Wraps

The use of fabric and neoprene rubber joint wraps is a protective measure common to most bodybuilders. Wraps are most frequently used around a part of the body that has previously been weakened by injury. Many women use wraps simply as a protective measure—particularly around the knees or wrists—to prevent the possibility of an injury.

Elastic fabric bandages measuring about 4 inches (12 centimeters) wide and 3 feet (slightly less than 1 meter) in length are the type most commonly used. The more stretch to the fabric, the better. In some sporting goods stores, wraps are available specifically for use on the knees of Olympic lifters and powerlifters. In America the most popular of these lifters' wraps is called Superwrap—the best-made wrap for bodybuilders because it provides the most support.

Superwrap (as well as the wraps of several competitors) can be ordered through advertisements in the monthly magazine *Powerlifting USA*. A one-year subscription costs $26.95, and it can be ordered from *Powerlifting USA*, P.O. Box 467, Camarillo, CA 93011.

You will find many other products bodybuilders need advertised in this excellent magazine, plus plenty of technical articles on how to develop strength and muscle mass. It's certainly not a sexist magazine, because women are featured quite prominently, even many women bodybuilders who lift competitively in the off-season. The most prominent of these is Mary Jeffrey, who has won class and overall honors at the Ms. America event. She's won about 10 world titles and set scores of world records as a powerlifter. Her bench press of 275 pounds, performed when she lifted in the under-123-pound weight division, is simply mind-boggling.

I'd suggest buying four sets of wraps, so you can always have a clean, dry pair when others are in the wash. When not in use, they should be rolled loosely (so they don't lose elasticity) and stored in your gym bag. When ready for use, they should be rolled as tightly as possible before you wrap a joint.

Most iron game devotees consider rolling up their wraps to be a tedious process at best. Some lifting genius has invented a wrap roller that attaches to the gym wall and rolls a wrap very tightly simply by the turn of a crank that rotates a spindle around which the bandage rolls up. If there's one of these handy little tools available in the gym where you train, you'll love using it, particularly on heavy squatting days when you have to wrap your knees before every set, unwrap them, and then get the wraps rolled up while you're breathing like a locomotive on an uphill grade—and then wrapping them again for another set.

Let's use wrapping a knee as an example of how to correctly wrap up. (Other joints are smaller but are wrapped in the same manner.) Sit at the end of a flat exercise bench with your leg bent at about a 20-degree angle. Start the wrapping process by taking two full turns—one over the other—just below your knee joint. Then wrap a tight spiral upward, being sure that the fabric overlaps enough so there are at least two layers over the joint. You should run out of cloth at about the time you have made two final, tight turns just above the knee.

Some fabric wraps come with little metal clips. They may be handy for invalids to use, but they are worthless for iron athletes. They simply tear up the cloth and fail to anchor the wrap. The fastest, safest, and most functional way of anchoring a wrap is to pass the loose end under one or two of the top spirals and then pull it as tightly as you can. Friction will effectively anchor your cloth wrap in this way, and it can be freed in an instant at the end of your set.

Neoprene rubber (the type used in scuba-diving wet suits) is also used for wraps. It is shaped into tubes of varying lengths and diameters that provide a minimum of actual support, but they are excellent at keeping a therapeutic damp heat over and around an injury-weakened joint. They are even made in sizes large enough to fit around your waist. While waistbands won't melt off fat—as some of their promoters promise—they do keep the lower back soothingly warm.

Some women with persistent knee pain use both rubber and fabric wraps for maximum protection. They slide on two knee bands, one on each leg, and then put on a pair of warm-up pants. Then they use the elastic fabric wraps on the outside, over the pants. I don't personally recommend going to these extremes, even though I've seen national-, international-, and pro-level women bodybuilders using this wrapping technique.

If your knees are chronically so painful that you have to use two types of wraps—and often chemically addictive painkillers, too—you should schedule a visit to an orthopedist or another physician specializing in sports medicine. Small bone and cartilage fragments can be removed arthroscopically and almost painlessly. You will actually be back in the gym within a week of your surgery, and probably doing a leg workout after a second week. The three scars made during arthroscopy are so tiny that you'll have trouble seeing them yourself 6–8 weeks after surgery, so they won't distract from your appearance onstage.

Podiatrists can also be quite helpful, because they can help you compensate for feet that are a bit out of line. With a pair of orthotics in your workout shoes and another for everyday wear, any knee pain caused by mechanically imbalanced feet will soon be a thing of the past. I know a woman bodybuilder who used to suffer excruciating pains in her back until she visited a podiatrist, who discovered that one leg was a half-inch (about 2 centimeters) shorter than the other. After a few days of using orthotics, she felt as if her back had undergone a miraculous cure.

Straps

As you become stronger in the pulling exercises you do for your upper body (e.g., chins, lat pull-downs, dumbbell bent-over rows, seated pulley rows, T-bar rows, barbells rows, and deadlifts), you will invariably reach a point at which you

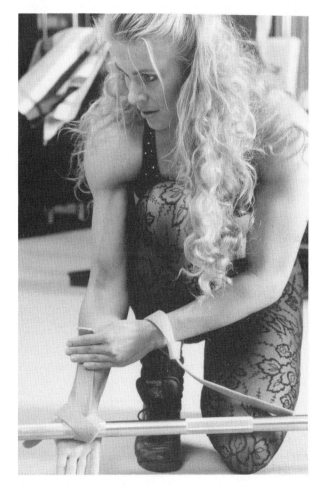

Old-fashioned straps work well if used correctly.

Even Superman can't break this grip!

A lower tech—but vastly more popular—grip reinforcer is a simple length of fabric webbing that runs through a very small loop to form a larger loop that fits around your wrist. To use it, simply pull on the free end to tighten the loop around your wrist. Place your palm over the bar and pull the loose end of the strap under the bar so that your hand is snugly up against the barbell or pulley handlebar. Wrap the strap one more full turn around the bar and then close your hand over the loops of webbing. As long as you keep your hand closed over the webbing, even Superman won't be able to break your grip.

The foregoing descriptions of how to use a wrap undoubtedly will be much clearer to you if you glance at the accompanying photos, which illustrate correct use of a grip strap. Certainly these straps are old-fashioned and low-tech, but almost all top bodybuilders use them. Oh, yes, they also cost between 50% and 75% less than the straps with the metal hooks on them.

Outdoor Workouts

Because we Germans live in a northern climate that gives us plenty of gloomy, snow-blown days each winter, we love being out of doors in the sun as often as possible. To live in a constantly sunny environment like California's would be a dream come true for me, but I could never stay away from my family and friends for long. But I do go off to southern California (where Venice Beach is the center of world bodybuilding) for a couple of weeks now and then when our weather is particularly gloomy.

German travel agents make a fortune setting up Mediterranean, Caribbean, and South Pacific vacation packages for sun-hungry men and women like myself. But I don't wish to paint too dark a picture of the German climate, because we have lovely summers and quite acceptable autumns and springs.

will need to reinforce your grip to get the most out of each set. Without reinforcing straps, your grip can give out and terminate a heavy and potentially very productive set of barbell bent-over rows before you receive maximum benefit from the movement.

You will see various types of fabric webbing wrist straps with metal hooks attached to them advertised in various muscle magazines. These straps work well in maintaining your grip on pulling movements. The hooks rotate out of the way as you do pushing exercises, which is a plus when you are performing a chest-back superset consisting of dumbbell low-incline presses and lat machine pulldowns behind the neck.

One good company that has this type of strap-hook is Lift Master, P.O. Box 6576, Folsom, CA 95630. You should write for information and a current price list.

My favorite outdoor activity, as I've mentioned, is pedaling my mountain bike. I'm certain that I've been up every steep hill in Stuttgart at least 50 times in the past year. The combination of sun and exercise is absolutely irresistible to me. I love it!

It's now becoming fashionable to train with weights outdoors, too. This movement began about 1980 when Joe Gold opened his famous World Gym in Santa Monica, California. That gym had an outdoor deck with plenty of heavy and varied equipment. The original World Gym was a couple of miles north of the famous Muscle Beach outdoor workout area. Even though Joe was charging 30 times more than the $10 yearly dues for members of the Muscle Beach Weightlifting Club, scores of Muscle Beach types trekked up to World Gym for their workouts. There were so many other members who also enjoyed pumping iron in the sun and fresh air that the outdoor gym deck was becoming exces-sively crowded at certain times of day.

About five years later, Joe's membership list had reached the point at which he was forced to look for a larger building. He found a nice lot in Venice, south of the original gym, and built his own custom-designed facility there. Arnold Schwarzenegger has his own perpetually re-served parking space under the structure. Of course, a new sun deck was included for out-door-training enthusiasts—a far larger and better equipped outdoor area than the one at the orig-inal World Gym.

This movement toward building outdoor train-ing areas has mushroomed, and they are pop-ping up everywhere, even here in Germany. If you have your own home-gym equipment, drag the portable pieces out into the backyard and have a sun-and-fun bodybuilding workout. That way you'll not only have an impressively muscled physique but a great natural tan to go with it!

6
Intermediate-Level Exercises and Routines

In Chapter 4 you learned the 26 most basic weight-training movements, which you will be using in one form or another for the rest of your involvement in bodybuilding. Now here are 25 more exercises to master, bringing your total to 51, probably more than most women perform day in and day out. Eventually I'll get you up to more than 70 training movements, so you can become a true master bodybuilder.

The process of learning the movements in this chapter is somewhat different from that in Chapter 4. You have already learned the basics, and everything presented in this chapter is an elaboration of one sort or another on these basics. Therefore, you won't have to stand in front of a mirror and pantomime the movements before picking up a weight. You can probably start right out with moderate poundages on each new movement and will have the exercise down pat in a matter of two or three practice sets.

I'll also give you three more training programs that you can follow, each one more difficult than the one before. But these will be the last ones suggested in the book, because you'll be able to make up your own individualized routines past this point. I will give you examples from my own

personal training programs in Chapter 13, but they will be presented only as *examples* on which you can model your own unique routines.

Leg Exercises

HACK SQUATS
Areas Emphasized—This unique machine movement places stress almost totally on the quadriceps muscles of the frontal thighs. Unlike ordinary barbell squats, there is little involvement of the gluteal muscles and even less emphasis on the spinal erectors. Most bodybuilders do hack squats primarily to increase the outer sweep of their thigh development.

Starting Position—Back into the sliding part of a hack machine, placing your shoulders under the padded yokes of the slide and your back against the movable back pad. There are several foot stances that can be assumed, but let's take the most basic one with feet set about shoulder-width apart, toes angled slightly outward. Straighten your legs to assume the weight of the slide, and reach up beside your shoulders to rotate the stop bars to release the slide for use.

Hack Squats—start and finish

Hack Squats—midpoint

Movement Performance—Keeping your hips somewhat forward throughout the movement, slowly bend your legs as completely as possible. Without bounding in the bottom position, slowly reverse the movement and straighten your legs to return to the starting point. Repeat the movement for the requested number of repetitions.

Common Mistakes—Bouncing in the bottom position of the exercise is a no-no, because it can have a harmful effect on your knees. Allowing your hips to come too far forward throws weight too much toward your toes, which can also strain your knees.

Training Tips—The main variations of this movement are accomplished by using different foot stances. The most commonly used alternative foot stance involves placing the heels very close together and rotating the feet outward, so there is a 90-degree angle between them. This stance greatly increases the amount of stress placed on the outer sweep of the quadriceps muscles. You should also experiment with placing your feet farther forward on the foot platform than usual, which tends to transfer stress onto the teardrop (vastus medialis) head of the inner thigh, just above the knee.

STANDING LEG CURLS

Areas Emphasized—When performed with a flexed foot, this movement almost completely isolates the biceps femoris muscles at the back of each thigh. If you allow your toes to point as you do the movement, however, you increasingly add to the stress absorbed by your calf muscles.

Starting Position—Let's do the right leg first, and you can merely do the mirror image of this description (and of the photo that illustrates it) when you do the left leg. Stand next to the

Standing Leg Curls—midpoint

lever arm of the machine so that it is to the right of your right leg. Hook your right heel under the roller pad attached to the end of the lever arm. Stand with your left foot on the little platform provided for it, which elevates your body sufficiently for your right leg to clear the floor as you do the movement. Keep your left leg straight throughout the exercise. Flex your right foot and keep it flexed for your entire set.

Movement Performance—Use biceps femoris strength to slowly curl the roller pad upward in a semicircular arc until it is as high as you can get it. Hold this peak-contracted point of the movement for a moment and then slowly lower your leg back to the starting point. Repeat the exercise for the require number of reps.

Common Mistakes—When you're locked into a machine like this, it's difficult to make mistakes. Most commonly, a bodybuilder will begin to jerk the weight upward, rather than moving it slowly and smoothly over its arc. Jerking any weight is hard on the joints, in this case the knee joint, which is the one being flexed as you perform the movement.

Training Tips—You can stress different heads of the biceps femoris muscle group by angling your foot in different directions. Foot straight ahead works the muscle group in general; angled outward at about 45 degrees tends to put more stress on the outer head of the two-headed muscle group; angled inward at about 45 degrees tends to place more stress on the inner head.

OUTWARD CABLE KICKS

Areas Emphasized—Cable kicks can be performed in four different directions. This one, in which the leg is raised outward to the side under resistance, stresses the muscles at the sides of the hips and upper thighs.

Outward Cable Kicks—start and finish

Starting Position—Attach a padded cuff to your right ankle, rotating it so the ring on the cuff is facing inward toward your left leg. Attach the cuff to the end of the cable running through a floor pulley. Position yourself so that your left side is a few feet away from the pulley. Stand erect with your left hand braced against something to keep your body from moving as you do the exercise. You can either let your right hand hang down or place it on your hip. I've illustrated both of these positions in the photographs; pick whichever one feels more natural. Allow the weight to pull your right leg as far across the midline of your body as is comfortably possible. Keep both legs straight as you do the movement.

Movement Performance—Slowly move your right leg so your foot travels in a semicircular arc out to the side and as high as possible.

Outward Cable Kicks—midpoint

Hold the peak-contracted point of the movement for a moment; then slowly move your leg back along the same arc to the starting point. Repeat.

Common Mistakes—Although this is called an outward cable "kick," it's actually a leg abduction. Therefore, the movement should not be a kick but a slow, smooth, and controlled work of art. Don't allow your toe to point out to the side as you perform the movement. Instead, the working foot should be oriented so your toe points forward throughout the exercise.

Training Tips—Many gyms have a leg abduction machine in which you can move both legs simultaneously in this type of arc while you are in a seated position. The most commonly used abduction machine is manufactured by Nautilus, although several other equipment companies have similar machines on the market. I've

chosen to illustrate the cable version of this movement, because virtually all gyms have the cable setup, while some don't have the much more expensive abduction machine.

Back Exercises

CLOSE-GRIP FRONT LAT MACHINE PULLDOWNS

Areas Emphasized—This variation of lat pulldowns tends to work the upper and outer sections of the latissimus dorsi muscles, with secondary emphasis on the biceps, brachialis, and forearm flexor muscles. Done with a close-grip parallel-hands handle, the movement places your arms in a very favorable pulling position (as opposed to, let's say, wide-grip front lat machine pulldowns). This position allows you to push your lats even harder than in most other pulldown variations.

Starting Position—Attach a handle to the end of the cable running through an overhead pulley that gives you a parallel-hands grip with your hands set close together. Grasp the handle with your palms facing inward, extend your arms fully, and sit down on the seat of the machine. Be sure to wedge your knees beneath the restraint bar to keep your body from rising off the seat to meet the pulley handle as you pull it downward. Relax your lats so the weight of the machine can fully stretch them. Arch your back and keep it arched.

Movement Performance—Being sure that your elbows are traveling down and to the rear as far as possible, slowly bend your arms and pull the handle down to lightly touch the upper part of your chest. I find it easiest to look forward during the first half of the movement and then up during the second half, as the handle comes down to my chest. Hold this peak-contracted position for a moment and then slowly return to the starting point. Repeat the movement for an appropriate number of repetitions.

Common Mistakes—Failing to keep your back arched will prevent you from completely contracting your lats in the bottom position of the movement. Be sure to feel the pulling movement as completely as possible in your latissimus dorsi muscles rather than in your biceps, since it's easier to isolate your arms out of the movement when using this type of pulley handle.

Training Tips—The more you incline your torso backward as you do this movement, the lower on your lats the stress seems to be felt. You'll sometimes see a unique variation of this movement being done in the gym, with a bodybuilder placing his or her feet on the restraint bar and sitting on the floor behind the seat, angling the torso backward at about a 45-degree angle. This variation is often used as a finishing-off movement for an upper-back routine, since only light weights can be handled in such a position without coming up off the floor to meet the pulley handle.

Close-Grip Front Lat Machine Pulldowns—start and finish

Close-Grip Front Lat Machine Pulldowns—midpoint

SEATED PULLEY ROWS

Areas Emphasized—This movement not only stresses the lats for both width and thickness but also places a great deal of emphasis on the spinal erectors and trapezius muscles. Secondary stress is placed on the biceps, brachialis, and forearm flexor muscles.

Starting Position—Attach a handle that allows you to use a parallel-hands narrow grip to the end of the cable running through a machine pulley. Sit down on the machine seat and place your feet against the restraint bar, with your legs almost completely bent. Incline your torso forward at the waist and straighten your arms. Then

Seated Pulley Rows
—start and finish

Seated Pulley Rows
—midpoint

Seated Pulley Rows (variation with wide-grip parallel handle)—start and finish

straighten your legs to assume the weight attached to the end of the cable. Be sure your legs are kept slightly bent, as illustrated, throughout the movement in order to protect your lower back from harmful stress.

Movement Performance—Starting from a position in which your lats are fully stretched, simultaneously sit erect and pull the handle slowly in to touch the middle of your abdomen.

As you pull the handle toward your torso, be sure that you keep your elbows in tightly against your sides. Hold this peak-contracted position for a moment and then slowly return to the starting position. Repeat the movement for the required number of repetitions.

Common Mistakes—Leaning too far backward, past the point at which your torso is perpendicular to the gym floor, tends to transfer

Seated Pulley Rows (variation with wide-grip parallel handle)—midpoint

excessive stress to the trapezius muscles, which in turn robs the middle-back muscles of much of the benefit they should be receiving from the movement. Similarly, leaning too far forward at the start of the movement tends to place excessive stress on the erector spinae muscles of the lower back.

Training Tips—A variety of other handles can be used when you perform seated pulley rows. I've illustrated one of them, the wide-grip parallel-hands handle, which has a somewhat different effect on the middle-back muscles. A straight bar handle is also occasionally used, with which you take a shoulder-width under- or overgrip on the bar. Some gyms have a type of handle that is actually split into two individual loop handles that are in turn attached to the main cable by two shorter cables. Each handle stresses the back differently.

MACHINE ROWS

Areas Emphasized—This movement totally removes any stress from the lower back while placing heavy stress on the latissimus dorsi (mainly for thickness rather than width), rear deltoids, biceps, brachialis, and forearm flexor muscles.

Starting Position—Sit on the machine seat with the vertical padded board firmly against your chest and abdomen. Reach forward as far as possible to grasp the machine handles, or have a training partner pull the apparatus back toward you far enough so you can grasp the handles. Your arms should be approximately parallel to the gym floor and your palms facing inward toward each other at the start of the movement.

Movement Performance—Concentrating mentally on pulling primarily with your middle- and upper-back muscles rather than your arms, slowly pull the handles to the rear as far as is comfortably possible. Be sure to keep your elbows in close to your sides as you perform the exercise. Hold this peak-contracted position for a moment, return to the starting point, and repeat the movement for the desired number of repetitions.

Common Mistakes—Pulling with your arms rather than your back muscles is a mistake, because you will be doing plenty of exercises that isolate stress on your arms. The object is to pull with the back muscles primarily. Never jerk the weight, particularly in the arms-extended position.

Training Tips—Many of the rowing machines available in large gyms have various sets of handles, all of which should be used at one time or another. A parallel-hands grip is illustrated with this movement; some machines allow a normal rowing overgrip on their handles.

Machine Rows—start and finish

Machine Rows—midpoint

BACK HYPEREXTENSIONS

Areas Emphasized—This exercise places almost equal stress on the spinal erector muscles of the lower back, the gluteus maximus, and biceps femoris muscles.

Starting Position—Stand within the machine, facing toward the horizontal pad (the roller pad or other restraint should be behind you at this point). Place your hands on the pad in front of you and lever your body up onto it so that it rests against your upper thighs and pelvis. As you lean forward keeping your legs straight, your heels will come up underneath the restraint behind you, which will keep you from tipping entirely forward. Flex your body at the waist until your torso makes approximately a 60- to 90-degree angle with your legs. Hold your hands behind your head and/or neck or underneath your chin, as shown in the photo, throughout the movement to prevent your swinging yourself upward with arm momentum.

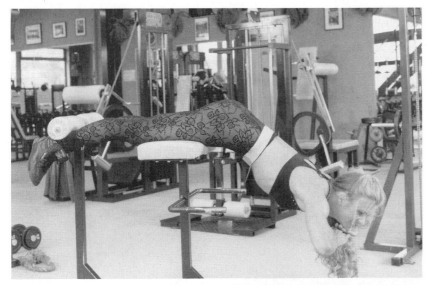

Back Hyperextensions
—start and finish

Back Hyperextensions
—midpoint

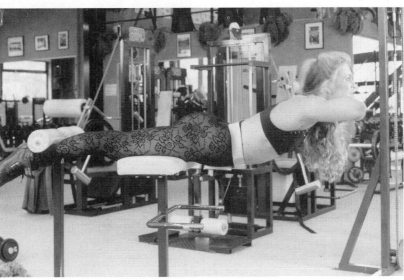

Movement Performance—Use lower-back, glute, and hamstring strength to raise your head slowly upward in a semicircular arc until your torso is parallel to the floor, as illustrated. Hold this peak-contracted position for a moment, go back to the starting point, and repeat for a sufficient number of repetitions to thoroughly stimulate the muscles you are working.

Common Mistakes—Arching your back so your torso comes up higher than the illustrated position parallel to the gym floor can actually injure your lower back. Avoid swinging your torso upward and downward. The movement should be slow and deliberate.

Training Tips—This is one exercise that allows you to work your lower back even when it is a little sore, because the movement tends to pull the vertebrae apart rather than crunching them together even tighter than they already are. When you get particularly strong in this back hyperextension movement, you can add weight by holding a loose barbell plate behind your head. The farther you slide your hips off the pad, the more stress you tend to place on your glutes and hamstrings at the expense of your spinal erectors.

Chest Exercises
. . . .

DUMBBELL INCLINE PRESSES

Areas Emphasized—As with barbell incline presses, this dumbbell movement places intense stress on the upper pectorals, the pec-delt tie-ins, the anterior deltoids, and triceps. Significant secondary stress is on the rest of the pectoral muscle complex, the medial deltoids, and the lats and other upper-back muscles.

Starting Position—Grasp two moderately heavy dumbbells and sit down on the incline-

bench seat. Sit back to rest your torso against the inclined pad, simultaneously pulling the weights up to your shoulders and pushing them to straight-arm's length directly above your shoulders. Rotate your upper-arm bones in your shoulder joints so your palms face each other at the starting point of the movement. Your feet can either rest on the gym floor, to balance your body in position on the bench, or on the bench seat, as I've illustrated. Resting your feet on the bench seat with legs fully bent makes the movement a bit more strict than if you rested your feet on the floor.

Movement Performance—Being sure to keep your elbows back, bend your arms and slowly lower the weights as far down as possible. As you lower the weights, rotate your wrists so your palms face forward in the bottom position. Without bounding at the bottom, slowly reverse the movement and press the weights back up to

Dumbbell Incline Presses—start and finish

straight-arm's length, rotating your hands again so your palms face inward in the finish position. Repeat the movement for the stated number of repetitions.

Common Mistakes—Be sure the weights don't travel too far out to the sides, or you'll lose one of them and possibly wrench a shoulder. If you rest your feet on the floor, don't use them to bridge your buns off the bench to improve pressing leverage. Never jerk or bounce the weights at any point along their range of motion.

Training Tips—You should experiment with different incline-bench angles. A bench at a 45-degree angle tends to place greater stress on the deltoids at the expense of the upper chest. A bench at 30 degrees is almost ideal. A bench with a low angle, achieved by merely slipping a block of wood under the head end of a flat exercise bench, tends to shift stress more onto the pectoral muscles themselves.

Dumbbell Incline Presses—midpoint

DUMBBELL DECLINE PRESSES

Areas Emphasized—As with barbell decline presses, this dumbbell movement stresses the lower outer sections of the pectorals and the triceps quite intensely. Strong secondary emphasis is on the anterior medial deltoids and the upper-back muscles, which impart rotational movement to the scapulae bones of the back.

Starting Position—Grasp two moderately heavy dumbbells and sit on the top part of the decline bench, the dumbbells resting on your knees. Place your insteps under the bench restraint and lie back on the decline bench, simultaneously pressing the dumbbells up to straight-arm's length, directly above your shoulder joints. Rotate your hands so your palms face inward at the start of the movement.

Movement Performance—Being sure to keep your elbows back, slowly bend your arms and lower the weights downward to as low a position as is comfortably possible. Simultaneously rotate your hands so your palms face toward your feet at the bottom point of the movement. Without bouncing at the bottom, reverse direction and slowly press the dumbbells back up to straight-arm's length, simultaneously rotating your hands so your palms again face inward toward each other at the finish of the pressing movement. Repeat.

Common Mistakes—Allowing your elbows to come in close to your torso on any dumbbell bench-pressing movement removes stress from your pectorals and places it more on your deltoids. Don't bounce or jerk the weights at any point along their full range of motion.

Training Tips—As with dumbbell incline presses, you can experiment with various degrees of bench decline, each of which will affect

Dumbbell Decline Presses—start and finish

Dumbbell Decline Presses—midpoint

your chest muscles differently. You should try a very low decline from time to time, a decline that is achieved by placing a thick block of wood under the legs of the bench at the foot end.

CABLE CROSSOVERS

Areas Emphasized—Depending on how you move your hands during this exercise, you can affect the entire pectoral muscle complex. Done in the standard manner, which I will describe here, the lower, outer, and inner sections of the pectorals get most of the emphasis, with secondary stress on the balance of the pectoral muscle complex and the anterior deltoids.

Cable Crossovers—start and finish

Starting Position—Attach loop handles to the ends of cables running through overhead crossover pulleys. Grasp the handle on one side and then grasp the other handle. Position yourself midway between the pulleys and slightly forward of an imaginary line drawn through each pulley. Set your feet a comfortable distance apart, either parallel to each other or with one a bit forward of the other. Bend your arms slightly and keep them rounded like this throughout the movement. Allow the weights attached to the cables to pull your arms up directly toward the pulleys, your palms facing the floor throughout the movement.

Cable Crossovers—midpoint

Movement Performance—Use pectoral strength to move your hands downward and slightly forward in semicircular arcs from the described starting point to a position at which they meet each other about 6 inches (18–20 centimeters) directly in front of your hips. Press your hands together in this position for a moment as you intensely contract your pectorals. Slowly return the pulley handles back along the same arcs to the starting point. Repeat for the suggested number of repetitions.

Common Mistakes—Standing too far forward places excessive stress on your shoulder joints. Doing the movement too rapidly or allowing your hands to gravitate out of their intended arcs of movement takes too much stress off your working chest muscles.

Training Tips—This movement is often performed in a kneeling position directly between the pulleys, something that tends to make the exercise somewhat more strict. You can do it with one arm at a time, holding onto something sturdy with your free hand to brace your body. The crossover movement in which the torso is kept erect is illustrated here, but you should also experiment with a movement in which your torso is inclined slightly forward at the top (head) end.

Shoulder Exercises

SEATED BARBELL PRESSES BEHIND THE NECK

Areas Emphasized—As with the standing version of this movement, direct stress is placed on the anterior deltoids and triceps, with strong secondary stress on the medial and posterior deltoids and the upper-back muscles, which impart rotational movement to the scapulae.

Seated Barbell Presses Behind the Neck—start and finish

Starting Position—Take an overgrip on a moderately heavy barbell, your hands set 4–6 inches (12–18 centimeters) wider than your shoulders on each side. Clean the weight up to your chest and push it over your head so it rests across the trapezius muscles behind your neck. Sit down on a flat exercise bench or on a bench with a back support that is perpendicular to the gym floor. Brace your feet flat on the floor or wrap them around the legs of the bench to steady your body in position throughout your set.

Movement Performance—Use shoulder and arm strength to slowly press the weight directly upward from your traps to a position at straight-arm's length above your shoulder joints. Flex your deltoids very hard in this straight-arm finish position. Then slowly lower the weight back to your shoulders, avoiding bouncing the

Seated Barbell Presses Behind the Neck—midpoint

weight off your traps. Repeat the movement for the required number of reps.

Common Mistakes—Bouncing the bar off your shoulders and traps is the error most common to this exercise. Allowing your elbows to drift forward reduces the direct stress you place on your anterior deltoids. Don't allow your torso to incline backward even one degree as you do this movement.

Training Tips—The main variation of this movement is to change the width of your grip on the bar, making it either wider or somewhat narrower. You won't, however, be able to make it much more than 3–4 inches (9–12 centimeters) narrower than the grip illustrated. You can, of course, also perform this movement while seated between the uprights of a Smith machine.

STANDING DUMBBELL PRESSES

Areas Emphasized—As with other forms of overhead pressing movements, dumbbell presses place direct stress on the front deltoids and triceps, with secondary stress on the medial delts and upper-back muscles.

Starting Position—Grasp two moderately heavy dumbbells and clean them up to shoulder level, rotating your wrists so your palms are directly forward as you begin. Be sure you keep your elbows almost directly under the dumbbells throughout the movement.

Movement Performance—Use shoulder and arm strength to slowly press the dumbbells directly upward from your shoulders to straight-arm's length over your shoulder joints, while simultaneously rotating your hands so your palms face inward toward each other at the finish. Reverse position and slowly lower the weights back to the starting point. Without bouncing in the bottom position, start your second rep and continue the set until you have met your repetition quota.

Common Mistakes—Inclining your body backward at the waist and/or kicking a bit with your knees to get the dumbbells started upward are little cheats that you should avoid. Never bounce the weights off your shoulders. The movement should always be performed slowly and deliberately.

Training Tips—Many bodybuilders do this exercise with their palms facing directly forward throughout the movement, rather than with the hand rotation I use. Either style of overhead dumbbell pressing is excellent. You can also do your dumbbell presses in a seated position to make the movement somewhat more strict, but don't expect to press as much weight seated as

Standing Dumbbell Presses—start and finish

Standing Dumbbell Presses—midpoint

standing. Many bodybuilders like to do dumbbell presses alternately, moving the weights in seesaw fashion, one going up as the other is descending. Regardless of the variation, overhead dumbbell presses are a truly great shoulder exercise that should frequently find itself in your shoulder routines.

TWO-ARM CABLE SIDE LATERALS

Areas Emphasized—As with the dumbbell side laterals described in Chapter 4, this movement isolates stress mainly on the medial heads of the deltoids, with secondary emphasis on the anterior delts.

Starting Position—The pulley cables you use in this exercise must cross in front of your body as you do the movement. Step to the right and grasp the floor pulley handle with your left hand. Move left and grasp the other pulley han-

Two-Arm Cable Side Laterals—midpoint

dle with your right hand. Then move to a position directly between the floor pulleys in which the weights pull your arms into a position in which they cross over each other in front of your chest. Place your feet at shoulder width or stagger them, with one foot in front of the other, as illustrated. Whichever way you choose to stand will put you in a position in which your body is braced solidly for the movement execution.

Movement Performance—Keeping your palms toward the gym floor, bend your arms slightly and keep them rounded like this for the entire set. Use deltoid strength to move the pulley handles in semicircular arcs out to the sides and slightly forward to a point just above shoulder level, as illustrated. Hold this peak-contracted position for a moment and then return your hands back along the same arcs to the starting point. Repeat the movement for the required number of repetitions.

Common Mistakes—Don't lean backward as you do the movement. Avoid jerking the weights. It's much better to use a moderate poundage and feel it in the working deltoid muscles than a heavier weight that you have to jerk upward in order to finish the movement.

Training Tips—This exercise is often done with one arm at a time, a movement that will be described in detail in Chapter 8. You'll find that you get more feel in your delts if you stand slightly behind an imaginary line drawn through the floor pulleys rather than directly between them or slightly ahead of that imaginary line.

ANJA DUMBBELL FRONT RAISES

Areas Emphasized—This is a very direct anterior deltoid movement that I use in many of my shoulder workouts. My coauthor has named it after me, because most other bodybuilders didn't start using it until they saw me doing it

Anja Dumbbell Front Raises—start and finish

regularly. But if the truth be known, I actually saw it first in one of his early books that was in the gym library when I started training. I tried the exercise out, liked the feel in my anterior deltoids when I did it, and stuck with it. I personally like to finish off a complete deltoid training session with dumbbell front raises.

Starting Position—Grasp a moderately heavy dumbbell by the handle with both hands, as illustrated. Be sure to bend your elbows about 30 degrees and keep them rounded like that throughout the range of motion of the exercise. Start with the dumbbell lightly touching your lower abdomen.

Movement Performance—Use deltoid strength to move the weight forward and upward in a semicircular arc to about eye level. Hold this

Anja Dumbbell Front Raises—midpoint

Seated Dumbbell Bent-Over Laterals—
start and finish

Seated Dumbbell Bent-Over Laterals—
midpoint

peak-contracted position for a moment and then slowly lower the dumbbell back to the starting point. Repeat the movement for an appropriate number of repetitions.

Training Tips—A similar exercise can be done with either an overgrip on a moderately heavy barbell or with two light dumbbells held in each hand. The second variation is described in detail in Chapter 8. All of these variations of forward raises can be made stricter if you perform them in a seated position.

SEATED DUMBBELL BENT-OVER LATERALS
Areas Emphasized—When it is correctly performed, this variation places isolated stress on the posterior heads of the deltoids, the traps,

and other upper-back muscles. Secondary stress is felt in the medial deltoids.

Starting Position—Grasp two moderately heavy dumbbells and sit down at the end of a flat exercise bench. Place your feet close together on the floor in front of you in such a way that your legs are bent at about a 90-degree angle. Incline your torso forward until it is below an imaginary line drawn at a 45-degree angle with the floor. Touch the dumbbells together directly beneath your legs. Bend your arms slightly and keep them rounded like this throughout your set.

Movement Performance—Use rear deltoid strength to move the weights slowly and directly out to the sides and upward until they reach shoulder level. Hold this peak-contracted position for a moment, slowly lower the weights back along the same arcs to the starting point, and repeat the movement.

Common Mistakes—Don't allow the weights to travel to the rear. It's preferable to have them go too far forward rather than to the rear of the shoulders. Don't raise your torso above the 45-degree established limit, or you will switch stress more to the medial deltoids.

Training Tips—If you have trouble with your torso moving upward and downward during the exercise, try pressing your chest against your upper legs throughout the movement. To feel the stress most strongly in your anterior deltoids, use light weights and move the dumbbells over their range of motion slowly and deliberately.

Arm Exercises
. . . .

SEATED ALTERNATE DUMBBELL CURLS

Areas Emphasized—Since the hands are strongly supinated in dumbbell curls, it should be clear that this is a direct biceps exercise. Minimum secondary emphasis is on the forearm flexor muscles.

Starting Position—Grasp two moderately heavy dumbbells and sit down at the end of a flat

exercise bench. Place your feet flat on the floor so that your upper body won't rock back and forth as you perform the exercise. Allow your arms to hang straight down at your sides, palms facing inward at the start of each repetition, and be sure to keep your upper arms in tightly against your sides as you do the curls. Slowly curl the weight in your right hand up to your shoulder, supinating your hand as you raise the dumbbell.

Movement Performance—Continue the movement in seesaw fashion, one dumbbell going up as the other descends. As each dumbbell comes down, be sure to pronate your hand so that your palm again faces inward when your arm is down at your side. Be sure to do an equal number of repetitions with each arm.

Common Mistakes—Rushing the exercise so that you begin swinging the weights and letting your upper arms travel outward robs your working biceps of much of the beneficial stress they should be receiving. Don't allow your torso to rock from side to side or forward and backward. Never fail to supinate your hand as completely as possible on each curling repetition, or you will be losing a lot of the effect you should be feeling in your biceps muscles.

Training Tips—I've seen some champion bodybuilders do this exercise a bit differently. They perform all of the reps on a set with one arm continuously, the other arm hanging down at their sides for balance. Then they repeat with the opposite arm. I personally don't have anything against this practice, but doing the exercise in seesaw fashion, as described, makes it significantly stricter. Obviously, you can also do this exercise with both arms simultaneously if you care to, but again a seesaw movement is stricter than curling both weights at the same time.

Seated Alternate Dumbbell Curls—midpoint

LUNGING ONE-ARM LOW-PULLEY CURLS

Areas Emphasized—I think I originated this particular exercise one day while fooling around with variations of pulley curls. At any rate, it's become a rather popular movement, because it gives a great stretch to the biceps before the curl is executed. Minimal secondary stress is on the forearm flexors.

Starting Position—Attach a loop handle to the end of a cable running through a floor pulley and grasp that handle in your left hand. Turn your hand so your palm is facing the floor at the start of the movement. Face away from the pulley and step forward far enough so you will have resistance on your biceps throughout the full range of motion of the muscle complex. Lunge forward with your right leg, keeping the left leg

Lunging One-Arm
Low-Pulley Curls—
start and finish

Lunging One-Arm
Low-Pulley Curls—
midpoint

relatively straight and bending the right to about a 75-degree angle, as illustrated. Incline your torso forward so it makes one long line with your rear leg. Rest your free forearm on your right knee, as I am doing. Keep your wrist straight and stiff throughout each repetition.

Movement Performance—Use only biceps strength to slowly curl the pulley handle forward and upward in a semicircular arc until your arm is as fully flexed as you can get it. Hold this peak-contracted position for a moment while intensely contracting your working biceps.

Slowly return your left hand back along the same arc to the starting point and repeat the movement for the correct number of repetitions. Switch over to the other arm and do a full set with it. Then alternate arms until you have done the same number of sets and reps with each one and have met your work-volume requirements for this exercise. When you do the movement with your right arm, do the mirror image of the description of the left-handed exercise.

Common Mistakes—It's fairly difficult to cheat on this exercise, but one way to do it is to allow your shoulders to twist toward the pulley and then jerk back to a more normal orientation to get the weight started. As with every other exercise I've described in this book, it's much better to perform a slow and controlled movement with plenty of mental concentration on the working muscles.

Training Tips—Your hand will already be supinated at the beginning of this movement if you get set up correctly, but be sure that you concentrate on keeping your hand supinated. You might even exaggerate the supinated wrist twist at the top of the movement. I've sometimes performed this exercise while seated on a flat exercise bench, but that doesn't give me quite the intense effect on my biceps that is achieved when I perform it in the illustrated lunging position. But if I hadn't been experimenting with variations of one-arm pulley curls in the first place, I wouldn't have evolved this key biceps exercise.

SINGLE DUMBBELL TRICEPS EXTENSIONS

Starting Position—Grasp a moderately heavy dumbbell in both hands so your palms rest against the underside of the upper grouping of plates when the dumbbell handle is hanging vertical to the gym floor. Be sure to encircle the

Single Dumbbell Triceps Extensions—start and finish

Single Dumbbell Triceps Extensions—midpoint

dumbbell handle with your thumbs to keep the weight from accidentally sliding out of your hands as you do the exercise. Raise the weight up to straight-arm's length directly above your head and sit down at the end of a flat exercise bench, bracing your feet solidly on the floor to balance your upper body as you execute each repetition of single dumbbell triceps extensions.

Movement Performance—Being sure to keep your elbows pointed upward at all times, slowly bend your arms and lower the dumbbell to the rear in a semicircular arc to as low a position down behind your neck and upper back as is comfortably possible. Without jerking at any time, reverse the movement and use triceps strength to slowly return the dumbbell back along the same arc to the starting point. Repeat the movement for the suggested number of repetitions.

Common Mistakes—The most common error in doing this exercise is to cut the movement short of its full possible range of motion. That always robs the working muscles of some of the benefit they should be receiving from the exercise. Be careful not to incline your torso backward as you complete this movement, because that's also a slight cheat.

Training Tips—You can also do this exercise while standing, but that makes it a little less strict, because you can jerk with your knees a bit to get the weight moving. There is also a variation in which you hold a dumbbell in one hand and do the exercise with one arm at a time.

BEHIND-THE-HEAD CABLE TRICEPS EXTENSIONS

Areas Emphasized—I particularly like this exercise because it stresses the meaty inner head of the triceps muscle more intensely than the rest of the muscle complex. At the start of the movement there is a beneficial stretch on the entire triceps muscle group. Obviously you can't totally isolate the medial and outer triceps heads from the movement, but proportionately greater

stress is placed on the longer inner head than on the other two.

Starting Position—Attach a short straight bar handle to the end of the cable running through an overhead pulley. I am illustrating the movement with a bar handle that angles downward slightly at each end, which is even better; a lot of gyms, however, don't have this type of handle in their equipment inventory. Take an overgrip on the handle, your hands set so your index fingers are about one palm's width from the middle of the handle where the cable attaches to it. I prefer to use a thumbless grip on this movement, with my thumbs (placed on the bar) going in the same direction as my fingers, but you can just as effectively encircle the bar with your thumbs if this makes you feel more secure. Turn away from the pulley and walk forward just enough so you keep constant tension on your triceps throughout the movement. Lunge forward with either leg to balance your body securely. Incline your torso forward so it makes approximately a 45-degree angle with the gym floor. Straighten your arms and assume the illustrated starting position with your arms somewhat higher than they would be if you were trying to keep your arms parallel to the gym floor as you do the exercise.

Movement Performance—Keeping your upper arms relatively motionless, bend your arms slowly and allow your hands to move in a semicircular arc back behind your head until your arms are as fully bent as possible. Use triceps strength to move the pulley handle back along the same arc to the starting point, and repeat the movement for the required number of repetitions.

Common Mistakes—There's a natural tendency to heave the weight forward from the bottom position by moving your torso upward and

Behind-the-Head Cable Triceps Extensions—start and finish

downward. Resist the temptation to do this. If you have a lot of trouble with this type of cheat, try doing the exercise kneeling on the gym floor, with your elbows braced on a flat exercise bench throughout the movement. This is a variation popularized by Larry Scott, the bodybuilder who won the first two Mr. Olympia titles, in 1965 and 1966.

Training Tips—You can experiment with different grip widths as well as with different torso angles in relation to the gym floor. Every slight variation of grip or torso angle will affect the triceps muscles somewhat differently.

Behind-the-Head Cable Triceps Extensions—midpoint

Barbell Wrist Curls—start and finish

Barbell Wrist Curls—midpoint

Barbell Wrist Curls (variation with palms facing down)—start and finish

BARBELL WRIST CURLS

Areas Emphasized—When executed with the palms facing upward, this movement places direct and intense stress on the forearm flexor muscles. When done with the palms facing the floor, stress is transferred to the somewhat weaker forearm extensor muscles. For a complete physique, you will need to work your forearms just as hard as all other areas of your body. I've seen a lot of competitors onstage with very weak forearm development, which might not have been the case if they had done enough wrist curls in workouts leading up to the contest.

Starting Position—I like to do each variation of this exercise kneeling on the gym floor and resting my forearms across a flat exercise bench to make the movement stricter. Assume an undergrip on the bar, your hands set at about shoulder, or slightly narrower, width. Place your forearms across the exercise bench, as illustrated, and keep them motionless throughout this movement. You can either encircle the bar with your thumbs, as illustrated, for this palms-up variation, or use a thumbless grip as I've illustrated for the palms-down version. In either case, allow the weight on the bar to pull your hands downward as far as is comfortably possible in order to stretch the forearm flexors.

Movement Performance—Use forearm muscle power alone to raise the weight upward in a small semicircular arc to as high a position as possible. Lower the weight back along the same arc to the starting point, and repeat the movement for the listed number of repetitions.

Common Mistakes—As with every other exercise, make the movement slow and controlled rather than jerky and out of control. Try to fight the tendency to raise your elbows up off the bench to assist you in finishing the curling

movement. The most common variation of this exercise is reverse wrist curls, which are the same movement performed with palms facing the gym floor rather than the ceiling. You can do both variations of barbell wrist curls while you are in a seated position at the end of a flat exercise bench, with your forearms placed on your legs, wrists extending off your knees to free your hands for movement. You can do wrist curls with dumbbells as well, or with a single dumbbell one arm at a time.

Calf Exercise

CALF PRESSES

Areas Emphasized—This movement directly stresses the gastrocnemius muscles of the calves and virtually none of the rest of the body. While the movement can be done on both horizontal and vertical leg-press machines, I'll describe and illustrate how to do it on the more popular 45-degree angled machine. From the description, you can easily infer how to do it on the other types of leg-press apparatuses.

Starting Position—Sit in the machine with your back firmly set against the angled backboard and your buns in the angle at the bottom of the board. Place just your toes and the balls of your feet on the bottom edge of the sliding platform of the machine, with your heels hanging off. Your feet should be set about shoulder-width apart, and they should be parallel to each other throughout the movement. Straighten your legs (you won't have to unlock the machine for the movement, so don't even think about it). Allow the weight on the slide to push your toes and the balls of your feet as far toward your face as possible, completely stretching the calf muscles at the start of each repetition. Keep your legs locked straight throughout the movement.

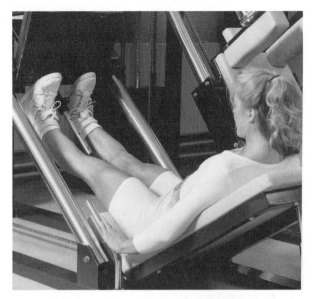

Calf Presses—start and finish

Calf Presses—midpoint

Calf Presses (variation with toes angled outward)—midpoint

Calf Presses (variation with toes angled inward)—midpoint

Movement Performance—Completely extend your feet, holding the pointed-toe position for a moment to increase the movement's peak-contraction effect, and then return slowly to the starting point. Repeat the movement for the required number of repetitions.

Common Mistakes—Unlocking your legs and kicking with them to get the weight out is a mistake that robs your working calf muscles of much of the resistance they should be receiving. Unless you are doing burns at the end of a set taken to positive failure, never bounce the weight when your feet are fully flexed.

Training Tips—I've also illustrated the two most common alternative toe positions for calf presses: toes angled outward at about 45 degrees on each side and toes angled inward at about 45 degrees on each side. Toes out works the outer part of the calf more, while toes in stresses the inner part of the calf more intensely. You can also experiment with various widths of foot placement on the platform, each of which will affect your calf muscles somewhat differently.

Abdominal Exercises

HANGING LEG RAISES
Areas Emphasized—Hanging leg raises stress the entire frontal abdominal wall (rectus abdominis), with perhaps slightly more emphasis on the lower than upper abdominals.

Starting Position—If you have elbow straps to dangle from, stand on a stool beneath the chinning bar and slide your upper arms into the straps, bending your arms enough so you can grasp the upper parts of the straps. Have a partner remove the stool. As long as you keep your upper arms parallel to the floor, you will be secure in this type of apparatus. If you don't have the elbows straps, jump up and take a shoulder-width overgrip on the chinning bar, allowing your body to hang straight down from your hands. Regardless of how you attach yourself to the chinning bar, bend your legs to about a 30-degree angle and keep them bent like this throughout your set to keep unnecessary stress off your lower back. Start with your thighs hanging straight down from your hips.

Movement Performance—Use abdominal strength to slowly raise your legs upward so

Hanging Leg Raises—midpoint

your feet travel in semicircular arcs from the starting point to a position on approximately the same level as your hips. Slowly lower your legs back to the starting point, and repeat the movement for the suggested number of repetitions.

Common Mistakes—There's a temptation to do this movement with the legs held straight, but you'll injure your lower back sooner or later if you insist on using such an exercise style. Never jerk or cut any movements short of their full range.

Training Tips—Particularly when you're hanging from your hands, you'll notice that your body has a tendency to swing a little. You can kill this swing either with the timing of each repetition of leg raises or by having a training partner hold your hips lightly as you do the exercise. You can also do a movement called frog kicks in this position. You simply pull your knees up to your chest while simultaneously flexing your legs fully. The frog kick movement does tend to place much more stress on the lower part of the frontal abdominal wall than on the upper section.

ELBOW PEDESTAL LEG RAISES
Areas Emphasized—This movement stresses the midsection muscles in much the same manner as hanging leg raises do, with emphasis on the entire frontal abdominal wall. With most types of leg raises, you will place some stress on the intercostal muscles at the sides of your waist, but most of the stress is on the rectus abdominis.

Starting Position—Directly under the pads on which you rest your forearms as you do the movement are a couple of steps that allow you to get into position in the apparatus very conveniently. Simply brace your back against the slightly angled back pad and grasp the handles, running your forearms down their pads. This

should put your upper arms in a nearly vertical position. Bend your legs slightly and keep them bent throughout the movement. Start with your legs hanging below your hips so your thighs make one line with your torso.

Movement Performance—Use abdominal strength to raise your legs slowly upward so your feet travel in a semicircular arc from the starting point to a position at the same level as your hips. Hold this peak-contracted point for a moment, and then return slowly back along the same arc to the starting point. Repeat the movement for the desired number of reps.

Common Mistakes—No jerking or swinging of the legs is permitted in this movement. The entire movement should be slow, deliberate, and controlled.

Training Tips—I've seen some women do this exercise in scissors fashion, raising their legs alternately. I've tried doing the movement that way, but don't get the same feel in my frontal abs as when I raise my legs together. But give this variation a try to see whether you like it.

Elbow Pedestal Leg Raises—midpoint

Free Floor Crunches—start and finish

FREE FLOOR CRUNCHES

Areas Emphasized—All variations of crunches intensely stress the entire rectus abdominis, particularly the upper half of the frontal abdominal muscle wall. Strong secondary stress is placed on the intercostal muscles at your sides.

Starting Position—Lie on your back on an exercise mat, place your hands behind your head for the entire movement, and raise your legs upward so your thighs are perpendicular to the floor. Cross your ankles and bend your legs

Free Floor Crunches—midpoint

slightly, as illustrated, and keep them in this position throughout the movement.

Movement Performance—All at one time, exhale forcefully, use frontal abdominal strength to curl your shoulders and upper back from the floor, and attempt to force your shoulders toward your hips, effectively shortening your torso for a moment. If you do these three functions simultaneously, you will be rewarded with an intense frontal abdominal contraction. Try to hold this peak-contracted position for a moment and then slowly return to the starting point. Repeat.

Common Mistakes—You can get your shoulders and upper back off the mat by throwing your arms forward rather than pulling with your abs, but that doesn't give you much frontal abdominal stimulation. Merely bending your head forward at the neck does nothing for your midsection unless you are also pulling hard with your rectus abdominis muscles.

Training Tips—Try twisting from one side to another on succeeding repetitions to place more stress on your intercostals. A variation of this exercise is done with your feet placed flat against a wall and your legs bent at 90-degree angles, your shins parallel to the gym floor. In this variation, be sure that you raise your hips off the mat using lower-abdominal strength rather than by pulling with your biceps femoris muscles.

SEATED TWISTS

Areas Emphasized—To tone your external and internal oblique muscles and intercostals, you can do seated twisting movements with a broomstick or unloaded barbell bar across your shoulders.

Starting Position—Sit down astride a flat exercise bench and intertwine your legs in the upright legs of the bench to restrain your lower body as you do the movement. (For photographic simplicity, I'm illustrating this movement sitting at an angle on one end of the bench. This is also a possible exercise position, as long as you press your feet firmly against the floor as you do the movement.) Place the broomstick or unloaded bar across your shoulders behind your neck and balance it in that position throughout your set, grasping the stick or bar out near the ends. Face straight forward at the start.

Movement Performance—Twist smoothly and powerfully as far in each direction as possible, using your lower spine as your pivot point. As long as you keep your pelvic structure stationary and twist at the lower part of your waist, you are doing the movement correctly. Continue twisting from side to side until you have done the required number of reps in each direction. One full cycle starts with you facing forward, then twisting fully to the left, fully to the right, and ends with you again facing forward.

Common Mistakes—If you twist your torso high in your spine (in the thoracic vertebrae), the exercise does little if anything for the obliques and intercostals. Cutting any motion short of its full range is another way of robbing the targeted muscles of some of the stress they ought to receive.

Training Tips—You can do a similar twisting movement in a standing position, locking your legs and pelvis and twisting from the lower back so your pelvis doesn't go with your torso. Another variation is done bent over at the waist so the torso is held parallel to the gym floor throughout the movement.

Seated Twists—start and finish

Seated Twists—midpoint (left)

Seated Twists—midpoint (right)

Suggested Intermediate-Level Routines
• •

I'll give you two types of split routines to follow in this section. The first two are four-day-per-week splits and the third one can be used for either three-on/two-off or three-on/one-off split routines. By the time you get to the intermediate level of weight training and bodybuilding, you will have 3–5 months of steady training behind you, so it's appropriate to move up to a split routine from a three-day-per-week full-body program. Each succeeding routine in Figure 6-1 is significantly more intense than the previous one.

Fig. 6-1. Intermediate-Level Routines

Routine 1

Monday/Thursday

Exercise	Sets	Reps
Hanging Leg Raises	2–3	15–20
Angled Leg Presses	4	15–8*
Hack Squats	3	10–12
Leg Extensions	3	10–12
Standing Leg Curls	3	10–12
Stiff-Legged Deadlifts	3	12–15
Seated Alternate Dumbbell Curls	3	8–12
Lunging One-Arm Low-Pulley Curls	3	8–12
Single Dumbbell Triceps Extensions	3	8–12
Behind Head Cable Triceps Extensions	3	8–12
Barbell Wrist Curls	2–3	10–15
Seated Calf Raises	4	10–15

Tuesday/Friday

Exercise	Sets	Reps
Elbow Pedestal Leg Raises	2–3	20–25
Seated Twists	1	50
Dumbbell Incline Presses	4	12–6*
Dumbbell Decline Presses	4	8–10
Seated Presses Behind Neck	4	12–6*
Two-Arm Cable Side Laterals	2	8–12
Seated Dumbbell Bent-Over Laterals	2	8–12
Close-Grip Front Pulldowns	4	12–6*
Seated Pulley Rows	4	8–12
Back Hyperextensions	2–3	10–15
Calf Presses	4	15–20

Routine 2

Monday/Thursday

Exercise	Sets	Reps
Free Floor Crunches	3	20–30
Seated Twists	1	50
Dumbbell Incline Presses	4	12–6*
Machine Bench Presses	3	6–10
Cable Crossovers	2	10–12
Standing Dumbbell Presses	4	12–6*
Anja Dumbbell Front Raises	3	8–12
Upright Rows	2	8–12
Lying Barbell Triceps Extensions	4	12–6*
Behind Head Cable Triceps Extensions	3	8–12
Standing Calf Raises	5	12–15

Tuesday/Friday

Exercise	Sets	Reps
Hanging Leg Raises	3	15–20
Squats	5	15–6*
Hack Squats	3	10–12
Leg Extensions	3	10–12
Lying Leg Curls	4	10–12
Outward Cable Kicks	3	10–15
Machine Rows	4	12–6*
Lat Pulldowns Behind Neck	3	8–12
Close-Grip Front Lat Pulldowns	2	8–12
Seated Alternate Dumbbell Curls	4	12–6*
Lunging One-Arm Low-Pulley Curls	3	8–12
Barbell Wrist Curls	2–3	10–15
Barbell Reverse Wrist Curls	2–3	10–15
Calf Presses	5	15–20

Routine 3

Day One

Exercise	Sets	Reps
Incline Sit-Ups	3	20–30
Machine Incline Presses	4	12–6*
Flat-Bench Dumbbell Presses	3	6–10

Exercise	Sets	Reps
Cable Crossovers	3	10–12
Seated Pulley Rows	4	12–6*
Parallel-Grip Front Lat Machine Pulldowns	3	8–12
Parallel-Grip Lat Pulldowns Behind Neck	3	8–12
Back Hyperextensions	2–3	10–15
Upright Rows	3	8–12
Standing Calf Raises	4–5	15–20

Day Two

Exercise	Sets	Reps
Incline Leg Raises	3	20–30
Seated Twists	1–2	50
Angled Leg Presses	5	15–6*
Hack Squats	3	10–12
Leg Extensions	4	10–12
Lying Leg Curls	4	10–12
Stiff-Legged Deadlifts	3	12–15
Seated Calf Raises	3–4	10–15
Calf Presses	3–4	20–25

Day Three

Exercise	Sets	Reps
Hanging Leg Raises	3	20–25
Seated Machine Presses Behind Neck	4	12–6*
Dumbbell Side Laterals	3	8–12
Seated Dumbbell Bent-Over Laterals	3	8–12
Standing Barbell Curls	4	12–6*
Seated Alternate Dumbbell Curls	4	8–10
Single Dumbbell Triceps Extensions	4	12–6*
Behind Head Cable Triceps Extensions	4	8–10
Barbell Wrist Curls	3	12–15
Barbell Reverse Wrist Curls	3	12–15
Seated Twisting	1–2	50

*Pyramid

A split routine works specific body parts more intensely by allowing you to spend more time and energy on each muscle group.

7
Advanced-Level Training Techniques

· ·

By now you've probably made some sensational gains in both strength and physical appearance. I'm sure you won't want to wrestle Godzilla, but trudging up a flight of stairs with a couple of heavy grocery bags is no doubt a snap. You also probably have a high degree of reserve strength to survive or handle—God forbid, you won't have to—some potentially life-threatening emergencies.

There are well-documented cases of untrained 90-pound (40-kilogram) women lifting cars off their children. You're in a class now in which you could probably lift the corner of a semi under similar circumstances. Even though the chance you might have to use your superwoman strength is a million to one, it still gives you a great degree of self-confidence to know that the extra power is there if you ever do need it.

I'm sure you have been checking yourself out in the mirror with increasing frequency and a more critical eye as time goes on. All of that cellulite you had in your upper legs, hips, and buns is now gone, isn't it? You bet it is. Your body-fat levels have fallen low enough so that you can easily show off the outlines of all the major muscle groups in your body whenever you

decide to selectively tense them. Face it, you've gone from being a mouse to being a lithe, tawny lioness.

Your muscles are much firmer to the touch, and most of them are larger and better shaped than when you started. You probably now have that ideal, feminine, hourglass figure you used to think existed only in the beauty magazines. Well, it's for real, and as long as you train fairly regularly and follow a good bodybuilding lifestyle, you'll keep it. Part of that lifestyle is a fat-restricted diet, which I will explain in detail in Chapter 11.

What I'm hinting at here is that many readers have come as far down the bodybuilding pathway as they ever intended. For those of you who have already reached your physical goals, more power to you as long as you continue to maintain this high grade of physical conditioning by training regularly and making a bodybuilding diet an integral part of your lifestyle.

You have my sincere admiration for coming this far with me. I love what you have done to reshape and strengthen your body and to improve your health to a degree that couch potatoes can never appreciate—or achieve.

If you train hard and consistently and eat the right foods, the results will motivate you to work even harder.

Many women have fallen by the wayside while you have persevered and made yourself into someone very special, someone with a seemingly limitless amount of personal energy. Do you realize how many women out there who are not in the bodybuilding world would almost kill for your physical appearance, physical fitness, energy levels, and positive outlook on life? The number is staggering.

Keep up the good work, and always be the best possible ambassador that our way of life could have. Be generous with your time and energy when an out-of-shape neighbor asks, "How did you ever get legs like that?" Tell her where she can train, make up a simple beginner's routine for her to follow, answer all of her questions, and please tell her where she can purchase her own copy of this book. If you lend it out, you'll probably never see it again.

Now what about the thousands of elite-level women who want to go even further? With the Anja approach you can change your body even more, build even greater overall strength, improve body flexibility, and develop absolutely tremendous self-confidence. You can get into such superb physical condition that with only a little specialized training, you could be entering—even winning—triathlons.

You might be so naturally strong that you'll choose to become a competitive Olympic lifter or powerlifter. I don't emphasize either of these competitive branches of weight training, since I am a professional bodybuilder, but I have great respect for female lifters. If you have the natural strength and physical durability for one or both of these sports, someone in your gym will have already noticed your potential and will have either begun to coach you or will have channeled you to another gym in your area that caters to lifters. I hope you set some national and world records! You already have developed a good foundation for a transition into either sport.

That leaves us with those elite women who wish to excel at bodybuilding. I know how excited you feel, because I was in your shoes at the ages of 16 and 17. At 18, the German bodybuilding federation sent me to Australia to compete in the Junior World Championships held each year for teenage athletes. I won my weight division and then had to reevaluate my goals and scale them upward. It had suddenly become obvious that I have much better genes than I had originally thought.

Just after my 20th birthday I won a qualification posedown to represent Germany in the heavyweight class at the European Championships, held that year in Warsaw, Poland. I wouldn't say that I was especially intimidated by the other heavyweights—I was the lightest and youngest woman in the division—but I didn't expect to win. I vividly remember my coauthor, Bill Reynolds (then editor of *Muscle & Fitness* and later editor of *Flex* magazine), coming up to me just after I weighed in. He politely introduced himself and asked me to promise him the first

interview after I won. I remember saying, "Okay, but I *won't* win."

Bill was right; I did win, beating out my teammate Suzanne Steurer and the great Dutch bodybuilder Peggy Ouwerling. The following weekend, I won the German Championship. About three months later, Bill's story was published, and suddenly I was a famous bodybuilder, much in demand for posing exhibitions and training-nutrition seminars.

Before delivering my son, I placed second in the IFBB Pro World Championships, plus fourth and then second in the Ms. Olympia. As my son grows, he needs my full-time attention, so my competitive bodybuilding career is currently on hold. But I believe it's safe to say that the bodybuilding world hasn't seen the last of Anja Langer as a competitor.

My rise in the sport was so quick that it makes me dizzy even to think of it now. Yours will probably go somewhat more slowly, but your burning desire to succeed will take you to the

Taking a break from the gym with my son, Elija, and Boy.

top. Certainly, you will keep improving quickly enough that you will be constantly setting newer and higher goals for yourself.

Most of the remaining chapters of this book will help you reach the level at which you can begin to take home first-place trophies and medals at local, state, and regional competitions. The chapter that you are reading now will teach you all of the advanced-level techniques you must master to become a successful competitor.

In Chapter 9 you will learn the importance of regular stretching to keep your body flexible, supple, and free of injury. Chapter 11 thoroughly covers the subject of bodybuilding nutrition—with proper nutrition you will win at least 50% of the battle during most of the year and up to 90% of the battle during the final two or three weeks before a competition. I have also included a discussion of the psychology of bodybuilding, in Chapter 12.

If you master all of these subjects, have at least average genetic potential, constantly monitor your nutrition, and put another year or two into hard gym training and aerobics, you *can* become a bodybuilding champion. You will have done it all on your own; no one will reap the rewards of your bodybuilding competitions but you.

I have frequently stated at training seminars and have written in magazine articles that you get out of bodybuilding exactly what you put into it. If you train hard and consistently, and if you eat the right foods every day, it will show, because you carry your sport around with you every day. Even the general public knows a great bodybuilder when it sees one.

Genetic Potential

Chapter 2 contains a few paragraphs about heredity factors and how they affect the degree of success you might expect to achieve by training with weights. Now it's time to get down to the real nitty-gritty and determine whether you are genetically gifted enough to become a serious competitive bodybuilder. If you want to know whether you have what it takes to be a winner, keep reaching. If you're afraid you might not have good genetic potential for bodybuilding, you can still take up croquet or backyard badminton.

Many negative things have been written about the role genetics play in bodybuilding. I've even read one pessimistic article that stated that only five or six individuals out of a hundred thousand have the genes to become world champion bodybuilders. And that author—himself a former world champion—went on to say that perhaps only one or two of those gifted five or six individuals would ever be exposed to the activity, and most of them probably wouldn't stick to a steady training regimen and appropriate diet. It seemed to him that one man or woman in one million would have optimum genetics, would train and diet diligently, and would ultimately triumph and take his or her destined position as a superstar.

Anyone who would believe this arrogant pap would probably be so discouraged that she would never set foot in a gym again! This author is so wrong about genetic potential in bodybuilding that they ought to lock him up in a dark room and throw away the key. The picture is not nearly as gloomy as he portrays it. Sure, some women have great genes and they reach the top of the pyramid very quickly. Others with lesser genetic gifts merely take longer and have to work harder to reach the top. Even a woman with the world's worst genes can develop a sensational body if she is persistent, trains hard and intelligently, and constantly monitors her diet.

It's foolish to view genetic potential as a limiting factor in bodybuilding. It's much more intelligent to be positive and think of it as an *enabling* factor. If you have great genes, you're just going to get there faster and more easily than many other women. And if you squander good genes, someone with markedly lesser abilities will mop the floor with you at your next competition.

It is best to assess your genetic potential for bodybuilding after at least one year of steady bodybuilding training. By then, every criterion of genetic potential should be obvious and vividly visible. I would suggest that you make your own assessment first and then consult with an experienced competitor or gym owner for confirmation of your evaluation. Be very careful to avoid asking the type of gym-rat friend who thinks you can do no wrong. She'll pat you on a muscleless shoulder and tell you you're ready to take on Lenda Murray at the next Ms. Olympia.

What should you look for? The answers to the following nine questions should give you a good idea of what your potential to become a competitive bodybuilder is:

• *How tall are you?* The bigger titles generally are won by taller, long-legged women, such as Cory Everson, who is 5′8″ tall and won six consecutive Ms. Olympia trophies. At 5′6″, I fall right into the middle range of better bodybuilders. You'll see some great physiques on women who are 5′1″ or 5′2″, but they seldom win overall titles, just titles in their weight class.

• *How intelligent are you?* Bodybuilding has evolved into a rather complicated scientific endeavor, and less intelligent women will fall by the wayside—the road to the top of the pyramid is littered with them. You will be require to understand such complex scientific disciplines as anatomy, kinesiology, biomechanics, biochemistry, exercise physiology, and every variety of sports medicine. Bimbos don't make the grade here.

• *How broad are your shoulders in relation to your waist-hip structure?* Ideally, you should have some indication that you are approaching the much sought-after hourglass figure after one year of training. The broader your basic shoulder structure, the better, because there is a limit to how much deltoid development you can add to each side to make them even wider. It's also nice to have a petite waist and hip structure and particularly good if you have a very narrow waist that accentuates latissimus dorsi flare and a feminine hip contour. If you have narrow shoulders, deduct a point from your optimum total. Ditto if you have a wide waist.

• *Do you have any glaring weak points?* After a year of steady workouts, any chronically weak point will become evident. Some of these problems are genetically determined and can't be corrected, regardless of how hard and systematically you go about it. Most weak points, however, will respond to specialized training if you use the muscle priority principle discussed in Chapter 5.

• *How large are your joints?* Small knees and ankles make even average calves look great, and small wrists are a good deal of help in displaying showy arms. Large joints, on the other hand, are a bit of a handicap, because you'll need to develop truly herculean muscles to offset them.

• *Are you making gains at an acceptable rate of speed?* If gains in muscle mass are coming so slowly that you become discouraged, you might give croquet and badminton a second thought. Or you might decide to train recreationally rather than for competition.

• *Are you relatively free of injuries?* All bodybuilders experience minor joint problems from time to time—particularly when in high-intensity precontest training—and they learn just to live with them. But if your horse happens to fall on you and mangles one of your knees, you might discover that you are limited as a bodybuilder. I hope it doesn't limit you so much that you can't find someone to sell the horse to. Similarly, chronically bad backs have nipped many potentially great bodybuilding careers in the bud.

• *Do you truly love the sport?* If you answer yes

to this question, you have the built-in drive and determination to become a champion. It will take time to learn about your body and how it reacts to training and dietary stimuli. Have the patience to allow yourself to mature gradually.

• *Can you afford the time and expense necessary to become a great bodybuilder?* You probably already have a good idea of how much time it takes each week to complete your weight and aerobics workouts. And that amount of time will certainly increase, particularly prior to a competition. Bodybuilding can also be costly. It's nothing out of the ordinary to spend $200–$300 per month on special food supplements, and probably even more on extra food that most individuals don't need to eat. Training attire can add to your monthly bodybuilding bill. Once you are competing, you'll need to figure in travel and hotel expenses. So it should be obvious that you either need a good job that is not physically taxing, an understanding spouse, or rich parents. Even with none of these factors going for you, however, you can still become a winner. Debby McKnight won an overall U.S. Championship as a single mother working 60 hours per week and still coping with the needs of two young children. If you want to win badly enough, no hurdle is too high for you to jump.

How It Should Feel

If you haven't already picked up on it, good bodybuilders are emphatically not weightlifters. Instead, we are weight*feelers*. You may read or hear that there is a direct, linear relationship between the amount of weight you can pump for 6–8 reps and the size and quality of the muscles that actually move that weight. This statement is misleading, because it is both true and false, depending on how you approach it.

For beginning and intermediate trainees, it's best to say it's true that there's a relationship between your strength levels in basic exercises and the mass and quality of the muscles that push or pull that iron. Once a novice bodybuilder has learned correct, strict form for all of the exercises she does, her next task should be to spend a year or two developing as much basic strength as possible. With each strength increase will come a noticeable increase in muscle mass.

In a very real sense, you are a weight*lifter* for the first couple of years you train as a bodybuilder. If you fail to pay your dues with heavy iron those first two years, you might be shortchanging yourself on what you will need down the road as you begin to prepare for your first competition. If you've pumped the heavy iron first, your physique will have a powerful, well-knit look that the pump artists never achieve. Before you begin to even think about refining your physique, build a good degree of general strength and muscle mass. Be sure to at least maintain these qualities as you seek better refinement by always keeping one or two heavy, basic movements in your routine for each body part.

I am arbitrarily setting it at the two-year mark, but a time will come when you reach the point at which emphasis must be shifted toward refining and perfecting your physique, leading up to the start of your competitive bodybuilding career. Then, and only then, you become a *feeler* rather than a lifter.

To sculpt every possible facet of a muscle, you will need to do plenty of isolation exercises for the area, using more moderate poundages and *feeling* the weight over the fullest possible range of motion for each exercise. Actually, you don't even notice the weight in your hands, but you feel the muscle being worked, powerfully and fully contracting and then extending completely as you resist the pull of gravity against the resilient strength of your working muscles.

At training seminars, I always talk about putting your mind into your working muscles. To feel the weight the way you should, you have to have developed an unbreakable, unwavering link between your mind and the working muscles. When you get it right, this mind-in-the-muscle process becomes almost mystical. I can personally feel so much physical pleasure during a good set that I feel like jumping around the gym on a pogo stick between sets.

We'll delve more deeply into mental concentration and a variety of other psychological techniques that will push your bodybuilding workouts into a new dimension when we reach Chapter 12. You'll be reading some really esoteric material in that chapter, but your mind is *everything* in serious bodybuilding. You are like a huge oil tanker that would be plowing through the ocean in random fashion except for that tiny rudder under the stern that makes the huge ship go where its captain wishes it to go. That small rudder is your mind, which gives total direction to all of your bodybuilding workouts and nutritional programs.

Now let's go back to how an advanced bodybuilder *feels* the weights as she trains. There are two subgroups of this type of feel. The first group is the way a heavy basic exercise should feel, because every good advanced body-part routine should have at least one basic movement in it.

As a beginner and intermediate trainee, your focus in a bench press was just to get that barbell up any way you could. You focused mentally on the bar going up, giving little or no thought to the way the muscles lifting it felt. As a serious bodybuilder, you need to focus your concentration on your pectorals, anterior deltoids, and triceps as you smoothly push the weight upward.

This is actually a rather difficult task—focusing on two or three muscle groups simultaneously. It was easy for me to accomplish this complex mental task from the very start, because I had an extensive dance background before I took up weight training. In classical ballet classes, I had to simultaneously concentrate on how each leg should be oriented and moved, how my arm should be positioned on the barre, and how the free arm should be positioned or moved. I always had to keep in mind my torso and head attitudes so that I looked like a dancer instead of a beginner in a first-level class.

If you compare this type of concentration to thinking only about chest, shoulder, and arm muscles as a bench-press movement is executed, you will understand that bodybuilding was very easy for me to master mentally. For most of you it will be much more difficult, however, and it will take time and practice to master the feel of a heavy basic exercise.

It's easiest to begin by concentrating on a single working muscle contracting and extending in an isolation movement. One good isolation exercise for your pectoral muscles is pec-deck flyes. It involves a little bit of anterior deltoid action, but most of the movement is performed with pectoral contractions alone. Work at this for a couple of weeks, and then give bench presses another try. Chances are good that you'll be able to feel your anterior delts and triceps contracting at the same time as your pectorals contract to initiate the upward stroke of the weight.

The second type of feel you should achieve in a muscle is that of a single muscle—or even part of a single muscle complex—contracting in an isolation movement. Obviously, this will be a piece of cake for you if you can already concentrate your mental energy on multiple muscle groups during a basic exercise. But you can add some refinements of feel that most bodybuilders ignore. Bodybuilders lose out on potential development when they ignore these refinements.

Different exercises feel differently at various points along their full range of motion, particularly exercises that isolate action of a single muscle. Let's use dumbbell side laterals, an excellent medial-head deltoid exercise, as an example. Starting with the dumbbells touching each other in front of your hips, you feel very little stress on your shoulder muscles as you begin to raise them out to the sides and upward toward a finish position in which the dumbbells are at shoulder level. In fact, the higher you raise each dumbbell, the more you feel your medial and anterior deltoids fighting to keep the weights moving upward. You feel the most stress on the delts at the top point of the movement.

An average bodybuilder would simply do her set of 8–10 reps in the dumbbell side lateral raise and be pleased to end her set by placing the dumbbells back on the rack. An intelligent, ambitious bodybuilder—that's you, if you've made it this far into my book—tries to get more out of the movement by emphasizing that top portion, where the deltoids are screaming for relief. So why not work them harder in this section of the movement? At the normal end of your set, rack the weights but immediately pick up a substantially lighter pair of dumbbells and use them to do as many strict half reps as you can, doing just the top half of the movement. When you finish this type of set, feeling the delts contracting progressively harder during each succeeding rep—actually crying out to you for mercy—you've done a real bodybuilding set of side laterals. You will have gotten 10 times as much out of your set than the woman who quit at her 8th or 10th rep.

The point I'm trying to make here is that every isolation exercise has a few inches in its range of motion during which you must exert your muscles to the max. Find it and then exploit it, either in the manner I described for side laterals or by doing several reps of burns (remember them from Chapter 5?) in that critical area. When you get to the point at which you have this type of feel in your muscles during a set, you can safely call yourself a bodybuilder, and no one would argue the point. It takes a *real* bodybuilder to train with this type of feel and intensity.

Instinctive Training

Training instinct can be one of the most useful tools in your bodybuilding arsenal. Once you get completely in touch with your body and can monitor and interpret all of the various signals it is giving you at all times during a workout, you can save months—even years—of stumbling down blind alleys and culs-de-sac. With good instinctive training ability, you can decide in a matter of hours or days whether or not a particular new training or dietary technique is working for you. Without instinctive training ability, you are flying blind through narrow gaps in the Alps. Sooner or later, you will crash.

What *is* instinctive training ability? It is an ability not only to interpret biofeedback that your body is constantly sending to you but also to use the information thus gathered to your advantage as a bodybuilder. Since your body is sending you hundreds of signals—some of them extremely subtle—it does require time and some effort in order to acquire this ability. But this will be time and effort well spent in the long run, because it will save you hundreds of hours of fruitless searching for solutions to your training and dietary problems.

To a bodybuilder, the most basic and revealing piece of biofeedback is muscle pump, that tight, blood-congested feeling you experience in a muscle group when you have trained it optimally. It's a pleasant feeling, which Arnold Schwarzenegger once described in the film *Pumping Iron* as something like sexual orgasm. If you get a good pump from a particular routine, stick with that program. You *know* it's working. But if a routine fails to produce any pump at all, regardless of how long you use it, forget it. You're never going to get anything out of that program.

The feel we talked about a few pages back is another good piece of biofeedback that you can use advantageously. With experience, you will know that one biceps training machine is working your bis to the limit, while a different machine is giving you only partial results.

Muscle soreness can tell you several things. If a muscle is pleasantly sore the day after you worked it, chances are good that you should stick with that particular routine for at least a few weeks longer. Chronic muscle soreness, however, can be an indication that you have become overtrained. Then you need to take a week or two off from the gym after which you should turn to a new and more challenging training program.

Hunger tells you that your body needs more food, which is fine until you have to short-circuit that particular sensor when dieting for a competition. Lack of appetite is another possible signal that you are overtrained.

A particularly fast weight gain usually means you've either consumed excessive sodium—which results in temporary water retention—or you have been hitting the ice-cream store a little too frequently lately. Even if the bathroom scale fails to show too-quick weight gains, you'll be able to see them in the mirror. With experience, you can spot water retention by pressing an area of your skin and seeing how fast it fades from pale to normal color. With even more experience, you'll be able to literally feel water retained in certain parts of your body.

I can give you a vivid example of feeling water in my body. I once flew for three or four hours to a competition, which I won. I had been eating foods very low in calories during the days leading up to the show in an effort to achieve a very lean body and had kept my sodium intake so low that I was retaining no excess water at all. What fluid I had in my body was in my muscles or was flowing through my prominent vascular system. I couldn't resist having a big victory dinner that night and had a typical continental

breakfast the next morning before flying home. As I sat in the airplane seat, excess water, which had entered my system after only two junk-food meals, gradually sank lower and lower. When I got up to leave the aircraft, I could feel this excess fluid squishing with every step I took. That was the last time I ever pigged out before a long flight.

Take a few minutes to mentally list as many additional biofeedback signals you can think of and what they mean to you. It's possible to compile a fairly impressive list in only a few minutes, because your body is sending you so much data to choose from.

The mere awareness of each type of biofeedback available to you is the first step in mastering training instinct. The second step is to begin relating various signals to muscle growth rates, speed of body-fat loss, and many other factors that concern you as a serious bodybuilder. Step-by-step, you will make references and counter-references as you truly get to know your body and what it has to tell you.

Ultimately your training instinct will become so acute that you can try a new exercise and tell in just one or two sets if it has any value to you. A new training program might take a day or two to evaluate totally and accurately. A new dietary variable can often be evaluated correctly in a matter of minutes, certainly within a 24-hour period. This training instinct will obviously save you a few months or years of groping in the dark. Having mastered it is one of a champion bodybuilder's greatest secrets to success.

How long should it take you to master instinctive training ability? Within 6–12 months you should be getting pretty good at it, and able to make quick and correct calculations about 90% of the time. After two years, you'll be a real pro at instinctive training, and you would really disappoint me if you weren't accurate in your assessments a full 100% of the time.

Muscle Confusion
· ·

In Chapter 5 we discussed how often a body-builder should change from one training program to an entirely new one. I hinted that some advanced bodybuilders change routines every time they work a particular muscle group, following a sort of nonroutine routine. This is the basis of the muscle-confusion training principle.

Many elite bodybuilders like to train differently each workout just to keep their muscles guessing what's going to be coming up the next time. When you constantly repeat the same workout—even though you are actually going up in intensity at all times—your muscles can actually adapt to that set workout and refuse to continue to improve in ultimate hypertrophy. So the object becomes to keep them constantly off-balance, confused about what is coming up next, and never to present them with a consistent type of stimulus, to which they are able to adapt. With this plan there is no way that they can get into a comfort zone where they don't have to adapt and improve. You keep them so confused that they are *forced* to improve in hypertrophy.

The technique for doing this is to constantly work in different exercises for each body part, even if they are just subtle shifts from, for instance, doing dumbbell incline presses at a 45-degree angle (for the chest) to doing the same movement on a bench set at a 30-degree angle. Or you could do barbell inclines one chest session and Smith machine inclines the next, changing not only the angle of the bench you're lying on but also the width of your grip on the bar.

Constantly vary set, rep, and weight combinations. For example, do 3 sets of 15 reps per back exercise with moderate weights one day, 5 sets of 5 with heavy poundages the next time you work your back, and then 4 sets of 10 with me-dium weights on each exercise the third time you return to your back.

Change training tempo frequently, going very quickly from one set to the next one time and then taking 2-minute breaks between sets another. Speed it up again with supersetted exercises, and perhaps still go quickly but do descending sets another time. Feel free to run through the entire gamut of available training principles over a period of time.

The object here would be never to repeat a workout even once in a year, if you ever repeat it at all. An intelligent and inventive woman could easily come up with a new leg-workout program every time she bombed her lower body for the next 10 years. This is not an exaggeration.

When you're really in your peak form as an instinctive trainer—totally in tune with your body and its exact needs from day to day—you can take muscle confusion training one step higher into a totally enjoyable and hyperproductive type of program my coauthor called freestyle bodybuilding in one of his previous books. You enter an almost Zen-like state in your workouts in which you are like a child at play, but the unique requirements of your body are nevertheless fully met.

I've used this freestyle bodybuilding technique very productively during periods between training partners—when one has left for whatever reason, and I still haven't found an acceptable new one. It's so enjoyable to be in such direct communication with your body that you can seemingly do nothing wrong or unproductive in any of your workouts. Perhaps you will soon reach a level in your instinctive training in which you can become a freestyle bodybuilder. When you do, you'll never enjoy your training sessions more nor get more out of them. Freestyle bodybuilding is the ultimate combination of art and athleticism in our great sport.

Aerobic Weight Training

Almost every woman who trains with weights to increase her strength and improve muscle contour also does some form of aerobic exercise to increase cardiorespiratory fitness. As I've said, my current favorite is mountain biking, but I've taken a lot of dance classes over the years and have taken more than my share of aerobic dance sessions in which we exercised to music with a leader. Others like to pedal a LifeCycle or pump up and down on a StairMaster, which simulates climbing stadium stairs. I have friends who swear by treadmill training and others who prefer brisk outdoor walking. Some like to jog a few miles per week around some lake or forest or park near where they live.

It is also possible to turn weight training—which most exercise physiologists cite as an ultimate example of anaerobic training—into an aerobic activity. To do this you set up a circuit of stations, performing one bodybuilding exercise at one station and then immediately moving on to another station at which a different area of the body is stressed. By moving rhythmically and steadily around your circuit, you can develop great combination of both strength and aerobic fitness.

It's rather difficult to set up your own circuit in a commercial gym and still have any friends left a week later, unless you have a key to the gym and happen to enjoy pumping iron in the middle of the night. Many schools, however, have so many students in a class that it can be conducted profitably only as a circuit training program. A coach blows a whistle every 30 seconds and everyone rotates to the next station and does 30 seconds of work at that station. Some students may rest 30–60 seconds and then jump back into the rotation.

If you've ever been in a situation like this—and you are usually *forced* into it when school enrollments are excessive—you probably look at circuit training as an ordeal to be avoided at all costs. In actuality, circuit training is an enjoyable way to go through a workout when it's carried out properly.

Let's assume you have a large, well-equipped home gym at your disposal, or you are lucky enough to have had a weight-training instructor more enlightened about circuit training than the harried type of teacher already described. Under these more ideal circumstances it might be possible to establish a circuit of 10–15 stations stressing every muscle group in your body. The best circuits are set up so you never do two exercises consecutively for related body parts. An example of a circuit is shown in Figure 7-1.

Figure 7-1. Sample Circuit Training Program

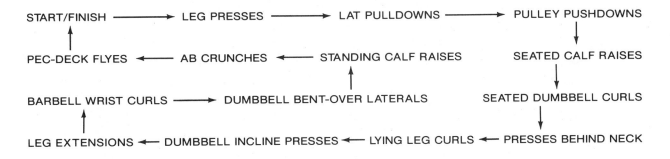

As you can see in Figure 7-1, each exercise in the sequence stresses a muscle group far removed from the previous one. Do your sets of 8–10 reps of upper-body exercises and 15–20 counts at leg and midsection stations as you progress around the circuit. Proceed at a comfortable pace until you have made one full trip. Rest for a couple of minutes to bring your breathing rate down to normal and then do another circuit. A complete workout involves 3–5 trips around the circuit, after which you should rest for a day or two to allow your muscles to recuperate. Then do another workout.

Pacing is important if you wish to keep within an aerobic heart-rate range, but there's no particular need to monitor your pulse rate. Just be sure to go around the circuit fast enough to keep your respiration accelerated but not so quickly that you couldn't keep up a normal conversation with a friend. This keeps you within the aerobic range, and you needn't do any complicated mathematics to determine precisely what your target pulse rate should be. After a few workouts, you'll know intuitively—here's that instinctive training principle again—when your weight training also qualifies as aerobics.

In circuit training, all of the normal workout procedures remain the same. Use strict form, particularly emphasizing a complete range of motion on each exercise. Periodically increase the resistance at each station incrementally as you grow stronger. And be sure to change the circuit around every few weeks—substituting new exercises at each station for the same body part—just to keep things interesting. You can train either alone or with a partner, and for safety's sake *always* have someone (even a cooperative family member) spot you when you do bench presses.

Very serious injuries—and even some deaths—have occurred when women training alone black out from holding their breath while bench pressing heavy weights. If you black out, with luck the weight would land on your chest or upper abdomen. With less luck, it could crash into your face, leaving you or your health insurance company with thousands of dollars in plastic surgery bills. With extremely bad luck, the bar could land on your throat and strangle you. It *has* happened, so remember to have a spotter, or do your bench presses with dumbbells and plenty of concentration on normal breathing patterns. Usually you black out only from exerting yourself while holding your breath. This is called the Valsalva effect, or the Valsalva maneuver.

If you stick to circuit training for 2–3 months, you will become fit and strong at the same time. So don't be too surprised to notice you are taking less and less time to complete a full circuit, and your poundages will easily go up at regular intervals. This is the best of both worlds. You increase both strength and aerobic fitness and develop a fabulous body in the process!

Maximizing Training Intensity

Assuming at this point that you have aspirations to compete as soon as possible in a bodybuilding show, this is not the time to go on cruise control. You should make every effort to continually increase the intensity of your gym workouts. You should still be gradually increasing your training poundages in each basic exercise—and even on many of the isolation movements—but *not* at the expense of good form and the right feel of each repetition in every set.

Your intensity at this point will be generated more by your mental commitment, which in turn will generate greater physical intensity. When you want and need to be the best, every workout is like fighting World War III. You will completely exhaust a muscle group when you bomb and blitz it, but with proper nutrition and sufficient time to rest between training sessions for that body part, you will come back a little better developed and a little stronger for your next nuclear attack on the muscle complex.

Let's go through a shoulder workout to show how hard, heavy, and intensely you could and *should* be training at this point. We'll start out with a light warm-up and then blast through highly intense pre-exhaustion supersets, with a training partner even giving you forced reps at critical points in each superset. Then you have only a few sets of various delt isolation exercises to finish off before you hit the shower room, get dressed, and head home for a solid, high-protein meal.

For your warm-up choose a light barbell, one that weighs about 50% of what you would normally use for presses behind the neck. Do a set of 15 reps of standing presses behind the neck and then shift the bar to a position across your upper thighs. Take a narrow overgrip on the bar to complete a superset of 15 reps of upright rows. Rest 30–45 seconds and repeat this warm-up superset. Unless you live in Siberia, your shoulder muscles should be warmed up after two of these supersets, but don't be embarrassed if your instincts tell you to do a third superset to optimize your warm-up and completely prevent any chance of injury during your shoulder training session.

It's important to set up your equipment in advance for the pre-ex part of your shoulder workout. In addition to a flat exercise bench, you will need three pairs of dumbbells and three barbells, all in graduated weight increments. You'll have to experiment for a couple of weeks to determine exactly what weights you need to set out. To help you get started, I'll give you a couple of rules. Choose the dumbbells on a percentage basis, with 100% being the maximum amount of weight you can lift in a strict set of 8–10 reps of standing dumbbell side laterals. The same rule applies for a maxed-out set of 8–10 reps of seated presses behind the neck with a barbell.

To illustrate the intensity factor of this series of pre-exhaustion supersets, choose dumbbells and barbells that are 60%, 70%, and 80% of your max. This is somewhat arbitrary, but if you discover that you like the delt workout I give you here, you'll gradually work out the right weights for all three pairs or dumbbells and all three barbells. If you're ready, let's let 'er rip!

Grab the lightest pair of dumbbells and sit at the end of the exercise bench with your feet firmly anchored. Do a set of 10 *seated* dumbbell side laterals. After the 10th rep, drop the DBs and have your partner quickly place the lightest barbell across your shoulders and behind your neck where you immediately set your grip at the correct width and blast out 10 solid reps of seated presses behind the neck. That wasn't so bad, was it? Well, tighten your lifting belt, because you're going to fry those puppies with the next three pre-ex supersets. This was just the opening salvo of an artillery battle you'll be going through for the next few minutes.

After no more than 60 seconds of rest after the first superset, grab the middle pair of dumbbells. On your own, do as many strict reps as you can of dumbbell side laterals. Then have your partner give you just enough help to do forced reps until you reach 10. Drop the dumbbells and immediately get to work with the middle barbell, steadily pushing it all the way up from a position low on your trapezius muscles to straight-arm's length overhead. If you can get 10 reps on your own, great; but otherwise your training partner will give you just enough of a boost to force out whatever number of reps you need to reach that magic 10 again. Give yourself the entire 60-second rest interval between supersets before embarking on the third one.

I have to interject a comment here about how

much time should elapse between the laterals and the presses so that you still will get the full benefit from the pre-exhaustion part of this workout. The amount of time between laterals and presses must be as close to zero seconds as humanly possible—try to get a fast-moving training partner. If you allow more than five seconds to elapse between the end of your side laterals set and the beginning of your presses, you are losing too much of the developmental value of the pre-ex part of the workout. So get those dumbbells on the deck and the barbell moving in its first rep as quick as you can blink your eyes.

Okay, you've had your 60-second rest interval after the second pre-ex superset, so grab the heaviest pair of dumbbells and again get as many strict reps of seated side laterals as you can, plus forced reps to get the set up to 10. Drop the DBs, grab the heaviest barbell, and immediately do as many overhead presses as you can manage on your own, plus enough forced reps to reach the 10 level again. You'll really need your 60-second rest interval between the third and fourth pre-ex supersets.

While you're in the middle of 60 seconds of bliss, you need to decide whether you're going to be a lioness or a mouse. The mouse would drop back down to the middle pair of dumbbells and the middle-weighted barbell on the final pre-ex superset. The lioness would stick with the upper sets of weights, no matter how much it hurt her physically. I'd stay with the heavy set myself, and I hope you will, too. Do big lions eat little mice, or is it too much trouble to chase the little critters down?

Now do the fourth pre-ex superset—the hardest, most painful, and most productive. Grab the heavy dumbbells and get as many reps as you can on the laterals. Regardless of how psyched up you are, you'll be lucky to get 5–6 good ones on your own. But get 'em any way you can, and

have your partner give you the absolute minimum amount of help you require to get your forced reps and finish at 10. By now you'd swear that two husky welders are playing their torches over your shoulders, but you're tough enough to get the heaviest barbell moving on your own. Then with a little boost here and there, you reach the magic number of 10.

You've just fried your anterior and medial delts at a higher level of heat than they've ever felt before, and you'd probably like to call it a day and head home, but you still have to do something drastic and painful to your posterior deltoids. So let's get four sets of dumbbells arranged to do a descending set for rear delts using bent-over lateral raises, but with a bit of a painful twist, of course. For the sake of illustration, let's say you need to get DBs weighing 50%, 60%, 70%, and 80% of your maximum for 10 reps of dumbbell bent-over laterals.

You will do your laterals *seated*, with your chest resting on your thighs at all times to make sure that the movement is performed as strictly as possible and that only the rear delts get the brunt of the action. If you're naturally big-breasted—or you've seen your friendly neighborhood plastic surgeon—you'll have a bit of an advantage here. The rest of us have to keep our somewhat flatter chests pinned to our quads at all times.

Start with the heaviest pair of dumbbells and get as many repetitions as possible in seated bent-over laterals. The number of reps really isn't important here, as long as you go to failure in strict form. I won't even torture you with the forced reps. But as soon as you drop the heaviest pair of dumbbells, grab the next heaviest set and immediately do as many reps as you can with them in strict form, again going to failure. Drop those and pick up the next pair, again going to failure. Finally drop those DBs and pick up the lightest pair—no fair resting yet—and do as many reps as you can until you literally can't move the dumbbells more than 5–6 inches out to the sides. Then you can take a 60-second break. You've finished attacking rear delts, and you're about finished with your shoulder routine.

I'm a big believer in having good deltoid-trapezius tie-ins—although I do think that heavy, sloping traps look awful on a woman. So you can finish off your shoulder workout with only three sets of 8–10 reps of upright rows. You could use a barbell for these, but I think it's too easy to cheat that way. So attach a bar handle to the end of a floor pulley, hike your exercise bench up toward the pulley, and do your three sets of slow, controlled *seated* cable upright rows. There's no way you can cheat on these, but I will give you a 30-second rest interval between sets, so you can change the pin in the weight stack without throwing up between sets.

Start out with the heaviest poundage that you can handle for 8–10 reps. Rest 30 seconds while you reduce the weight by about 10%. Do a second set, reposition the pin so your last set is another 10% lighter, and finish off your last deltoid set for the day. Then you can rest as long as you like, have a drink of water or a gulp of your carbohydrate-replacement drink, and remind yourself that you've just done 15 total sets of inhumanly intense deltoid work, and those babies need a few days of rest before you go back at them again.

A lot of elite women bodybuilders have complimented me for my high level of shoulder development over the years. Do you really think my delts look that good? If you do, you also know what it takes to get your own shoulder-girdle muscles up to the same level.

It's a very demanding routine, but I never promised you this would be easy. Nothing really worth having in life is that easy to get, is it? If others tell you it's easy to develop world-class muscle in a particular body part, thank them politely and never bother with them again. *You* know how to get there, and they don't have a clue!

Stress Management

For most women, following a bodybuilding lifestyle on a regular basis is one of best means of managing everyday stress. But for a few of the more tense and mentally hyperactive women bodybuilders, competitive bodybuilding can become such a serious endeavor that it in itself becomes an agent of extreme stress. If you are one of these women, you need to learn how to manage the excess stress in your life. Read on—we don't want you to die trying!

Stress is negative—everyone knows that. It causes you to experience a complex series of emotions that can harm both the mind and the body. But did you know that something as pleasurable as deeply kissing your lover can elicit exactly the same physiological responses as losing your home or, worse yet, losing that contest you've been preparing for 24 hours per day for the past year!

Whether something is stressful or pleasant, then, is merely a matter of how you view it. Stress researchers look in a person's life for what they call stressors, agents that cause harmful stress, and they suggest replacing them with the positive types of things that elicit the identical physiological response as the stressors.

Managing stress begins with writing down everything that causes you stress during the day—you keep, as it were, a stress diary. Every time you feel stressed, write down what time of day it is, what caused you to feel stressed, and how your mind and body reacted negatively (or possibly positively) to that stress. Keep this diary for a couple of weeks, and you'll have a good handle on those things that cause the most stress in your life.

By adding such techniques as muscle confusion, visualization, and instinctive training to your workout, you can achieve dramatic results in strength, muscle definition, and self-confidence.

If you're a committed competitive body-builder, you obviously can't eliminate daily bodybuilding activities because they cause stress. But you can begin to look at them in a new way that is less negatively stressful to you. Here's an example: Having to follow a very strict diet is negatively stressful to most women. But can there be a way to somehow switch some type of internal dial and make it positively stressful? In point of fact, you can actually do this, just as long as you realize how and why you are turning a negative stressor into a positive one.

Let's follow through on that horrible old diet. Sure, it's a pain to have to prepare the food, and it's not in the least enjoyable to have to choke it down day after day in order to get into the type of shape required to be a winning bodybuilder. But if you look at the end result more than at the process toward that end, it becomes much easier to cook and eat those pieces of dry fish or poultry breasts—skinned prior to preparation, of course—and those dry baked potatoes, dry rice, dry sweet potatoes, and salads with nothing on them for dressing but perhaps a squeeze of lemon juice.

Start thinking of all of these negatives in our diet as positives. There are yuppies who are paying big money to eat the way you do, and for no other reason than to be trendy. You're doing it in order to quickly climb the ladder of success in bodybuilding, to speed the day when you get your IFBB pro card and are well on your way to your first Ms. Olympia placing.

In addition to switching your mental dial, you can schedule positive stressors. Make love to your husband or boyfriend more frequently, and make it a big production, something you can both look forward to throughout the day. If that doesn't perk you up, nothing will.

Perhaps you're overlooking the relaxing nature of repetitive tasks you used to enjoy when you were younger—sewing some of your own cloth-ing (why spend money on posing suits when you can make them yourself and end up with better quality?), needlepoint, embroidery, and God only knows what. Actually, you know what, too, because you can search your memory and come up with plenty of relaxing hobbies that you can take up in modified forms to distract yourself from the rigors of contest preparation.

It really doesn't take much more than aware-ness of the problem to reduce stress in your bodybuilding life. Once aware of the problem, solutions almost automatically seem to present themselves to you. Pick up on a few of them, and you'll significantly reduce the stress of a precom-petition bodybuilding lifestyle. Manage that ex-cess stress, and you'll end up placing higher in the contest than you might have if you had al-lowed the harmful stress to dominate your life.

Increasing Personal Energy Levels

During the precompetitive cycle in serious bodybuilding your energy reserves are at a min-imum. But for the most part, merely following a solid bodybuilding lifestyle—weight training, aerobics, stretching, and maintenance of a healthful, low-fat diet—will go a long way to-ward increasing your daily personal energy lev-els.

Sometimes it's difficult to convince yourself of this fact, however, because the increase in energy levels comes almost as gradually as im-provements in your physique. There is one sure way to convince yourself that your energy levels have really peaked out. Simply take a one- or two-week layoff from the gym and discover all the energy you have to burn. You will have so much that you won't know what to do with it! What better proof could you have that serious bodybuilding and weight training dramatically increase personal physical and mental energy levels?

Five-and Six-Day Split Routines

· ·

I've already told you various ways to divide your body parts up to facilitate a split routine. We've already discussed a four-day-per-week split routine and both three-on/two-off and three-on/one-off splits. Now it's time to tell you about some other alternatives, both five-day and six-day methods.

For a five-day split, you will need to divide up your body parts into two somewhat equal groupings. You will find two alternatives for this in Figure 7-2. Of course, others exist, and I'm sure you'll be able to come up with many additional alternatives with a little thought.

A five-day split routine assumes that you will work out daily Monday through Friday and then take Saturdays and Sundays off each week. By alternating routines each weekday, you will do one of them three times the first week, twice the second and then invert the ratio the second week. If you label Day 1 "A" and Day 2 "B" in either example in Figure 7-2, here is how a five-day split routine would look for a four-week period of time.

Mon	Tues	Wed	Thur	Fri	Weekends
A	B	A	B	A	Off
B	A	B	A	B	Off
A	B	A	B	A	Off
B	A	B	A	B	Off

There are two distinct types of six-day-per-week split routines, each of which assumes that you will train Mondays through Saturdays, taking only Sundays off from the gym each week. In the least severe method, you will divide up your body parts into three groupings and do each of the three twice per week. Following is a typical example of such a six-day split routine:

Mon/Thur	Tues/Fri	Wed/Sat
Chest	Quadriceps	Shoulders
Upper Back	Hamstrings	Biceps-Triceps
Calves	Abdominals	Forearms

In this and most other split routines, we won't need to include direct neck training, since that muscle group comes up quite nicely simply as a result of training such peripheral body parts as the trapezius, upper pectorals, deltoids, and so forth. Besides, why try to develop a thick neck, which tends to diminish a woman's feminity? Of course a very thin neck also tends to look a bit silly on a woman.

Figure 7-2. Alternative Ways of Dividing Up Body Parts into Two Groupings

Alternative 1

Day 1	Day 2
Legs	Chest
Upper Arms	Back
Forearms	Delts
Calves	Abs

Alternative 2

Day 1	Day 2
Chest	Legs
Shoulders	Back
Upper Arms	Calves
Forearms	Abs

The second—more severe—type of six-day-per-week split routine is also based on the alternative splits outlined in Figure 7-2. The body is divided in some way into two somewhat equal halves, with the first half trained on Mondays, Wednesdays, and Fridays, the second on Tuesdays, Thursdays, and Saturdays. Sunday is the only day off from the gym, and even then some women like to go in and do some sort of aerobic training, such as riding a stationary bike, stair climbing, or walking on a treadmill set at a rather high angle, which more directly affects the tush muscles, rounding them out better than almost any other form of aerobic training.

For the most part, six-day-per-week split routines—and even five-day splits—are a bit too strenuous for most women bodybuilders. These routines simply don't allow sufficient recovery time between sessions for each body part, and recovery is increasingly important as you become more advanced and reach the point at which you are seriously thinking about entering some competitions.

For most women I'd suggest either the three-on/two-off or three-on/one-off split. These splits do allow sufficient recovery time between workouts for each body part, which induces accelerated muscle hypertrophy.

Double-Split Routines

For very brief periods of time, some competitive bodybuilders successfully follow double-split routines, which are normal split routines subdivided so that half of one day's program is done in the morning and the other half later in the day. If you take a nap between sessions, this will work well in elevating your BMR (basal metabolic rate) for short periods of time.

Actually, most bodybuilders *do* double-split, if you choose to count the aerobics they do as one of the halves of the double-split. Every time you work out for at least 30 minutes—be it with weights or aerobically—your BMR remains elevated for as much as an hour after you have begun to rest. When you're trying to burn off stubborn body fat close to an important competition, this can sometimes make the difference between being successful and not.

The downside of double-split routines is that it is impossible to hold down even a halftime job when following such an elaborate routine. But a high-level (usually pro) bodybuilder who follows double-splits considers training to be her job, so it's nothing for her to do two or more workouts daily for several weeks in a row leading up to a competition.

It is also relatively easy to overtrain when double-splitting, even if you have an optimum diet and you rest at all times that you aren't actually working out. At a minimum, a double-split is mentally dulling. At a maximum, you use up so much energy that you can't recover completely enough between sessions to keep from overtraining.

As hinted, the most basic form of double-split is one in which you perform your workout with weights—usually following a three-on/one-off split routine—in the morning and then go back later in the day for one, possibly even two, aerobics sessions of varying lengths. Throw in posing practice, and you're probably actually exercising in some form three or four times per day.

Speaking strictly about weights, the most basic form of double-split routine involves doing the major body parts early in the day, taking a long nap during the early afternoon, and then going back at night to finish up on such minor groups as abdominals, calves, and perhaps forearms. Following is such a basic double-split, formed around the normal three-on/one-off split routine:

	A.M.	P.M.
Day 1	Chest	Abdominals
	Back	Calves
Day 2	Quadriceps	Abdominals
	Hamstrings-	Forearms
	Lower Back	
Day 3	Shoulders	Abdominals
	Upper Arms	Forearms

Rest on the fourth day—or perhaps do at least a somewhat extended aerobics session—and then begin the double-split again on Day 5. Survive a couple of weeks of this, and you can actually consider yourself either a veteran double-split training bodybuilder or some kind of exotic nut.

Advanced Training Intensification

We still haven't gotten around to six advanced-level training intensification techniques: trisets, giant sets, peak contraction, continuous tension, rest-pause training, and quality training. You might well be ready for one or more of these techniques, so let's get at them.

TRISETS AND GIANT SETS

Supersets were discussed in Chapter 5. You no doubt remember that they consist of two movements performed with little or no rest between them. They are generally followed by a rest interval of 1–2 minutes and then usually another is performed. The easiest of the two types of supersets combines movements for antagonistic muscle groups, such as biceps and triceps (barbell curls + pulley pushdowns) or quads and hamstrings (leg extensions + leg curls).

A much more intense form of superset involves combining two movements for the same body part, such as barbell preacher curls and standing barbell curls—for the biceps. If you have that madwoman-type of personality, you might have given the second and more intense form of superset a trial in your own workouts. Well, you can take this madness several steps farther up the ladder of training intensity.

Much more intense than either type of superset is a triset, which is a compound of three movements—no rest between exercises, of course—followed by a normal rest interval of 1–

2 minutes, and, sometimes, another triset. Trisets work best for muscle groups that have three distinct aspects to them, such as the triceps. Following are trisets for various muscle groups, which you might like to try out in your own routine (then again, you may elect *not* to try them out):

Triceps
Incline Barbell Triceps Extensions (inner head)
Lying Barbell Triceps Extensions (medial head)
Pulley Pushdowns (outer head)

Deltoids
Standing Barbell Presses (anterior head)
Dumbbell Side Laterals (medial head)
Dumbbell Bent-Over Laterals (posterior head)

Arms
Standing Barbell Curls (biceps)
Pulley Pushdowns (triceps)
Standing Barbell Wrist Curls (forearm flexors)

Even more intense than trisets are giant sets, which are series of 4–6 combined movements (again, no rest between exercises), followed by a longer-than-normal rest interval of 2–3 minutes and perhaps by further giant sets. Obviously, four-exercise giant sets are more intense than trisets, five-exercise giant sets are more intense than four-exercise giant sets, and six-exercise giant sets are more intense than five-exercise giant sets. Following are examples of all three types of giant sets, which you may or may not choose to give a trial in your own workouts:

Four-Exercise Giant Set (Chest)
Dumbbell Bent Presses (lower outer pectorals)
Incline Dumbbell Flyes (upper pectorals)

Cross-Bench Dumbbell Pullovers (serratus)
Pec-Deck Flyes (inner section of pectorals)

Five-Exercise Giant Set (Back)

Medium-Grip Front Lat Pulldowns (lower lats)
Seated Pulley Rows (lat thickness)
Cross-Bench Dumbbell Pullovers (inner lats)
Wide-Grip Pulldowns Behind Neck (upper lats)
Dumbbell Bent-Over Laterals (upper-back cuts)

Six-Exercise Giant Set (Chest + Back)

Dumbbell Incline Presses (upper outer pecs)
Seated Low-Pulley Rows (lat thickness)
Parallel Bar Dips (lower outer pecs)
Wide-Grip Pulldowns Behind Neck (upper lats)
Pec-Deck Flyes (inner sections of pecs)
Barbell Bent-Arm Pullovers (inner sections of lats)

It should be quite obvious that these hyper-advanced training techniques will not work for every woman who wants to try them, but you should at least consider experimenting with one or more of them from time to time. Perhaps you have the degree of personal between-workouts recuperative power necessary to profit from one of them. I personally don't use any trisets or giant sets in my own general training and have never missed them!

PEAK CONTRACTION

Anatomically speaking, each major muscle group is made up of long bundled strands of individual muscle cells set end to end, somewhat like canoes tied together end to end. Each cell either contracts under a load or doesn't contract at all. Exercise physiologists call this the "all or nothing model" of muscle-cell contraction.

In practice, you will have the maximum number of individual muscle cells contracted when you have a muscle group—such as your biceps—completely flexed. That does make sense, because that *is* when the muscle mass itself is shortest. For optimum development, it makes good sense to have a peak load on the muscle when it is completely contracted (i.e., when the maximum number of individual cells have fired off).

Placing a load on a completely contracted muscle group is called the peak-contraction principle, and it's an advanced training technique I often use in my own workouts. You can be sure you are using peak contraction simply by choosing exercises for each muscle group that guarantee that the muscles are fully tensed at the top point of the movement.

The value of most exercise machines is that they guarantee that you place a peak-contraction effect on your muscles during each repetition. Following is a list of peak-contraction-oriented exercises, using free weights, for each major muscle group:

Quadriceps

Leg Extensions
Sissy Squats

Hamstrings

Leg curls (lying, standing, seated)
Hyperextensions

Spinal Erectors/Glutes

Hyperextensions

Trapezius

Shrugs (barbell, dumbbell, machine)
Upright Rows (barbell, dumbbell, cable)

Latissimus Dorsi

Chins (all variations)
Lat Machine Pulldowns (all variations)
Rows (all variations)

Pectorals
Pec-Deck Flyes
Cable Crossovers

Deltoids
Side Laterals (dumbbell, machine, cable)
Front Raises (dumbbell, machine, cable)
Bent-Over Laterals (dumbbell, machine, cable)
Upright Rows

Biceps
Barbell Bent-Over Concentration Curls
Dumbbell Bent-Over Concentration Curls

Triceps
Dumbbell Kickbacks
Barbell Kickbacks
Cable Kicks

Forearms
Standing Wrist Curls (barbell, dumbbell)

Calves
Standing Calf Raises
Seated Calf Raises
Donkey Calf Raises
Calf Presses (45-degree, vertical, seated leg-press machine)

Abdominals
Crunches
Hanging Leg Raises

Simply include these movements in your bodybuilding routines—particularly during a precontest peaking cycle—and you will automatically get a peak-contraction effect in your muscles. To intensify this peak-contraction effect, try holding the top point of the movement for a slow count of three, constantly trying to contract the muscles even harder, before you return to the starting point.

CONTINUOUS TENSION
Another advanced technique used by many con-

test bodybuilders is called continuous tension. With this method, you simply slow the bar or machine down in its upward and downward cycles until it is traveling about half as fast as usual. As you slow down the bar, try to feel the weight more, being certain that you keep your working muscles continuously contracted. It's impossible to cheat up the bar when you are using continuous tension, so it's also a good off-season technique if you have a problem maintaining strict body mechanics.

QUALITY TRAINING
A final precontest training technique used by some top bodybuilders is called quality training. In it, you consciously reduce the length of rest intervals between sets while still attempting to keep your training weights up as high as possible. Obviously, when you are dieting for a show and low on energy, it becomes impossible to keep your weights up when you also insist on incrementally decreasing rest intervals between sets. But the object is to try as hard as you can to keep your poundages up. After all, everything is relative—as long as the weights feel heavy to you, they are heavy, regardless of how heavy they actually happen to be.

I've personally never seen much point in quality training, because I've been able to achieve a true contest condition merely by training hard with weights, manipulating my diet so I gradually consume fewer and fewer calories, and increasing the length and/or frequency of aerobics sessions. You'll be taking on quite a full plate when you do just this—without also trying to reduce the length of rest intervals between sets—and you will find my method quite effective anyway.

If you train heavy, diet, and do lots of aerobics, but still end up a bit short when it comes to the shape you desire for a competition, you might want to give quality training a try. I'm not sure you can avoid the funny farm if you do, however!

The Drug Question

Women's competitive bodybuilding has been tainted as a sport in recent years by the consistent suspicion that we "get that way" through the use of tissue-building drugs and other types of chemical preparations that stimulate the BMR. I'd be the first to admit that a few misguided women have gone the drug route, but everyone you see onstage at a major IFBB bodybuilding competition is drug free, and I can prove it.

The International Federation of Bodybuilders is made up of more than 120 member federations, making bodybuilding one of the more popular participatory sports in the world. As a result, we have been trying for many years to gain entry into the program of sports in the Olympic Games. We have consistently been rejected, but I'm sure someday soon bodybuilding will find its rightful place as an Olympic sport.

One way in which we prove our legitimacy to the International Olympic Committee (IOC) is by supporting drug testing at major competitions as well as randomly at other competitions throughout the year. I dare say that in no other sport on earth are competitors drug tested so rigorously as in bodybuilding. A Ms. Olympia competitor, for example, might be tested two or three times with only 24 hours notice during the off-season to ascertain whether she takes drugs to enhance her training. Then she is tested again on the eve of the competition to ensure that she is free of drugs as she steps onstage.

The type of testing program is modeled strictly after that of the IOC. In fact, Dr. Manfred Donike (director of the IOC program) also oversees drug testing within the IFBB. The samples are taken according to IOC rules and are tested only at approved IOC labs. In America, the lab is in Los Angeles; in Germany, it is in Cologne.

With such rigorous testing, a woman occasionally is caught. The penalties are severe. For a first offense, she is suspended from the competition. For a second positive test, she is suspended from competition for one full year and is forced to return all prize money she might have won while on drugs. A third positive test results in a lifetime ban from the sport. As severe as these penalties are, I still don't find them severe enough. I think a single positive test should result in a lifetime ban from competitive bodybuilding.

I have been tested repeatedly and have never had the slightest suspicion attached to my name when it comes to drug taking. My stand on drugs is well known—they ruin femininity, they are immoral, and they hurt a sport I love. I've never taken them and never will, and I am willing to be tested at any time to prove this assertion.

Some bodybuilding federations actually encourage drug use among female competitors, and I don't think you could look at many of these bodybuilders and still consider them females. They look like something that might come teetering out of Dr. Frankenstein's mythical lab along with the monster that was assembled from parts robbed from local graves.

Not only do women who indiscriminately take drugs to "improve" their appearance end up with the muscles of men, they also have the beards of men (they all shave regularly) and the voices of men. Many develop male pattern baldness, and some have secretly had hair transplants to restore some semblance of femininity. Some suffer from clitoral enlargement. All of these side effects from steroids are irreversible, too.

If a woman is foolish enough to allow herself to become pregnant while on steroids, the effects on her unborn child can be disastrous. Under the circumstances, how can anyone condone the use of "bodybuilding" drugs among women, or among men for that matter?

Bodybuilding should be a healthy, enjoyable sport that enhances women's femininity. If done correctly—without the taint of drugs—it does just that. Can you look at my body and deny it?

8
Advanced-Level Exercises

With the addition of the 21 new resistance exercises precisely illustrated and completely described in this chapter, my book offers you a pool of more than 70 movements from which to choose in making up your own routines. In Chapters 4 and 6 I provided suggested beginning- and intermediate-level routines, but I won't be giving you any more sample programs, except for my own personal training program that is outlined in Chapter 13. There's no reason for me to continue making up routines for you, because you now understand how to do it for yourself. Besides, I can't determine what is best for you after you have passed the intermediate stage of weight training.

Don't give up searching for and mastering new exercises beyond this point, however, because scores more exist that should become an integral part of your general training procedures. You'll discover these new movements in many places—from other bodybuilders in the gym, in iron-pumping magazines, and in weight-training and bodybuilding books. Give each new one a reasonable trial in your own workouts, keep the effective ones, and discard those that are less useful.

Leg Exercises

LUNGES

Areas Emphasized—Lunges can be done in various ways to place intense stress on the quadriceps, buttocks, and hip flexor muscles. In general, you'll be putting the most stress on the glutes of the leg that is in the front and on the quads and hip flexors of the leg that is in the rear. But this can vary as you try different styles of lunges, since each one feels a bit different from the others in your lower-body musculature.

Starting Position—Essentially, you assume the same starting position as for squats, although I've illustrated an alternative arm position in the accompanying photographs. Rather than grasping the bar out near the collars, as I do in performing squats, I wrap my arms around the bar and grasp the edges of the plates to help steady the bar across my shoulders behind my neck. You can either take the weight off a squat rack or merely clean it up to your chest; then push it overhead to rest across your trapezius muscles. Since the weight you will use in lunges is rela-

Lunges—start and finish

Lunges—midpoint

tively light, you won't have much trouble dispensing with the squat rack. Stand erect, your feet set at about shoulder width and toes angled so your feet are parallel to each other. Look straight ahead during the entire movement and attempt to keep your head up. Note that I am wearing a lifting belt to protect my lower back and abdomen while doing my lunges.

Movement Performance—Step forward with your right foot and set it about 3 feet (1 meter) in front of the left one and a bit to the right of center. Bend both legs and lunge forward, as illustrated. Push hard with your right leg and return to the erect position, repeating the movement with your left foot forward. Continue the exercise by alternating legs until you have performed the required number of repetitions with each leg.

Common Mistakes—Not stepping forward enough or merely dipping into a squat between narrowly spread feet places excessive strain on your knees. Keep the movement smooth and steady, even when pushing off with your forward leg to return to the erect position. There is no reason to jerk at any point during the exercise.

Training Tips—Some trainees like to keep their back leg a bit straighter than I do, which transfers a bit more stress to the hip flexors of the rear leg. You can increase the stress on your glutes by lunging up onto a thick block of wood that has been wedged securely against something so it doesn't slide forward as you perform the movement. All variations of lunges can be performed while you are holding a pair of moderately heavy dumbbells in your hands rather than balancing a bar behind your neck.

REAR CABLE KICKS

Areas Emphasized—This is a direct and intense gluteus maximus exercise that will give your buns a nicely rounded look if you stick with it long enough. Secondary stress is on the lower back and upper hamstrings.

Starting Position—Attach the ankle cuff to your left leg, rotating it so the ring is on your shin. Attach the end of the cable leading through a floor pulley to the ring and face the pulley. You should be standing back from the pulley far enough so you have resistance on your leg even when it is extended directly toward the pulley, as it should be at the beginning of the movement. Brace your upper body to keep it steady throughout the movement, making sure that your torso is not angled forward much more than mine is in the illustration. Keep both legs straight throughout your set.

Movement Performance—Use the strength of your gluteal muscles to slowly move your right leg directly to the rear and upward to as high a point as is comfortably possible. Hold this peak-contracted position for a moment and then slowly return your leg to the starting point. Repeat the movement for the suggested number of repetitions. Switch legs and do the same number of reps with your right leg. Alternate back and forth between legs until you have performed the same number of repetitions and sets with each leg.

Common Mistakes—Although I call this exercise rear cable kicks, you should not make an abrupt kicking type of movement. Raise your leg to the rear slowly and steadily; if you don't, you will lose much of the developmental benefit of the movement—and you will run the risk of a back injury if you move the weight with a kick or jerk.

Rear Cable Kicks—midpoint (right leg)

Rear Cable Kicks—midpoint (left leg)

Training Tips—In well-equipped commercial gyms, there are machines that duplicate this movement, and you should try them if they are available. Every gym has a floor pulley, however, which is the reason I've suggested doing the movement with that apparatus.

INNER-LEG CABLE KICKS

Areas Emphasized—When correctly performed, this exercise intensely and directly stresses the adductor muscles of the inner thighs, particularly the sartorius muscle, which, incidentally, is the longest muscle in the body.

Starting Position—Attach the ankle cuff to your left leg and rotate it on your ankle so the ring is pointed outward, away from the midline of your body. Take the cable running through a floor pulley and hook it to the cuff, standing with your left side pointed directly toward the pulley. Brace your upper body in position with your left hand, resting your right hand on your hip, as illustrated. Plant your right foot firmly on the gym floor and keep both legs straight throughout your set. Allow the weight attached to the end of the cable to pull your left leg directly toward the pulley until it is in the starting position illustrated.

Movement Performance—Use leg adductor strength to slowly move your leg from the starting point across the midline of your body in front of your right leg, terminating the movement only when you can no longer move your leg any farther. Return your leg slowly to the starting point and repeat for the required number of repetitions. Switch legs and do the same number of repetitions. Alternate back and forth from one leg to the other until you have done the required number of sets and reps with each leg.

Common Mistakes—Actually I should have called this exercise cable leg adductions rather than cable kicks, but the second term is in

Inner-Leg Cable Kicks—start/finish

Inner-Leg Cable Kicks—midpoint

much more common use. As with the previous movement, you should avoid kicking or jerking the weight at any point along its intended arc. If you always think about moving your leg slowly and smoothly against the resistance supplied by the weight at the other end of the cable, you can't go wrong.

Training Tips—You will find many commercial gyms with machines that place stress on the working muscles as you do leg adductions. Give them all a trial in your workouts, and pick the one that works best for you—if that isn't actually this cable movement.

Back Exercises

FRONT CHINS

Areas Emphasized—If you work long enough at lat machine pulldowns and get your body-fat percentage down far enough, you will be able to include chins in your back routine. When you can, you will be doing the best width-building movement for your lats. Very intense stress is placed on the lats, rear delts, biceps, brachialis, and forearm flexor muscles when you do a set of chins.

Starting Position—Jump up and take an overgrip on a chinning bar in which your hands are set 4–6 inches (12–18 centimeters) wider than your shoulders on each side. Bend your legs at about a 90-degree angle, cross your ankles, and maintain this leg position throughout your set. Fully straighten your arms and allow your body weight to pull your torso down far enough to completely stretch your lats in the bottom position of the movement.

Movement Performance—Being sure to pull primarily with your lats (which means keeping your elbows back as you do the movement), slowly chin yourself until your nose

Front Chins—start and finish

Front Chins—midpoint

reaches bar level. Be sure to arch your back in the top position of the movement, or you won't get as much out of the exercise as you should. Try to hold this peak-contracted position for a moment and then slowly lower yourself back to the starting point. Repeat the movement until you have completed the assigned number of repetitions.

Common Mistakes—The most common error in doing chins is to include them in your routine before you are strong enough to do a decent set. Unless you can do 8–10 reps on your first set of chins, you simply aren't strong enough to include them in your back routine. Remember not to swing or jerk your body upward.

Training Tips—When you are doing front chins, as described, you are placing more stress on the lower lats than on the upper part of the muscle group. To stress the upper lats more intensely, you will have to do chins behind the neck, pulling yourself up to the bar so it touches the upper part of your trapezius muscles. Whether you are doing front chins or chins behind the neck, you can experiment with various grip widths from time to time. With front chins, you can also use an undergrip on the chinning bar. If you become particularly strong in this movement and reach the point at which you can do more than 15 repetitions in a set, you should begin to add weight to the exercise. This is done by hanging a dumbbell between your legs at the end of a loop of nylon webbing draped around your waist. Don't be surprised, however, if it takes you a few years to get strong enough to perform the exercise this way.

ONE-ARM CABLE BENT-OVER ROWS

Areas Emphasized—This is a good movement for increasing your back thickness. It is very similar to one-arm dumbbell bent-over rows, yet it is sufficiently different in effect on the lats that it should be occasionally included in your back routine. One-arm cable bent-over rows place direct stress on the latissimus, posterior deltoid, biceps, brachialis, and forearm flexor muscles. Minor secondary stress is on the lower trapezius muscles.

Starting Position—Attach a loop handle to the end of the cable running through a floor pulley. Station a flat exercise bench about 3 feet (a bit under 1 meter) back from the pulley, with the end of the bench pointed directly at the pulley itself. Grasp the cable handle with your right hand and place your left knee about midway down the bench. Brace your upper body by straightening your right arm and placing your right hand over the end of the bench, as illustrated, and rest your right foot on the floor behind you. Allow the weight at the other end of the cable to pull your hand toward the pulley until your right arm is completely straight and your right shoulder is rotated downward a bit toward the pulley. You should feel a definite stretch in your upper-back muscles on the right side of your torso in this position.

Movement Performance—Pulling primarily with the lats (you actually don't have to bend your working arm that much), slowly pull the pulley handle from the described and illustrated starting point of the movement to a position at the side of your right hip. Hold this peak-contracted position while intensely flexing your upper-back muscles for a moment, being sure that your right shoulder is rotated back, as shown in the exercise photo. Then slowly move your right hand back along the same path to the starting point. Repeat the movement for the required number of repetitions. Alternate back and forth between arms until you have done the same number of sets and reps with each arm.

One-Arm Cable
Bent-Over Rows—
start and finish

One-Arm Cable
Bent-Over Rows—
midpoint

Common Mistakes—Don't position the bench too close to the pulley, because that makes your pulling angle too similar to that of one-arm dumbbell rows. At the beginning point, your working arm should be extended forward at about a 45-degree angle down from the level of your torso. Do the movement slowly and correctly, or you risk losing too much of the benefit you should be receiving. In other words, do it right or don't do it at all!

Training Tips—As you can see from the two photos illustrating the start and finish positions, I keep the palm of my hand facing inward toward my body throughout the movement. You might want to play around with different hand positions. Try doing some sets with your palm pointed down at the floor throughout the movement; then try some with your palm pointed directly up toward the gym ceiling. For a really interesting effect, start the movement with your palm down but supinate your hand as you do the pull, so your palm is facing up when your hand reaches your hip. Then pronate your hand as you return to the starting point.

SEATED ONE-ARM PULLEY ROWS

Areas Emphasized—This movement stresses the same muscle groups as seated pulley rows with two hands—but the angle of the body differs. The muscle groups most effected are the latissimus dorsi, posterior deltoids, biceps, brachialis, and forearm flexor muscles. Secondary stress is on the trapezius and erector spinae muscles.

Starting Position—Attach a loop handle to the cable running through the low pulley on a rowing machine. Grasp the handle in your right hand and sit down on the seat, bracing your right foot against the restraint. You should keep your right leg slightly bent, as illustrated, throughout the movement in order to keep potentially destructive stress off your lower back. Bend your left leg at about a 90-degree angle and rest your left foot on the floor beside you. Place your left hand on your hip and keep it there throughout your set. Twist to the left and extend your left arm toward the pulley, while keeping your torso relatively upright, to stretch the right lat. Start with your right hand twisted in such a manner

Seated One-Arm
Pulley Rows—
start and finish

that your thumb is facing the floor. Your thumb can be rotated inward and upward during the movement.

Movement Performance—Simultaneously twist your torso about 90 degrees to the right, pull the handle parallel to the floor and straight to the rear until your hand touches the side of your waist; then rotate your working hand so your palm is facing inward toward your torso in the finish position. Hold this peak-contracted position for a moment and then slowly reverse the movement and assume the starting position. Repeat the exercise slowly until you have completed the suggested number of reps.

Common Mistakes—Since this movement involves torso twist, you *must* do it slowly and in a very controlled fashion. Otherwise you will run a great risk of injuring your lower back. Never jerk or pull the weight so fast that it goes ballistic.

Training Tips—Try doing this exercise with the pulley set at different heights. Each incre-ment of height increase will stress your back muscles completely different from the increment below it. You can also experiment with other hand positions—palm facing down throughout the movement, up throughout the movement, or toward your torso throughout the movement.

Chest Exercises

CROSS-BENCH DUMBBELL PULLOVERS

Areas Emphasized—All types of pullovers stress the entire muscle complex that rotates the scapulae, particularly the lats and rhomboids. Equal stress is placed on the pectorals and the serratus anterior muscles at the sides of the rib cage.

Starting Position—Place a moderately heavy dumbbell on its end on the surface of a flat exercise bench, being sure it is close to either end of the bench. Back up to the bench and sit down so the dumbbell is right behind you. Position your upper torso so you are lying

Seated One-Arm
Pulley Rows—
midpoint

Cross-Bench
Dumbbell Pullovers—
start and finish

Cross-Bench
Dumbbell Pullovers—
midpoint

across the bench with your shoulder blades in contact with the flat surface. Place your feet on the floor, with your legs either partially bent or straight (I've illustrated the second position). Reach over and take a grip on the dumbbell. The palms of your hands should be against the underside of the upper group of plates, and your thumbs should encircle the dumbbell bar to keep it from sliding out of your hands. Pull the weight upward to a position at straight-arm's length directly above your chest.

Movement Performance—Simultaneously bend your arms to about a 30-degree angle and lower the dumbbell backward and downward to the rear in a semicircular arc to as low a point as is comfortably possible. Without bouncing in the bottom of the movement, slowly move the weight back along the same arc as the one in which you lowered it until you reach the starting point again. Repeat for the desired number of repetitions.

Common Mistakes—Don't hold your breath as you do this movement, breathing only between reps. This could cause you to black out. It's best to breathe as you lower the weight and as you raise it. Never bounce the weight in the bottom position, because that can put a great amount of stress on your shoulder joints. I know a bodybuilder who actually dislocated her shoulder when she bounced the weight. If you do the movement slowly and in a controlled fashion, you will have no need to worry about injuries.

Training Tips—To stretch the working muscles in the bottom position of this movement, make it a habit to slightly dip your hips as the weight reaches the low point. A similar movement can be done lying lengthwise on a flat exercise bench, either with a dumbbell grasped in both hands (as in this exercise) or with a narrow overgrip on a light barbell handle.

CABLE CROSSOVERS (MIDDLE-CHEST VARIATION)

Areas Emphasized—This variation of cable crossovers places more stress on the muscles of the inner pecs, down in the cleavage between the muscles where they go in along the sternum. Minor secondary stress is on the anterior deltoid muscles.

Starting Position—You should assume the same starting position as for regular cable crossovers. Attach loop handles to the ends of two cables running through high pulleys. Grasp the handles and stand midway between the two pulleys, slightly forward of an imaginary line drawn between the pulleys. Your feet should be set either about shoulder-width apart, to balance your body rigidly in position as you do the movement, or set in a slight "fore-and-aft" split, to accomplish the same purpose. (I personally

Cable Crossovers (middle-chest variation)—midpoint

favor the second foot position.) Start with your palms facing downward toward the floor, your arms extended out to your sides. Bend your arms slightly and keep them rounded like this throughout the movement.

Movement Performance—Move your hands forward and slightly downward in semicircular arcs until they touch each other directly in front of the middle of your chest. Press your hands together tightly while intensely flexing your pectoral muscles for a moment. Relax slightly and allow the handles to travel back along the same arcs to the starting point. Repeat.

Common Mistakes—Although you should lean slightly into this movement from your waist, be sure that your torso angle doesn't exceed about 20 degrees from the vertical. Don't jerk at any point in the movement and don't cut it short.

Training Tips—You can do this exercise with one arm at a time while holding onto a sturdy upright with your free hand to additionally brace your body in position. In this case, you should actually pull the handle as far past the midline of your body as possible before holding the peak-contracted position.

CABLE CROSSOVERS (UPPER-CHEST VARIATION)

Areas Emphasized—Using this variation of cable crossovers, you can transfer most of the stress to the upper pectorals and anterior deltoids.

Starting Position—Assume the same starting position as for the previous exercise.

Movement Performance—Slowly move your hands in semicircular arcs forward and upward until they come together about 18 inches (about 45 centimeters) in front of and slightly above the level of your head. Press your hands together tightly in this position and hold the

Cable Crossovers (upper-chest variation)—midpoint

peak-contracted point for a moment as you intensely flex your upper pectorals. Relax slightly and slowly return the pulley handles back along the same arcs to the starting point. Repeat the movement for the required number of repetitions.

Common Mistakes—You won't be able to use as much weight in this variation of cable crossovers as in others. A common mistake is to select a heavier weight than you can handle, and then you find you have to horse the pulley handles up to the finish point with extraneous body movement. You should perform pulley crossovers for your upper pectorals in a slow and controlled manner.

Training Tips—As in the previous variation of crossovers, you can do the movement with one hand at a time while holding onto a sturdy upright with your free hand to brace your body in position. In this case, you should again pull the handle as far past the midline of your body as possible before holding the peak-contracted position.

Shoulder Exercises
. . . .

DUMBBELL ALTERNATE FRONT RAISES

Areas Emphasized—All variations of front raises will place the most intense stress on your anterior deltoid muscles, with secondary emphasis on the medial delts.

Starting Position—Grasp two light dumbbells in your hands and stand with your feet set about 6–8 inches (18–24 centimeters) apart and parallel to each other. Your hands should be

Dumbbell Alternate Front Raises—midpoint

down at your sides. Bend your arms slightly and keep them rounded like this throughout your set. I like to start every rep with my palms facing toward the rear of my body.

Movement Performance—Start with your right arm by raising the weight along the midline of your body in a semicircular arc up to shoulder level. As the weight in your right hand begins to descend, simultaneously raise the dumbbell in your left hand along the same type of arc as was described with your right hand. Keep moving the weights in seesaw fashion like this until you have completed the desired number of repetitions with each arm.

Common Mistakes—Swinging the weights is a common error. You should also avoid allowing the dumbbells to deviate out to the sides, away from the midline of your body. Arnold Schwarzenegger loved this exercise when he was a competitor, and he always recommended raising the weights slightly *across* the midline of the body in order to keep them from deviating out to the sides.

Training Tips—Similar movements can be performed while you hold a single dumbbell in both hands (see the Anja dumbbell front raises already described and illustrated in Chapter 6) or with an overgrip on a light barbell handle.

ONE-ARM CABLE SIDE LATERALS

Areas Emphasized—This is a truly intense isolation exercise for the medial head of the deltoid. Minimal stress is concurrently placed on the medial head of the working deltoid muscle.

Starting Position—Attach a loop handle to the end of the cable running through a floor pulley. With your left side toward the pulley, grasp the handle with your right hand in such a way that the cable runs diagonally across the front of your body as you do the exercise. Set

One-Arm Cable Side Laterals—start and finish

your feet close together, as illustrated, and brace your body with your free hand so your torso doesn't move during each repetition. Bend your right arm slightly and keep it rounded like this throughout the movement. Start the exercise with your right hand about 6 inches (18 centimeters) directly in front of the middle of your pelvic structure.

Movement Performance—Move the handle in a semicircular arc slightly forward and out to the side and then upward until your hand reaches approximately eye level. Throughout the movement, the palm of your right hand should face toward the floor. Hold this peak-contracted position for a moment to more intensely stress the medial delt and then move the handle along the same arc to the starting point. Repeat the movement for the desired number of repetitions. Repeat the exercise with your left arm. Be sure

One-Arm Cable Side Laterals—midpoint

to complete the same number of sets and reps with each arm.

Common Mistakes—Don't allow your hand to come forward more than about 4 inches (12 centimeters), since going beyond this distance with your hand removes concentrated stress on the medial deltoid and transfers it to the anterior section of the muscle complex. Never jerk or cut a movement short.

Training Tips—Two distinct variations of this exercise exist, and each stresses the medial head of your working deltoid completely differently from the others. In the first variation, run the cable behind your back rather than diagonally across the front of your body. In the second variation, stand with your working arm toward the pulley, so you pull more directly upward against the weight as you complete the movement.

ONE-ARM CABLE BENT-OVER LATERALS

Areas Emphasized—This is a fairly isolated rear deltoid movement that places only a minor amount of stress on the upper-back muscles.

Starting Position—Attach a loop handle to the end of the cable running through a floor pulley. Grasp the handle in your right hand and stand with your left side toward the pulley. Bend your left leg at about a 45-degree angle and rest your left hand or wrist on your knee, as shown. You can split your right leg out to the side (my personal preference), or keep it about shoulder-width away from and parallel to your left foot. With the cable passing beneath your torso, which is held parallel to the gym floor throughout the movement, allow the weight attached to the opposite end of the cable to pull your right hand across the midline of your torso. Bend your working arm to about a 30-degree angle and keep it rounded like this throughout your set.

One-Arm Cable Bent-Over Laterals—start and finish

Movement Performance—Use posterior deltoid strength to move the pulley handle in a semicircular arc directly out to your right side and upward until it is approximately at eye level. Hold this peak-contracted position for a moment and then lower the handle back along the same arc to the starting point. Repeat the movement for an appropriate number of repetitions. Repeat the exercise with your left arm. Be sure that you do an equal number of sets and reps with each arm.

Common Mistakes—The most common mistake is to rotate your torso with your arm, rather than merely articulating your arm in your shoulder socket. Rotating your torso removes considerable stress from the rear deltoid muscle, although it does allow you to use a much heavier weight on the movement. Don't allow your arm to travel toward the rear, which will lessen the stress on the part of the shoulder you are trying to work the hardest. The movement should always be directly out to the side.

One-Arm Cable Bent-Over Laterals—midpoint

Arm Exercises

ONE-ARM CABLE CURLS

Areas Emphasized—This is a direct biceps movement that helps bring out the peak in the middle of the muscle complex. Only minor secondary stress is on the forearm flexor muscles as you execute each repetition.

Starting Position—Attach a loop handle to the end of the cable running through a high pulley. Grasp the handle in your left hand, your left side toward the pulley and about a body length away from it. Brace your torso in position with your free hand. Rotate your left hand so it is fully supinated (palm toward the gym ceiling) and extend your left arm directly upward toward the pulley. Your working arm should be straight at the beginning of each repetition.

One-Arm Cable Curls—midpoint

One-Arm
Cable Curls—
start and finish

Movement Performance—Use biceps strength to move your hand in a semicircular arc from the starting point to a position as close to your shoulder as possible, while keeping your upper arm motionless. Hold this peak-contracted point for a moment and then slowly return your hand to the starting position. Repeat the movement for the required number of repetitions. Do the same number of reps with your other arm. Be sure you complete the same number of sets and reps with each arm.

Common Mistakes—The most common error in doing this exercise is to allow your upper arm to waft all over the place as you bend and straighten it. Your arm should always remain as motionless as possible, with the entire movement coming from bending the elbow joint just by tensing your biceps muscles. Another common mistake is to do the movement without fully supinating your working hand. Always keep in mind that the biceps both flex and supinate your arms.

Training Tips—You can do this movement with both arms simultaneously by first attaching another loop handle to the end of the cable running through the other overhead pulley and then standing midway between the two pulleys. As you perform the movement, you will look as if you are doing a double-biceps pose onstage at a bodybuilding competition. It's also possible to execute the one-armed variation of this movement while facing the pulley rather than with your side toward it.

WIDE-GRIP PULLEY PUSHDOWNS

Areas Emphasized—All variations of pushdowns directly stress the triceps muscle complex, with minimal additional emphasis on the forearm flexors. This particular variation places more stress on the middle head of the muscle. Outer head stress is felt when you do the exercise with the more common narrow grip.

Wide-Grip Pulley Pushdowns—start and finish

Wide-Grip Pulley Pushdowns—midpoint

Starting Position—Attach a lat pulldown bar to the end of the cable running through an overhead pulley. Take an overgrip on the bar so your hands are set 4–6 inches (12–18 centimeters) wider than your shoulders on each side. With your arms down at your sides and pressed firmly against your torso throughout the movement, start with your arms bent as fully as possible, the bar running along the upper line of your pectorals.

Movement Performance—Use triceps strength to slowly straighten your arms and move the pulley handle in a semicircular arc from the starting point to a position in which the bar is running across your upper thighs. Hold this peak-contracted position for a moment, move the bar along the same arc back to the starting point, and repeat the movement for the suggested number of repetitions.

Common Mistakes—Leaning too far into the movement takes a lot of the stress off your triceps. Don't jerk the weight or cut any movements short.

Training Tips—You should try grips incrementally narrower than the one illustrated and described. You might find that a shoulder-width grip places more direct stress on the areas of your triceps that you're trying to hit.

REVERSE-GRIP PULLEY PUSHDOWNS

Areas Emphasized—Doing this movement with an undergrip on the pulley handle places the most intense stress on the medial triceps head, with proportionately less emphasis on the inner and outer lobes of the muscle complex. Minimal secondary stress is on the forearm flexor and extensor muscles.

Starting Position—Attach a short bar handle to the cable running through an overhead

Reverse-Grip Pulley Pushdowns—start and finish

Reverse-Grip Pulley Pushdowns— midpoint

pulley. Set your feet close together and about 1 foot (about 35 centimeters) back from the pulley. Take a relatively narrow undergrip on the pulley handle, pin your upper arms to the sides of your torso for the entire set, and fully flex your arms.

Movement Performance—Use triceps strength to slowly straighten your arms and move the pulley handle in a semicircular arc from the described starting point down to a position across your upper thighs. Hold this peak-contracted position for a moment; then move the handle along the same arc back to the starting point. Repeat.

Training Tips—You won't be able to use as much weight with this type of grip as with the more common overgrip. A common mistake is to try using the same weight and forcing yourself to horse the weight down, using excessive body English. Don't push the weight straight down but rather describe a distinct semicircular arc with it.

Training Tips—Try different grip widths to determine whether one of them is better for you than the others. You can also do this movement with one arm at a time (as in the next exercise description) by attaching a loop handle to the end of the cable running though an overhead pulley.

ONE-ARM PULLEY PUSHDOWNS

Areas Emphasized—One-arm pulley pushdowns emphasize the entire triceps complex. When done with the hand supinated, as illustrated, the movement places the most intense stress on the medial deltoid head.

Starting Position—Attach a loop handle to the end of the cable running through an overhead pulley. Take an undergrip on the handle with your left hand. Press your left upper arm

One-Arm Pulley Pushdowns—start and finish

One-Arm Pulley Pushdowns—midpoint

Advanced-Level Exercises | **209**

against the side of your torso and keep it there throughout the movement. Start with your left arm fully flexed. Brace your torso in position by grasping a sturdy upright with your right hand.

Movement Performance—Keeping your hand fully supinated throughout the movement, use triceps strength to slowly move the handle forward and downward in a semicircular arc until it reaches a position slightly behind your left buttock. Hold this peak-contracted position for a moment and then move the handle along the same arc back to the starting point. Repeat the movement for an appropriate number of reps. Do another set with your other arm. Be sure to complete the same number of sets and reps with each arm.

Common Mistakes—Avoid having to use body English by selecting a relatively light poundage. Don't allow your upper body to move all over the place as you do the pushdown movement. Never let your upper arm drift away from your torso during the exercise.

Training Tips—You can do one-arm pulley pushdowns with your hand fully pronated as well. That type of hand position transfers the stress more to the meaty inner head of the triceps.

DUMBBELL KICKBACKS
Areas Emphasized—This is a direct triceps movement that hits the entire muscle complex. It is especially good for using peak contraction, since all of the weight is still on your muscles when the movement has been completed.

Starting Position—Grasp a light dumbbell in your right hand. Place your left knee and left hand on a flat exercise bench, as illustrated, with your right foot on the floor to brace your torso in a position slightly above an imaginary line drawn parallel to the gym floor. Press your right

Dumbbell Kickbacks—start and finish

upper arm against the side of your torso and keep it there throughout the entire movement. Bend your left arm to a bit more than a 90-degree angle, making sure that your hand is oriented so your palm is facing inward toward your body throughout each set.

Movement Performance—Use triceps strength to slowly straighten your arm, moving the dumbbell in a semicircular arc from the described starting point to a position level with your shoulder joint. Hold this peak-contracted position for a moment before moving the weight along the same arc back to the starting point. Repeat the movement for the correct number of repetitions.

Training Tips—You can also do kickbacks with both arms simultaneously by holding a dumbbell in each hand and standing with your feet close together and your torso held parallel to the gym floor.

Dumbbell Kickbacks—midpoint

Calf Exercise

. . . .

ONE-LEGGED STANDING CALF RAISES

Areas Emphasized—All standing calf raises place direct stress on the gastrocnemius, as long as the working leg is held straight throughout the movement.

Starting Position—Face a standing calf machine and place your shoulders beneath the padded yokes. Position the ball and toes of your right foot on the calf block, being sure that your heel hangs off. Hold your left leg either forward or backward, bending your left knee to keep that leg out of the movement. Straighten your right leg and torso to bear the weight of the machine. Allow the weight to push your heel as far as is comfortably possible beneath the level of your toes, which fully stretches your calf muscles.

Movement Performance—Use gastrocnemius strength to slowly extend your right foot as you rise up as high as is humanly possible on your toes. Hold this peak-contracted position for a moment and then slowly return to the starting point. Repeat the movement for the suggested number of repetitions. Repeat the exercise with the other leg, alternating legs until you have done the required number of sets and reps with each leg.

Common Mistakes—Bending and then kicking with your working leg to get yourself up into the finish position is inappropriate. Using your free leg to assist your working leg in the movement robs your calves of some of the stress they should be getting from this exercise.

Training Tips—If there is not a standing calf machine available, you can do a variation of this movement. Simply hold a light dumbbell in your right hand down at your side as you do the movement with your right leg, balancing your body in position by grasping a sturdy upright with your left hand. Hold the dumbbell in your left hand when you do the exercise with your left leg.

One-Legged Standing Calf Raises—start and finish

One-Legged Standing Calf Raises—midpoint

Floor Crunches—midpoint

Abdominal Exercises
. . . .

FLOOR CRUNCHES
Areas Emphasized—All variations of crunches place the most direct stress on the entire rectus abdominis muscle wall, with perhaps the most intense stress on the upper abs. Significant secondary stress is on the intercostal muscles at the sides of your midwaist.

Starting Position—Lie on your back on a mat on the gym floor. Bend your legs at an angle that is slightly more than 90 degrees. Place your feet flat on the floor about shoulder-width apart. Place your hands behind your head and neck and keep them in this position throughout your set.

Movement Performance—Simultaneously exhale forcefully and use upper abdominal strength to curl your shoulders off the floor and toward your hips. Hold this peak-concentrated position for a moment and then slowly lower

your shoulders back to the starting point. Repeat the movement for an appropriate number of repetitions.

Common Mistakes—Never merely throw your head and shoulders off the mat. Use abdominal strength to slowly curl them up off the floor. Don't just pull with your hands and lift your head off the mat—that does little, if anything, for your abdominals.

Training Tips—For a greater amount of stress on your lower abs, you can use lower-ab strength to also raise your hips from the floor as part of this movement. I use the hip movement as an upper-ab isolation exercise.

END-OF-BENCH LEG RAISES
Areas Emphasized—This movement stresses the entire rectus abdominis muscle wall but places the most intense stress on the lower half of the frontal abdominals.

End-of-Bench Leg Raises—start and finish

Starting Position—Sit at the end of a flat exercise bench and recline your torso backward at a 45-degree angle with the floor, gripping the sides of the bench, as shown, to brace yourself throughout your set. Bend your legs to about a 20-degree angle and keep them rounded like this throughout the movement. Extend your legs forward and a few inches above the level of the bench.

Movement Performance—Use lower-abdominal strength to move your legs upward and downward over about a 30-degree arc of motion. Keep the movement slow and totally under control, repeating it until your abdominal muscles are pleasantly fatigued.

Common Mistakes—You should keep your legs pressed together as you do bench leg raises. Allowing your feet to drift apart lets a discordant note into the music you are making. Never jerk while you are doing this exercise and don't do it with straight legs, since both of these common mistakes will place harmful stress on your lower back.

Training Tips—There are two variations of this movement. To do the first one, lie back on the bench and grasp its sides behind your head. Raise and lower your legs out in space off the end of the bench. In this variation, you can do a long, sweeping, smooth movement instead of the shorter one described earlier. Another variation, commonly called knee-ups, begins in the same position described for end of bench leg raises, but your knees are pulled up to your chest as you simultaneously bend your legs fully. The movement is finished by slowly returning your knees and legs to the starting point.

End-of-Bench Leg Raises—midpoint

PULLEY CRUNCHES

Areas Emphasized—Your position dictates which parts of your midsection muscles are most intensely stressed. If you do the movement facing straight ahead, you place the most intense stress on the upper half of the rectus abdominis. If you do it facing off to one side, the intercostals will get considerable stress, while at the same time emphasis is also placed on the rectus abdominis muscle wall.

Starting Position—Attach a straight bar handle to the end of the cable running through an overhead pulley and place an exercise mat beneath the pulley. Grasp the pulley handle with a narrow undergrip and kneel down on the mat. Bend your legs slightly, as illustrated, and keep them bent at this angle throughout your set.

Bend your arms a little past a 90-degree angle and maintain that arm bend for the entire movement. Start with your torso almost erect and your hands at about chin level.

Movement Performance—Simultaneously exhale forcefully, bend over about 30 degrees at your waist, and intensely flex all of your abdominal muscles. Hold this peak-contracted position for a moment and then return slowly to the starting point without allowing stress to come off your midsection. Repeat this short movement for the suggested number of reps.

Common Mistakes—Failing to exhale forcefully will completely negate the effect of this exercise. Bending over too far at the waist doesn't actually improve the quality of the stress placed on your abdominals.

Pulley Crunches—start and finish

Training Tips—If you bend a bit to each side alternately as you do this movement, you will intensely involve the intercostal muscles and less intensely stress the obliques. If you can find a rope handle (a short length of rope with knots in the ends of it, the middle of which passes through a ring attached to the pulley, allowing you to take a parallel-hands grip on the ropes), try using the handle as you do the pulley crunches. For a direct effect on your intercostals, attach a loop handle to the end of the pulley cable and hold it just in your right hand, bending directly to the right as you crunch. Then take the loop handle in your left hand and perform the movement. Be sure to do an equal number of sets and reps with each arm.

Pulley Crunches—midpoint

9 Stretching!

All members of the cat family spend a great deal of time stretching the skeletal muscles of their bodies. I'm sure you have observed this behavior in a pet Siamese or tabby cat, particularly after these relatively small members of the cat family arise from a nap or an all-night sleep. Sometimes a cat's instinctive stretching program can last for as many as five minutes before the beautiful little animal strolls gracefully away from his or her bedding place to see what food is available.

Even the largest cats of the world—tigers, lions, panthers, cheetahs, and leopards—are veteran stretchers. If you observe them when they are incarcerated in animal prisons (some people call these zoos), you will see the big cats do plenty of stretching. In fact, since they are no longer allowed by the prison wardens to run at will or climb high up into trees, feline prisoners actually stretch more thoroughly and for longer periods of time than their brothers and sisters in the wild. It's the only true exercise they get, yet they remain in incredible physical condition, with no excess body fat and sinewy muscles clearly visible beneath their skin. Even in captivity big cats are magnificent creatures!

Humans should take a lesson from these feline beasts and include regular stretching sessions in their overall physical-fitness and appearance-enhancement programs. With sufficient daily stretching, you can have the long, supple, powerful-appearing muscles of a jungle cat.

Did you know that the animal kingdom's fastest runner (perhaps she cross-trains to build up her sprint speed) is the cheetah, which is capable of short bursts of speed of up to 60 miles (100 kilometers) per hour when trying to run down prey? Interestingly, most of the kills for food are made by the female of the species. Nature has made her more cunning in her tactical approach to a gazelle or other food source, a faster runner than her lazier spouse, and a more efficient killer when it is necessary for her to bring home food to her cubs and mate. Perhaps there is a second lesson we should be learning from the large predatory cats of the world.

Stretching: Where It Fits In

Performed correctly and consistently, stretching exercises will make your entire body more supple and resistant to injury. If you make daily stretching a part of your lifestyle, something you do because you love it rather than because you know you are "supposed to do it," you will be far more likely to have the long and more sensuous muscles of a swimmer than the bunched-up musculature of a gymnast, bodybuilder, or weightlifter.

Did you know that yoga is actually a rigidly stylized form of flexibility training, which is frequently done to promote a spiritual tranquility? The type of flexibility program I will outline in this chapter can also give you a feeling of consistent tranquility, to say nothing of the same degree of physical suppleness as possessed by a yoga devotee. When done in the right frame of mind, my program might even give you the same feeling of spirituality experienced by yoga practitioners.

Yogis may practice no other form of physical exercise, yet they are uniformly lean of body and very fit. If some extraordinary situation occurs to keep you away from your weights for a few weeks or months—such as that extended stay in Antarctica you've been planning—stick with your flexibility routine. It will keep your fitness levels high enough that you'll experience little difficulty in the weight room when there is one handy again.

Cross-training, a popular buzzword these days, means the combining of several types of exercises into one fitness regimen. Competitive bodybuilders are the ultimate cross-trainers, because they place almost equal emphasis on strength-building workouts in the gym, flexibility sessions (particularly as part of every warm-up before a weight-training session), and consistent aerobics (stationary cycling, stair climbing, walking, running on the treadmill—or my personal favorite, mountain biking), and a variety of physically taxing outdoor activities.

Because we competitive bodybuilders are such fanatic cross-trainers—and we pay strict attention to our diets—we become unbelievably

physically and mentally fit. I dare say that we have become a race of superwomen! But for now, all you need to know is that stretching is one vital factor in the equation for developing thousands upon thousands of superwomen.

Stretching: Values and Benefits

When you assume the exaggerated postures illustrated in this chapter—and hold them for periods ranging from 30 seconds up to 2 minutes and more—you are stretching the muscles, connective tissues, and joints of your body in a therapeutic and productive manner. While it will require some time and persistence, you eventually will increase the suppleness of your muscles and the range of motion over which you can bend and extend each body joint.

The process of becoming flexible by stretching is relatively slow, particularly when compared to the speed at which you can increase the strength of selected muscles with normal weight training—or with an accelerated form of the activity called "strength training," or "power training." You can improve visible muscle strength much more rapidly than you can enhance cardio-respiratory efficiency and muscle endurance. But improvements in body flexibility and suppleness come even more slowly.

How long will it take to see improvement in flexibility? If you are consistent and persistent, you will see gains in body suppleness within six months to a year. But it will probably require 3–4 years of effort to tap all of the reserves of flexibility and suppleness hidden within your body. If by some misfortune you are forced to suspend flexibility workouts for any extended period of time, you will discover that your own body rebels very quickly and becomes stiff and unyieldingly tight virtually overnight.

As a side note, it is well known that teenage

girls—particularly those who have not yet reached puberty—can develop full-body flexibility much more quickly than mature women can. The older you get, the more difficult it becomes to reach higher flexibility levels.

My mother made sure I began dance classes at the age of eight. I continued to stay heavily involved in dance until I was in my late teens, when I switched all of my concentration over to trying to become the world's greatest female competitive bodybuilder. Still, most of my own body flexibility—particularly in my legs, hips, and lower torso—is the result of daily dance classes.

If you are particularly inflexible, or easily bored with the stretching program presented in this chapter, I strongly recommend that you sign up for adult-level beginning dance classes. There are many available in urban areas. Simply consult the Yellow Pages under a category such as "Dance Studies/Instruction," and make a couple calls to see who can take you on as a beginning student.

I particularly recommend taking classic ballet classes for added flexibility, much of which will come during basic dance movement work at the barre. Or if competitive bodybuilding is a strong interest, I'd suggest enrolling in jazz dance or contemporary dance classes, which will be an enormous help whenever you need to choreograph a new free-posing routine. Most of my own transitional movements that link my static poses onstage were learned on the dance floor or were improvised from well-known dance movements.

One of the most immediate benefits of consistent flexibility training is the fact that it makes your body more resistant to all types of injuries, from those tiny microtraumas that might ultimately result in long-term sore joints to truly traumatic problems such as muscle pulls, joint sprains, and even muscle tears, broken bones, and joint dislocations. The last three types of injuries are almost nonexistent in weight train-

ing, but since they occur in competitive sports contests I thought it was important to mention that flexibility training can protect various types of athletes from serious injuries.

In Chapter 2, I talked about how to thoroughly warm up your body prior to a weight-training session, and stretching exercises were an integral part of this type of warm-up. Stretches are included in all warm-ups mainly because they so efficiently act to protect your body from injury.

A second major benefit of consistent flexibility training is that it can actually improve your muscular development. At first glance, this probably seems like a fatuous statement, but I assure you it is true. Flexibility in your joints and muscles will actually improve the ultimate shape and quality of a bodybuilder's musculature. But how can this possibly occur?

When your joints and muscles are highly flexible, you will find that you can move your limbs—even your torso—over more exaggerated ranges of motion. That means you can do the same thing with a weight in your hand—you are able to place resistance on a muscle over a far greater-than-normal range of motion. It doesn't take a rocket scientist to conclude that exercising a muscle over an exaggerated range of motion will stress it more thoroughly and from a greater number of vectorial angles. And *that* is what causes the muscle to gradually assume a more pleasing shape.

A final major benefit of having a markedly flexible body is visual—and it is a quality that is evaluated subjectively. It is something that will accrue from consistently practicing your flexibility exercises. This final benefit is greater grace of movement. Whether you are just out for a walk around a park or a shopping mall or are competing seriously onstage, it will be universally acknowledged, and it will give you great advantages.

All in all, I know you will agree that setting aside regular periods of time to practice stretching exercises is highly beneficial. Yet I see few women actively involved in this superb form of movement training. They somehow don't consider stretching to be that important, so they let it slide for a few days, then weeks, and then months, until they ignore the activity altogether.

Convince yourself of the supreme importance of regular and consistent stretching training, and then *make time in your busy schedule for stretching sessions*. You'll never be sorry that you made such a decision, and you'll never doubt the value of full-body flexibility once you have it.

I personally stretch prior to every workout, before both aerobics and weight sessions. I also do 20 minutes of slow, languorous stretching at any time during the day when I am feeling agitated, overstressed, or otherwise out of sorts. Invariably, stretching completely calms my nerves and helps to center me. Despite the fact that I frequently lift extremely heavy weights in my gym sessions, my body flexibility has helped me remain completely free of injuries.

PNF—The Wrong Way to Stretch

Proprioceptive Neural Facilation (PNF) has enjoyed a brief vogue as *the* way to most efficiently improve body flexibility. PNF has been particularly popular in athletic circles, largely among athletes engaged in combative sports such as football, soccer, and wrestling. For fitness purposes, however, PNF can be counterproductive. Certainly, it will not give you the same safe flexibility that you can attain by using slow, gentle, yogalike stretches.

PNF is a relatively violent form of stretching that requires a partner who forces the subject into fully stretched positions, holds him or her at full stretch—or usually well *past* the most efficient stretching zone—for a few seconds, releases the subject, and then forces the person back into the stretch. Many reps of each stretch are done in this manner in the PNF technique.

A small body of literature outlining studies of PNF indicates that PNF is a highly efficient means of inducing great body flexibility relatively quickly. No studies have yet been conducted to show whether there is any harmful effect on connective tissues when PNF is regularly applied. But we strongly suspect that the PNF process does cause tiny tears in connective tissues, tears that can accumulate and ultimately result in more serious movement-limiting injuries.

Other recent research concludes that cold muscles and joints should never be stretched, not even in a gentle manner. Stretching cold does result in microtraumatic injuries. This has been scientifically demonstrated and verified in follow-up studies.

Researchers today recommend warming up prior to stretching, the same way you would warm up before beginning a heavy weight workout (except that the warm-up before the weight workout also includes systematic stretches). Before you begin a stretching program, researchers recommend about 5–8 consecutive minutes of light aerobics (e.g., stationary cycling, jogging in place, walking on a treadmill, and/or skipping rope). Begin at a slow pace, with minimal limb movement. Gradually increase both pace and movement toward the end of the aerobics warm-up. This activity may be followed by a few minutes of either calisthenic exercises or light, high-rep weight work *before* you begin to stretch.

If researchers recommend a prestretching warm-up this extensive to prevent tissue breakdown, it should be obvious that connective tissues—tendons, cartilages, and ligaments—are a bit more fragile than most people would suspect. Certainly, they do heal very slowly once injured, because their deficient blood supplies limit the speed with which the connective tissues can repair themselves.

Let's take three examples of how quickly three main types of body tissues heal. If you suffer a severe muscle tear, the injury will heal itself in about three weeks. Some 3–4 additional weeks of physical therapy will be required to return the function of that muscle to normal (*all* injuries require at least as much physical therapy once an injury has healed).

As a second example, let's say you broke your wrist in a basketball game. Depending on the severity of the injury, a sports physician would put your wrist in a cast to immobilize the area for 6–8 weeks while it healed. A bone injury takes approximately twice as long to heal as a comparable muscle injury. In both cases, the physical therapy time is about equal.

For our final example, let's say a woman fell on your knee in a field hockey match and tore the medial knee ligament (the band of fibrous tissue on the inner edge of your knee that gives the knee lateral stability). Such an injury would require immediate and relatively serious surgery during which stainless-steel staples would be used to permanently reattach the torn portion of the ligament to the bone. The joint would then be immobilized in a plaster cast, which would stay in place for up to 12 weeks, the length of time depending on how quickly you heal. This means that a serious connective-tissue injury requires twice as long to heal as a comparable injury to a bone, and four times as long to heal as a serious muscle injury. Physical therapy for the injured knee would take even longer; in this case it would be 6–8 weeks before you would again be cleared by a physician to practice hockey.

Given the extremely slow rate of healing of connective tissues, why would you ever want to risk injuring any of them (even if the tears might be visible only under great magnification) by having a training partner forcefully and often violently ram you into a stretched position using the PNF technique? I don't believe you would want to take such a risk, and there is an alternative for you that can increase your full-body flexibility in a much more gentle and feminine manner.

The Right Way to Stretch

The method of stretching I wish to teach you in this chapter has much in common with yoga asanas (stretches), which have been actively creating extremely flexible bodies for hundreds of years. The main reasons I teach this type of stretching are:

• Above all, it is a gentle type of stretch and yet an immensely effective method of improving flexibility.
• Exercises can be chosen to stretch every joint and skeletal muscle group in your body.
• This type of stretch has both active (dynamic) sections and passive (static) areas, with most of the stretch benefit coming from the static part of the exercise.
• When you do these stretches your flexibility sessions can ultimately include a spiritual, as well as a physical, component.
• This form of stretching can also be physically pleasurable.

A word about stretching mats is in order before a discussion of the correct way to stretch. Along with a small ladderlike dance barre (actually several barres set at graduated heights), the mat is the only piece of equipment you will require to carry out a solid stretching program.

The mats are made of polyurethane, a type of plastic that permanently traps thousands of small bubbles of air that give the mat both a soft and a relatively firm surface. It's soft enough to protect your knees, tailbone, and other bony projections yet firm enough to actually keep these bones from contacting any unyielding gym or dance-studio floor. Dance/stretching mats are so flexible that they can be rolled up between periods

Seated
Forward Stretch
—midpoint

Seated
Forward Stretch
(variation with
flexed feet)
—midpoint

of use and stored in relatively small spaces.

A mat of standard size is a bit over 3 feet (about 1 meter) long and about two feet (60 centimeters) wide. Most are approximately 1 inch (3–4 centimeters) thick. You can find them for sale in any dance supply shop as well as in many gymnasium equipment emporiums. Cost is nominal (about $10–$15 each), and the mats will last indefinitely if well cared for. Be sure to run a damp cloth or sponge over the mat's entire surface prior to storage in order to remove any perspiration residue. This rule also applies at home, even if you are the only person who ever uses the mat.

The barre can also be found at dance supply shops. Even though wood is the traditional material for barres in dance studios, I'd suggest buying a sturdy plastic or fiberglass model, both of which usually have a metal frame for rigidity. The synthetic horizontal bars won't split under consistent use, they always have dependable joints that don't come apart, and they will invariably give you many more years of trouble-free performance than the wood versions. They even come in many attractive designer colors that can be matched up effectively with mat colors.

In order to teach you the optimum way to stretch, I've chosen a typical stretching exercise, which is described in detail—and illustrated—later in this chapter. It is a basic movement, a seated forward stretch that primarily affects the hamstrings, buttocks, and spinal erector muscles.

Sit at one end of the mat, with your legs extended straight forward from your hips so that your buttocks, backs of your legs, knees, and calves are in contact with the mat. Press your legs together and hold them straight throughout the stretch. Begin with an erect posture. Your spinal vertebrae should be in perfect vertical alignment, as though they were a stack of coins balanced one on top of the other but held in line by the paper or plastic wrapper the bank places around a roll of coins.

Attempting to keep your spine as straight as possible, bend forward only at the hips and waist until you can reach ahead and place your hands flat on the mat on either side of your ankles. Note in the first photo illustrating this stretch how straight I keep my arms as I reach forward to place my palms on the mat.

In both photos, you can easily see what I mean by bending "only at the hips and waist." While my middle and upper spine describe a gentle, natural curve, above my hips my back is held as straight as humanly possible. In the first photo (the one showing the greatest forward bend), you can see that more than 90 degrees of my forward bend is achieved just in the hips, while the rest of it is achieved in the lower third of my spinal vertebrae (specifically in the lumbar vertebrae).

As you bend farther and farther forward, you will begin to feel a somewhat pleasant stretching sensation first in your hamstrings, then in your lower spine, and, after a few additional degrees of bend, in your hip-girdle muscles. Push even farther, and this stretch sensation will quickly become one of pain as you reach an over-stretched position.

The key to using any stretch most effectively is to discover the *stretching zone* through experimentation and then locating the *pain edge* at which comfort changes abruptly to discomfort. As long as you stay within your stretching zone, you will accrue all of the benefits of a stretching workout. But if you grow excessively enthusiastic about your flexibility program and push past the pain edge, you will cease to gain benefits from your stretch and begin to risk injury to stretched tissues.

Now back to the example of the seated forward stretch. Slowly bend forward until you begin to sense the pain edge approaching. Back off a couple of degrees and hold this stretched position for a minimum of 30 seconds. Backing off correctly from the pain edge should keep you several degrees of amplitude away from an injury that could occur if you pushed the stretch too far; yet you will be in a position at the upper end of the productive stretching zone. After 30 seconds, release the stretch just as slowly as you assumed it, rest for a minute or two, and then either repeat the stretch or move on to execute a stretch for a different area of your body.

At first your stretches will be easiest to maintain if you hold them statically. It's nothing to be embarrassed about, however, because all neophyte stretchers' first efforts are performed statically. I had such a solid dance background before I took up bodybuilding that my joints and muscles were hyperflexible, and I was already an expert stretcher (all experienced dancers are). I had long since learned to "work" a stretch, moving slightly into and out of it according to my internal body rhythms, which makes each stretch more interesting to do and more productive in the long run.

Superior body flexibility doesn't come overnight, but once it does, you'll discover ways of intensifying each stretch in your flexibility program. Because of my dance background, the initial seated forward stretch was a little too tame for me, so I set about finding ways to intensify it. If you look carefully at the second photo, you will see the accommodations I made.

The first of these was to move my hands forward to grasp my heels, so I could pull myself into a more exaggerated position that intensely stretched my hamstrings, glutes, and spinal erectors. Note how I have flexed my feet rather than pointing them, as I did in the first illustration. Foot flexion in this position adds to the stretch intensity in the hamstrings and also brings the gastrocnemius, soleus, and tibialis anterior muscles of the lower legs strongly into the overall stretch.

A Note on Nomenclature

After many years of stretching, I have developed my own personal terms in German for each of the stretches illustrated and described in this chapter. When Bill Reynolds, my coauthor, and I tried to translate some of them into English, I discovered that a large portion of my stretching movement terminology was somewhat whimsical and could not be meaningfully translated into precise English. So for the English-language edition of the book, we have opted to name the exercises primarily according to which areas of the body they tend to stretch. When two or more exercises stretch the same area, we have added small refinements to the names (whether the exercise is performed seated or standing, what equipment is used, etc.) to distinguish between one stretch and another.

At any rate, each named exercise also has at least one (and in many cases three) photos accompanying it, so confusion should be kept to a minimum. You are certainly free to call these individual stretching postures anything you like. The resistance exercises within this book have highly standardized names, which you'll need to stick to when talking bodybuildingese. But with the stretches, you can feel free to be as whimsical in your choice of exercise names in English as I was in German.

My Favorite Stretches

I have chosen the exercises to be illustrated and described in this section mainly because they are among the most basic of all flexibility postures. All of them find their way into my own stretching programs quite regularly, but so do many others that I simply can't include for lack of adequate space.

Master this group first, because you, too, will always come back to many of them due to their fundamental nature. Then as your interests expand, you can gradually add more esoteric flexibility movements to your catalog of stretching exercises. This way, you can rotate new ones in and out of your overall program to prevent any sort of boredom from creeping in.

CIRCULAR FORWARD STRETCH

This is a good one to start with, because it stretches almost all of the muscles at the rear of your body. Particular emphasis is on the glutes, hamstrings, spinal erectors, external obliques, and upper-back muscles, but you will also place a lesser degree of stretch on your shoulder-girdle muscles and even the sides of your hips and calves. As with all of my favorite stretches, there are static sections; with this one there are transitions between stopping points.

Start out by setting your feet on your mat somewhat wider than shoulder width, toes

Circular Forward Stretch—midpoint (right) (position 2)

Circular Forward Stretch—start and finish (position 1)

Circular Forward Stretch—midpoint (left) (position 4)

angled outward on each side by about 30 degrees. Stand erect and then bend forward with your knees locked until your torso is approximately parallel to the floor. Extend your arms directly forward parallel to the floor. This is position 1 (which also becomes positions 3, 5, etc., as you perform the stretch). Stretch forward at the waist, allowing your hips to shift slightly to the rear to maintain balance as your arms and torso move forward. Hold this pleasant stretched position for 30–60 seconds.

Keeping your hips level and oriented as closely as possible to the way they were in position 1, slowly move your torso to the right as far as is comfortably possible, which is position 2. This will cause you to sense more of a stretch in the muscles at the sides of your hips and waist. Hold this stretched position for another 30–60 seconds.

Move back to position 1 (which by now is position 3), hold that position for 30–60 seconds, and then slowly rotate into position 4, the mirror image of position 2. Hold for another 30–60 seconds.

Perhaps you will want to repeat this series more than once. After a couple weeks of consistent stretching, feel free to do so.

BALLET SIDE STRETCH

This is an adaptation of a classical ballet barre movement. For those readers unfamiliar with ballet, barre usually makes up the first half of a class and comprises the thorough warm-up your entire body must undergo before you are ready for the adagio portion of the class where everything is done in the middle of the dance floor. The barre is the horizontal wooden bar attached to the wall parallel to the dance floor at about waist level. It is used for gripping during intricate foot and leg movements and is also a stretching aid. In this case, an actual barre is not necessary, but this type of stretch is commonly done during the barre section of a ballet class.

The ballet side stretch emphasizes stretching those muscles at the sides of the hips, waist, and upper torso. I start out with my feet set on the mat in ballet foot position 2. (For the layperson, this involves setting the feet about 6–8 inches—35–40 centimeters—wider than the shoulders. Your toes should be pointed almost directly out to the sides, but rotation for this type of turnout, as it is called in dance circles, *must* come from your hips rather than your knees.)

Stretch the left side of your hips and torso first. Extend your left arm directly upward from your shoulder, but round it by bending the arm slightly as illustrated. Keep it rounded like this throughout the stretch. Your right arm should pass in front of your torso and also be held rounded throughout the stretch (although this rounded-arm position is more clearly visible for the lower arm in the second photo of this stance).

Keeping your legs locked throughout the stretch, slowly bend to the right, until you feel you have reached the stretching zone. You will find that both of your arms cross the midline of your body quite naturally as you assume the stretch, although how far you actually can bend in either direction will depend on relative body flexibility, not on arm movement. Once in the stretching zone, hold the stretched position for 30–60 seconds before again standing erect.

Reverse your arm positions and repeat your ballet side stretch to the left. Since this stretch is the mirror image of the first one that was described in detail, you should be able to handle it with no additional instruction. Hold the fully stretched position for the same length of time that you hold the stretch to the other side. You may wish to alternate sides one or two times before you sense that you have completely stretched the sides of your hips and torso.

One common mistake made in doing this type of side stretch is to allow your hips to travel

Ballet Side Stretch—midpoint (left)

Ballet Side Stretch—midpoint (right)

outward to the side away from the direction you are stretching. Fight this tendency. Your hips should remain stationary and directly over a point midway between your feet in order for you to receive maximum benefit from ballet side stretches.

LOWER-BACK STRETCH

This posture will stretch the muscles of your lower back and serve to ensure a healthy spinal column by maintaining correct alignment of lumbar, thoracic, and cervical disks. You will sense a secondary stretching sensation in your glutes and hamstrings.

I start out this stretch lying on my back lengthwise on the mat. Throughout the stretch my arms are kept in the same position, held straight and down at my sides, the palms of my hands pressed flat against the mat. This arm and hand position is important, because it provides you

with leverage to get comfortably into the fully stretched position.

I personally like to hold my legs straight and my toes pointed like a ballet dancer's during the entire movement and stretched position. You can feel free, however, to bend your legs slightly at the knees and/or flex your feet. It makes little difference in terms of how effectively this stretch does its job.

Pressing down with your hands against the mat, slowly raise your legs off the floor as though you were doing the leg-raise exercise common to many weight-training abdominal routines. Usually you would halt this movement when your feet reach a position directly above your hips and then reverse direction, returning to the starting point. But this time I want you to keep moving your legs farther and farther—allowing your buttocks to come off the mat—until your knees reach a position directly above your face. This is clearly illustrated, as is the maxi-

Lower-Back Stretch—midpoint

mally stretched finish position of the posture in which my toes actually rest lightly on the exercise mat above my head.

It is vitally important as you slowly enter this stretch that you keep all of your back muscles as fully relaxed as possible. And don't tense up once you are fully into the stretch, or you'll lose much of the benefit of this movement. Hold the fully stretched position, staying as relaxed as possible, for another 30–60 seconds. Then slowly unroll yourself and return to the starting point. Perhaps after a 60-second break, you will want to repeat your lower-back stretch.

SEATED HAMSTRINGS AND LOWER-BACK STRETCH

This is a variation of the seated forward stretch I used to illustrate proper stretching procedure earlier in this chapter. It is a bit more intense way of stretching the muscles of your hamstrings and lower back, with secondary emphasis on the glutes and upper-back musculature. For some reason, I find this to be a particularly calming stretch to perform whenever I've had a mentally or emotionally hectic day. And for that reason, I will often begin my stretching program with this posture.

Seated Hamstrings and Lower Back Stretch— midpoint

Seated Hamstrings and Lower Back Stretch (variation with flexed feet) —midpoint

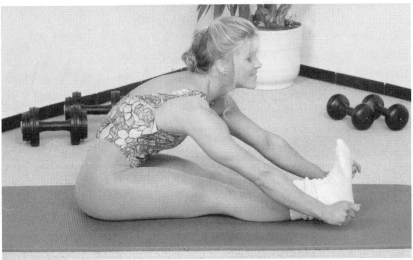

I start by sitting erect on my mat, my legs extended directly forward. I press my legs together, straighten them, and keep them in the same position throughout the stretch. Normally I start out with my toes pointed, but as you will see I sometimes like to flex my feet as well.

Attempting to keep my spine straight and bending mainly in the lumbar region, I reach forward with both hands and simultaneously bend forward as slowly and as far as is comfortably possible. At first you will find it difficult to bend very far forward, but soon you'll be able to comfortably rest your torso along your thighs with your knees locked out so your legs are straight. Whatever distance it takes for you to reach your stretching zone, assume it slowly, and hold that position for 30–60 seconds.

Relax and then return to the starting point. After a brief break, you may wish to do the stretch a second time. With this—and almost all other stretching exercises—you will notice that your stretching zone has extended out a bit past where it was the first time. This is a result primarily of a warm-up effect from the initial repetition of the exercise, and it is one reason why I usually suggest doing repetitions of each posture.

With time, you'll find this stretch easy to do, and you'll need to push it a little harder. The easiest way to accomplish this is to grasp your ankles or heels and pull yourself more deeply into a stretched position. You will also discover that you can intensify the stretch sensation in your hamstrings with this movement by flexing your feet rather than leaving your toes pointed.

I'm all for variety in stretching—as I am when pumping iron—so I like to play around with subtle variable such as changing between pointed toes and flexed feet when doing my seated hamstrings and lower-back stretches. Every little variation in a stretch makes it more interesting mentally and changes the way in which the exercise affects your muscles and joints.

STANDING HAMSTRINGS AND LOWER-BACK STRETCH

This exercise is equivalent to the seated variation, but it also allows me to illustrate how to "roll up" from a fully stretched position to maximally relax all of the spinal erector muscles and perfectly align the vertebrae. When I'm training hard for a bodybuilding competition, my back will sometimes feel tight after doing squats and heavy back movements. Whenever this happens, I'll take a brief time-out and do this standing stretch with roll-ups to alleviate the tight feeling and prevent any chance of injury.

I start my standing hamstrings and lower-back stretch on my exercise mat, although the mat is really optional since you don't have to sit or lie

Standing Hamstrings and Lower-Back Stretch—midpoint

on a cold, dirty gym floor to do this exercise. I place my feet together, which means they must assume a position parallel to each other, lock out my knees so my legs are held straight, and maintain this foot and leg posture throughout the movement.

Usually, I will extend my arms straight upward from my shoulders, although that part of the movement is not illustrated. Keeping my back flat, I slowly bend forward at the waist until my palms are flat on the floor directly in front of my feet (the heels of my hands actually touch my toes). At first you probably won't be able to touch much lower than the middle of your shins with any degree of comfort, but soon you will be able to place your palms flat on the mat or gym floor. Regardless of where you find your stretching zone, hold it for 30–60 seconds, back off, and perhaps repeat the stretch.

I've also illustrated a more difficult form of

this stretch (see the second photo) in which I've walked my hands to the rear to induce a forward bend of greater amplitude. If you want to push it even further, you can grasp the backs of your lower legs and pull your head closer and closer to your knees. I'm actually flexible enough at this point that I can press my nose to my knees quite comfortably without even having to pull myself into such an exaggerated position. It's just that I didn't want to show off and perhaps discourage a less flexible woman from using this stretching movement on a regular basis.

How you come out of this stretch is also important. The idea is to allow your spine to curve and then slowly roll up, releasing one vertebrae at a time, beginning with your lumbars and ending with the cervical vertebrae of your neck. Just be certain to make this roll-up movement slow and gradual, perhaps taking as much as a minute to accomplish it.

Standing Hamstrings and Lower-Back Stretch (variation with hands behind feet)—midpoint

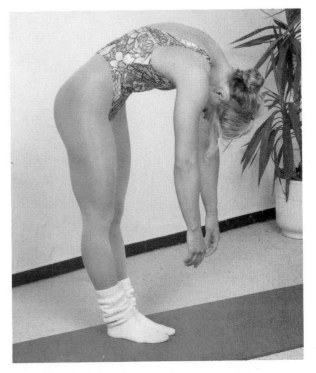

Standing Hamstrings and Lower-Back Stretch—rolling up

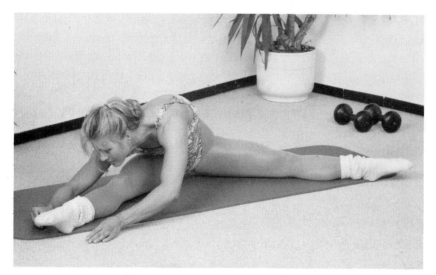

Seated Hamstrings
and Inner-Thigh Stretch—
midpoint (right)

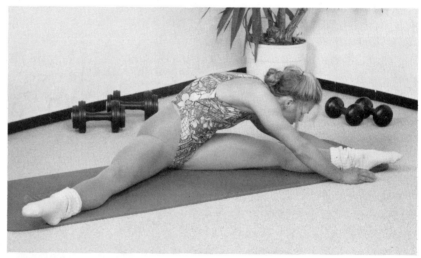

Seated Hamstrings and
Inner-Thigh Stretch—
midpoint (left)

Seated Hamstrings and
Inner-Thigh Stretch—
midpoint (center)

SEATED HAMSTRINGS AND INNER-THIGH STRETCH

This is a more advanced type of stretch than those I've given you so far. Primarily it stretches all of the muscles of the hamstrings, inner thighs, and lower back—and to a lesser extent, the upper-back musculature.

I begin this stretch sitting erect in the middle of my exercise mat with my legs spread as wide as possible. I can still do side splits even though I haven't had direct dance training since my late-teenage years, but for the sake of illustration I have assumed a leg position more in line with what most women will be able to comfortably achieve. Even if you can assume a leg position in which there is only a 90-degree angle between your legs, that is a good beginning. With time, patience, and work, you'll be able to appreciably increase this angle. Regardless of leg angle, keep your legs straight throughout the stretch.

There are three stretching positions. In the first, I twist my torso to the right so my shoulders directly face my right leg, place my hands on the floor on either side of my ankle, and then slowly lean forward at the hips as far as I can comfortably manage. For me, it's no problem to rest my chest right along my lower thigh, knee, and upper calf. Hold this stretched position for 30–60 seconds and then return to the starting point.

Part two of the stretch is exactly the same, except it's done facing toward the left leg. Again, hold the stretch for 30–60 seconds.

Finally, I face straight ahead and lean forward at the hips, walking my hands slowly away from my pelvis until I've reached a fully stretched position. I'm flexible enough to rest my upper torso directly on the mat in the fully stretched position. Hold this for another 30–60 seconds, return to the starting point, and repeat the series of three stretches as desired.

Obviously, you can make this stretch extremely long and intense as you gain greater flexibility in your hamstrings, lower back, inner thighs, buttocks, and the various other muscles attached to your pelvic structure. But be sure to do similar stretches for the same areas first as a warm-up before going into true attack mode. You'll prevent a lot of painful injuries that way. I'd have to say that this is my favorite overall stretching exercise most of the time.

SEATED TWISTING STRETCH

This is a good one for loosening up a tight lower back that doesn't untense itself when you do the lower-back stretch described earlier. That one tends to pull the vertebrae apart, while this torso-twisting stretch does the same thing in a lateral manner. It is reminiscent of the way a chiropractor cracks your lower back by twisting your torso in relation to your legs. The torso-twisting stretch has the added advantage of loosening up all of the muscles at the sides of your hips, waist, and upper back. If you've had a stressful day and your back feels tense from the stress, this stretch—which is based closely on a yoga asana—will very quickly relieve residual stress and muscle tension in your back.

Let's start out with your legs going to the right, your head and upper torso to the left. I sit crosswise on the exercise mat, slide my right leg across the midline of my body while keeping it flat against the mat, as illustrated, and pull my right foot up as close to my left gluteus maximus as possible, using one or both hands. My left leg is then bent at approximately a 90-degree angle and crossed over the right leg, so I can place my left foot flat on the mat with my left ankle snugly pulled up against my right knee.

Once my legs are correctly positioned, I place my left hand on the floor behind the plane of my hips, keep the arm straight, and use it to twist my torso as far to the left as possible. You can rest your left arm any place you like—it is inactive during this stretch. In order to achieve a more fully stretched position, rotate your head and

Seated Twisting Stretch—
midpoint (left)

Seated Twisting Stretch—
midpoint (right)

look in the direction you are stretching. Once you have reached the fully stretched position, hold it in a relaxed manner for 30–60 seconds before releasing and returning to a natural seated position on the mat.

Next perform the exact mirror image of the stretch just described, rotating your upper torso and head to the right rather than to the left. Hold the stretched position for 30–60 seconds, release, and repeat the left-facing and right-facing stretches a second time.

I know the body positions I've described for this stretch will seem quite complicated at first—particularly since you will have to do them in two directions—but after a few repetitions you'll be able to do them as automatically as you brush your teeth!

TORSO-TWISTING STRETCH

This is a good variation on the previous stretching exercise, but it has the added benefit of giving the quadriceps muscles at the fronts of your thighs a good degree of stretch as well. This torso-twisting stretch also loosens up all of the muscles at the sides of your hips, waist, and upper back.

I begin by lying lengthwise on my back on the exercise mat. Then, as illustrated, I look one way and rotate my bent legs in the opposite direction until I feel I have reached the stretching zone. You can do this movement with your legs pressed together at first; then try crossing your legs, one over the other, as you gain greater flexibility. In either case, hold the stretch for 30–60 seconds in each direction. Repeat as desired.

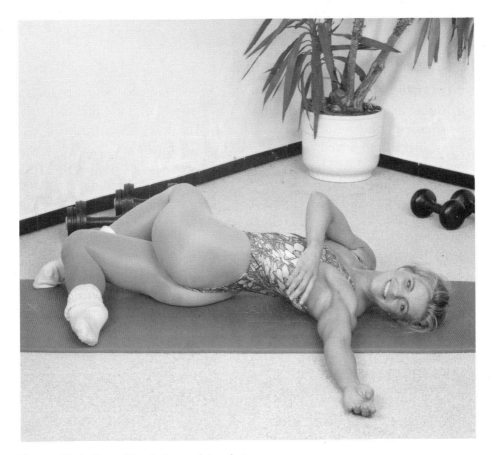

Torso-Twisting Stretch—midpoint

Standing Quadriceps
Stretch—midpoint

STANDING QUADRICEPS STRETCH

This is a simple, direct exercise for stretching out the quadriceps muscles on your upper legs. I personally picked it up from watching track sprinters warming up one day when I had opted to run around a 400-meter track near my home rather than run cross-country, which is my usual way of running when I'm not using my mountain bike. I always use this stretch in my warm-up prior to working my legs with heavy weights, as well as a between-sets stretch during hard leg workouts.

While I use my portable barre unit for balance during this stretch, you can just as easily balance yourself by grasping a kitchen table, countertop, or a doorknob. If you're in a gym, there are all sorts of exercise machines with vertical or horizontal bars or surfaces that you can grasp with your free hand to balance yourself.

Let's stretch the quads of the right leg first. I grasp the barre with my left hand for balance

and bend my right leg at the knee, curling my foot upward until it's high enough so I can grasp it by the toe by reaching back with my right hand, as illustrated. From this position, I pull upward and somewhat to the rear on my right foot until I feel the correct amount of stretch sensation in my right quadriceps muscles. When you've achieved a similar position, hold yourself in the stretch for 30–60 seconds before releasing.

It will quickly become obvious to you that the stretch becomes progressively more intense the higher up and farther to the rear you can pull your foot. Be careful about leaning too much forward with your torso as you pull on your foot. Forward torso lean negates the upward pull on your foot. The photo illustrates about the maximum degree of forward torso inclination permissible as you do a quad stretch.

Reverse legs to stretch the quadriceps of your left thigh for 30–60 seconds. Release and repeat stretches of both legs as desired.

Barre Quadriceps and Hip Flexors
Stretch—midpoint

BARRE QUADRICEPS AND HIP FLEXORS STRETCH

It takes a degree of suppleness and physical coordination to get into this stretch in the first place. But once you get it down pat, you'll find it to be quite rewarding. Properly performed, this stretching position will add flexibility to both the quadriceps muscles on the fronts of your upper legs and the hip flexors, which help to pull your knee upward as you bend your leg and try to touch your knee to your abdomen while in a standing position. You will also discover that you can stretch your lower abdominals and hamstrings with this exercise. (For the sake of reference, you'll stretch the quads and hip flexors of the upper leg and the hamstrings of the lower leg while performing this flexibility exercise.)

It will be most convenient if you have a portable barre for this stretch, because it allows you to assume positions in sequence with your rear foot set at a variety of heights from the floor. You can, however, improvise something similar with a chair, a few thick books, and/or a couple of seat cushions.

I start out facing away from my barre, which is placed on the solid floor at one end of the mat. Back up so you are 2–3 feet (60–90 centimeters) from the barre. Keeping both legs straight, bend forward at the waist and place your hands on the floor on either side of your feet to steady your body in position. Raise your right leg from the hip to the rear and upward in a semicircular arc and place the instep of your foot on the horizontal barre of your choice. It will be easiest to start out with your foot on one of the lower bars; incrementally raise your foot a bar at a time as you grow more supple.

Once in the correct starting position, you'll feel most of the stretch in the thigh biceps muscle of your plant leg (the foot of the plant leg is on the mat). To stretch your quadriceps and hip flexors of the rear leg, push upward with your arms to raise your head and shoulders. Once you've reached the stretching zone you're after, hold the position for 30–60 seconds before releasing.

Reverse legs in order to stretch the front of your right thigh. Hold the stretched position for 30–60 seconds, release, and repeat the stretch on both sides as desired. I'd suggest *always* preceding this stretch with the standing quadriceps stretch discussed a little earlier as a warm-up, because barre quad/hip flexor stretches are a highly advanced and intense exercise. Without a proper warm-up prior to executing this posture, you could run a greater risk of injury to the muscles and connective tissues. Why risk injury when it can be prevented with a simple warm-up stretch?

BARRE HAMSTRINGS AND INNER-THIGH STRETCHES

There are actually *three* stretches included in this category, but they are so similar that I'll group them together. The first variation stretches the hamstrings, inner-thighs, and the muscles at the sides of your torso. The second variation adds suppleness to the same areas, perhaps with a bit less emphasis on muscles at the sides of the upper torso. And the third variation stretches the hamstrings and to a lesser extent the gluteus maximus muscles and calves.

For all three stretches you'll need a portable barre unit set up near one end of your exercise mat. Or you can improvise with a footrest, a kitchen chair, thick books, and/or a seat cushion or two.

Variations 1 and 2 are performed with one side of your body turned toward the barre and 2-3 feet (60-90 centimeters) away from the unit. Keeping both legs straight, raise your left leg up

and rotate it in your hip socket so you can place your instep or heel over one of the horizontal bars. This rotation in your hip is called turnout by ballet instructors, and I can't think of a better term for it. You'll also need turnout on your plant leg during this stretching stance.

For variation 1, raise your right arm directly up from your shoulder, and round both arms as you did for the ballet side stretch discussed earlier in this chapter. Then simply execute the ballet side stretch in this position, with your left leg up on the barre, until you reach the stretching zone. Hold that position for 30-60 seconds, release, and repeat on the other side. Alternate sides a second time if desired.

For variation 2, assume the same leg starting position as described for variation 1. But this time, raise your left arm until it is parallel to the gym floor and stretch toward your raised foot, keeping your free arm down at your side. Hold the stretched position for 30-60 seconds, re-

Barre Hamstrings and
Inner-Thigh Stretches
(variation 1)—midpoint

Barre Hamstrings and
Inner-Thigh Stretches
(variation 2)—midpoint

Barre Hamstrings and
Inner-Thigh Stretches
(variation 3)—midpoint

lease, and repeat on the opposite side for the same length of time. Repeat the stretches as desired.

For variation 3, face the barre, your feet set 2–3 feet (60–90 centimeters) back from the unit. Turn out your right foot and leg and hold both legs straight throughout the movement. Raise your left leg up, moving your foot in a semicircular arc to a position high enough so you can hook either your instep or heel over one of the horizontal bars. Execute the stretch by leaning your torso forward until you can grasp the barre with both hands (which rung you grasp isn't important, but usually it'll be easiest to hang onto either the same one your foot is on, or the one above it). Pull with your arms until you have

your torso forward far enough to put the correct degree of stretch on your hamstrings. Hold this position for 30–60 seconds, release, and repeat on the opposite side for the same amount of time. Repeat as desired.

As a side note, my classical ballet training is so deeply ingrained that I automatically point my toes on all of my stretching exercises. This toe point, however, isn't necessary. You can flex your feet if you like, and you'll actually sense a somewhat different effect with alternate toe positions. You'll probably be better off if you alternate foot attitudes from time to time. But for photos, pointed toes look nicer, so you won't see flexed feet on any of the pictures used to illustrate this chapter.

Standing Hamstrings and Calf Stretch— midpoint (right)

Standing Hamstrings and Calf Stretch— midpoint (left)

STANDING HAMSTRINGS AND CALF STRETCH

This stance requires an advanced degree of suppleness and physical coordination. Once you master the stretch, however, you'll find that it rapidly increases the flexibility of your hamstrings, calf muscles, and buttocks.

Start by planting your left leg and keep both legs straight throughout the duration of the exercise. Bend forward at the waist and place your hands on the mat directly beneath your shoulders. Slowly raise your straight right leg with turnout until it makes one long straight line with your torso. When in the correct position, your raised leg will act as a counterbalance for your torso while you stretch.

To execute the stretch, continue bending forward at the waist until you sense the correct degree of stretch in the calf, hamstring, and buttock muscles of your plant leg. Hold yourself in the stretching zone for 30–60 seconds, release, and repeat on the opposite side for the same length of time. Alternate sides a second and third time as desired.

WIND-DOWN STRETCH

I like to use this wind-down stretch as the final exercise in my flexibility routine. It both contracts and stretches the beautifully sensuous muscles of your hamstrings, buttocks, and lower back. It's an easy, pleasant stretch to perform, making it a perfect way to end your routine.

I start out lying on my back on the exercise mat, my legs bent at approximately a 90-degree angle and my hands set on my hips so my arms are akimbo if viewed directly from above. (Although I'm looking at the camera—you know, eye contact makes you look so much more sincere—it's best to rest the back of your head on the mat and look directly up at the ceiling throughout the exercise.)

To execute the movement, contract your hamstrings, buttocks, and lower-back muscles to bridge your body off the mat, where you can support your hips in a comfortably stretched position with your hands for 30–60 seconds. Release and repeat as often as desired.

Be sure to fully relax your abdominal and lower-back muscles as you do this stretch. If you do, you'll feel tremendously relaxed when you've finished doing the movement.

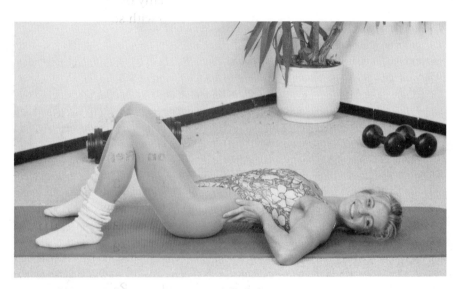

Wind-Down Stretch—start and finish

Wind-Down Stretch—midpoint

Suggested Stretching Routine

· ·

This flexibility program can be adapted for a woman at any flexibility level. Simply pick the two columns in Figure 9-1 that apply to your level of suppleness. Then execute the program with each repetition in the correct time-duration range and for the number of repetitions suggested. Perform exercises in the order in which they are listed in Figure 9-1.

If You Experience Pain

· ·

Pain is your body's signal that you are pushing something too far or that you have already either injured something or you soon will. The objective when stretching is to *avoid* pain. Stretch in that zone just short of the edge of pain, and you'll get a lot more out of each stretch without running the risk of actually overtraining. If you do overtrain and end up with sore muscles, take

Fig. 9-1. Suggested Stretching Program

Stretching Exercise	Beginning Level		Intermediate Level		Advanced Level	
	Reps	Duration	Reps	Duration	Reps	Duration
Circular Forward Stretch	1	30–60 secs.	2	60–90	3	90–120
Ballet Side Stretch	1	30–60	2	60–90	3	90–120
Lower-Back Stretch	1	30–60	2	60–90	3	90–120
Seated Hamstrings and Lower-Back Stretch	1	30–60	2	60–90	3	90–120
Standing Hamstrings and Lower-Back Stretch	—	—	1–2	60–90	2–3	90–120
Seated Hamstrings and Inner-Thigh Stretch	1	30–60	2	60–90	3	90–120
Seated Twisting Stretch	1	30–60	2	60–90	3	90–120
Torso-Twisting Stretch	—	—	1–2	60–90	2–3	90–120
Standing Quadriceps Stretch	1	30–60	2	60–90	3	90–120
Barre Quadriceps and Hip Flexors Stretch	—	—	—	—	1–2	60–90
Barre Hamstrings and Inner-Thigh Stretches—I	1	30–60	2	60–90	3	90–120
—II	—	—	—	—	1–2	90–120
—III	—	—	1–2	60–90	2–3	90–120
Standing Hamstrings and Calf Stretch	—	—	1–2	60–90	2–3	90–120
Wind-Down Stretch	1	30–60	2	60–90	3	90–120

this as a signal to back off the next time you stretch the same area. Otherwise, stretch and enjoy it!

Further Reading

. . . .

If you really get into stretching—and many bodybuilders do—you'll eventually run out of exercises to perform if this book is your main source. Since this is a resistance-training manual, I have included fewer than 20 stretching exercises. Through dance experience and other readings, I have mastered nearly 100 stretching postures, many of them admittedly quite esoteric. Where can you go from here if you desire to master many more stretches?

The best compendium of stretches in English that I have discovered is called *Stretching*, a book of drawings and detailed descriptions originally self-published by the author, Bob Anderson, and later published by Shelter Books in New York City. *Stretching* is available at larger book stores, and any book shop (regardless of size) can order and get a copy for you within a couple of weeks. It comes with my highest recommendation.

Anderson has also produced a series of plastic-coated wall charts of stretches for various physical and sports activities. These are intended as supplements to the book, but *Stretching* does stand quite solidly on its own. It's just that you will see these charts—as well as those of many imitators—posted on the walls of gyms, health spas, aerobics studios, and many other fitness-oriented institutions. But buy the book regardless of how many charts you see up on walls. There are hundreds of flexibility exercises illustrated in *Stretching*.

Your training program should always include a good stretching routine. Not only will it add to your flexibility, it will also make your body more resistant to injury.

10
Pregnancy and Bodybuilding

In January 1991 I delivered my baby boy. His name is Elija, and he's a real handful, bursting with energy most of the day. I'd like to share the questions I had and uncertainties I faced when I discovered my pregnancy in the midst of a highly intense preparation for a competition.

I was getting ready for the 1990 Ms. Olympia when I became pregnant. I was therefore in very good physical condition and had been following a well-balanced and healthful diet supplemented with extra vitamins and minerals. My main question I had is no doubt familiar to other bodybuilding mothers: what differences in my body and lifestyle would I experience in the near future? I didn't have the answers then, but I do now.

My first decision was to face all new situations in a relaxed and calm manner and with a consistently positive mental attitude. This made it possible to expand my mind and body awareness during my pregnancy rather than becoming depressed, as many women do.

It was necessary to shift my priorities in three main categories once I learned I was pregnant. I had to:

1. change my nutritional program, because my

Elija and I enjoy some time outdoors. By eating properly and exercising throughout my pregnancy, I was able to get quickly back into shape within a month after delivery.

previous diet was insufficient for both baby and myself—it was limited in calories in order to help me achieve a contest level of muscularity

2. alter my physical behavior, because certain muscles are strained unilaterally when one begins to move and eat for two rather than one

3. restructure my mental processes so I would begin to think for two—rather than just for myself, which is very common among competitive bodybuilders.

Nutrition

I had to understand that my body is a unique organism with individual needs, which would change with pregnancy. Eating for two meant altering my diet in several areas.

First of all, as a bodybuilder, I had been con-suming comparatively large amounts of protein in order to support (and hopefully increase) muscle mass. I gradually cut back on the amount of protein in my diet, which caused a moderate loss of muscle mass and made my pregnancy more comfortable.

I'm a big believer in making all nutritional and training changes gradually. Changing rapidly can be a harmful shock to the system.

Since I had been preparing for an Olympia, I was consuming a rather large quantity of vitally important vitamins and minerals. While many nonathletic pregnant women have to increase their intake of vitamins and minerals, I simply continued to take the special food supplements I was already consuming. To replace the protein calories I was no longer eating, I increased my consumption of complex carbohydrates. Many serious women bodybuilders will find them-

Eating fresh, healthful foods during pregnancy is good for both mother and baby.

selves in the same situation regarding nutrients when they decide to have babies.

Many women use pregnancy as an excuse to pig out and gain 30–40 pounds over their nine-month term. Much of this significant weight increase becomes stored body fat, which is very difficult to eliminate after giving birth. I kept my weight under control by sticking to healthful foods (no sweets or junk foods, no excessively fatty foods) and consuming about 10% more calories per day than my normal off-season maintenance level.

As you can see from the photos that accompany this chapter, I kept my body weight firmly under control. I gained only about 15 pounds while carrying my baby, very little of that in stored body fat. So I was back in good shape just one month after delivery. It took self-discipline and control, but every bodybuilder should pos-

sess these qualities anyway. If she doesn't, she has no hope of ever winning a high-level competition.

It almost goes without saying that all expectant mothers should avoid alcohol and tobacco, because the use of those substances can result in premature births, low birth weights, birth defects, and other negatives. As a bodybuilder, I consume very little alcohol—even though I'm European and was brought up drinking wine with dinner—and I am a nonsmoker, so I had few worries there. The main concern I had was avoiding passive smoke—I stayed clear of smokers.

Training

Bodybuilding training at a competition level is *not* an appropriate activity during pregnancy.

The series of photos on this and the following two pages shows four easy positions for stretching and relaxing your body that can be performed with or without leg weights.

Training twice per week with light weights is sufficient for maintaining muscle tone. Your strength and muscle tone will naturally decrease on such a light training regimen, so you should work more on flexibility than strength by practicing stretching and freehand exercises, which were covered in Chapter 9. The photos with this chapter will show you how the individual stretches—as well as freehand and weight movements—have been adapted for use during pregnancy.

Training seriously for a bodybuilding competition is by nature a very self-centered act, particularly if you are at the elite level of the sport. But when you are pregnant, never forget that you are carrying a human being inside you, one who needs constant attention, care, and love. This fact alone would be enough to deter you from hard, heavy workouts. Don't think for one; think for two.

I found getting back into shape after delivery easier to accomplish than some of my friends had suggested it would be. This is mainly because I was already in super shape before getting pregnant and was able to maintain my good condition with regularly scheduled training sessions during my pregnancy. Still, it's best to follow your doctor's directions as to when you can resume a certain training intensity level. Always be consistent in both training and diet when you are getting back into top shape after giving birth. Consistency is everything in this case, although it's something that is more difficult to achieve when you have a baby to care for.

Mental Approach

One of the most satisfying experiences of my life was relaxing and enjoying my pregnancy after 10 years of intense attention to my training and nutritional programs. I always intended to put aside my professional bodybuilding career to benefit my child in his first and most important years of development. My attitude toward pregnancy and childbirth enables me to look forward to reviving my former highly intense training periods with a positive and harmonious outlook.

Stretches

SEATED SIDE STRETCH

The seated side stretch emphasizes stretching those muscles at the sides of the hips, waist, and upper torso.

Begin by sitting erect in the middle of the exercise mat with your legs spread as wide as is comfortable. Keep your legs straight throughout the stretch.

Stretch the left side of your hips and torso first. Extend your left arm directly upward from your shoulder but round it by bending the arm slightly, as illustrated. Keep it rounded like this throughout the stretch. Your right arm should pass in front of your torso and also be held rounded throughout the stretch.

Keeping your legs locked throughout the stretch, slowly bend to the right, until you feel you have reached the stretching zone. You will find that both of your arms cross the midline of your body quite naturally as you assume the stretch, although how far you actually can bend in either direction will depend on relative body flexibility, not on arm movement. Once in the stretching zone, hold the stretched position for 30–60 seconds.

Reverse your arm positions and repeat the

Seated Side Stretch—midpoint

stretch to the left. Since this stretch is the mirror image of the first one that was described in detail, you should be able to handle it with no additional instruction. Hold the fully stretched position on this side for the same length of time as the other side. You may wish to alternate sides one or two times before you sense that you have completely stretched the sides of your hips and torso.

SEATED HAMSTRINGS AND INNER-THIGH STRETCH

This is a more advanced type of stretch. Primarily it stretches all of the muscles of the hamstrings, inner thighs, and lower back, and, to a lesser extent, the upper-back musculature.

I begin this stretch sitting erect in the middle of my exercise mat with my legs spread as wide as possible. Even if you can assume a leg position in which there is only a 90-degree angle between your legs, that is a good beginning.

With time, patience, and work, you'll be able to appreciably increase this angle. Regardless of leg angle, keep your legs straight throughout the stretch.

There are three stretching positions. In the first, I twist my torso to the right so my shoulders directly face my right leg, place my hands on either side of my ankle, and then slowly lean forward at the hips as far as I can comfortably manage. Hold this stretched position for 30–60 seconds and then return to the starting point.

Part two of the stretch is exactly the same, except it's done facing toward the left leg. Again, hold the stretch for 30–60 seconds.

Finally, I face straight ahead and lean forward at the hips, walking my hands slowly away from my pelvis until I've reached a fully stretched position. Hold this for another 30–60 seconds, return to the starting point, and repeat the series of three stretches as desired.

Obviously, you can make this stretch ex-

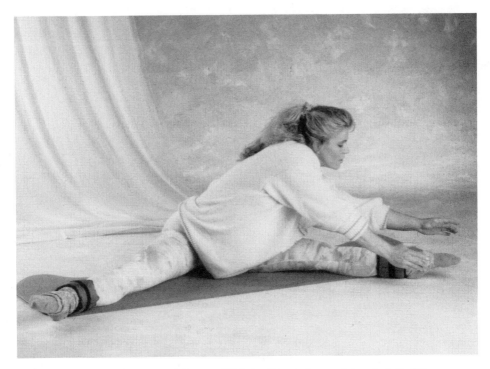

Seated Hamstrings and Inner-Thigh Stretch—midpoint (left)

tremely long and intense as you gain greater flexibility in your hamstrings, lower back, inner thighs, buttocks, and the various other muscles attached to your pelvic structure. But be sure to do similar stretches for the same areas first as a warm-up before going into true attack mode. You'll prevent a lot of painful injuries that way. I'd have to say that this is my favorite overall stretching exercise most of the time.

SEATED BACK AND INNER-THIGH STRETCH

This stretch works the inner-thigh, hip, and back muscles. Sit erect in the center of your exercise mat. Spread your legs as wide apart as is comfortable. Raise your hands up over your head. Your palms should be facing each other. Keep your legs and back straight throughout the movement.

Seated Back and Inner-Thigh Stretch— start and finish

Seated Back and Inner-Thigh Stretch— midpoint

Slowly lean forward with your hands and head along the same line as your back until you feel you have reached the stretching zone. Hold the stretch for 30–60 seconds and then slowly return to the starting position. You may want to repeat the movement in order to completely stretch your back and inner thighs.

Exercises

It is important to get your doctor's approval before beginning any exercise program, especially if you're pregnant. I recommend using light weights and doing 15–20 reps per set. Do only what you are comfortable with and avoid overexerting yourself.

LEG EXTENSIONS

Areas Emphasized—This is a strict isolation movement that places almost its entire stress quotient on the quadriceps muscles at the fronts of your thighs. Minimal stress is also shared by the forearm muscles (which help you grip the seat handles to brace yourself in the machine) and the trapezius muscles (which also help brace you in the machine).

Starting Position—Sit down in a leg-extension machine and hook your insteps beneath the roller pads attached to the end of the machine lever arm. Slide yourself backward until the backs of your knees rest firmly against the edge of the seat. Recline against the backrest. Reach down and grasp the seat handles, keeping your arms straight to help brace yourself in the machine.

Movement Performance—Using only quadriceps strength, slowly straighten your legs as fully as possible. Hold this top position for a slow count of two in order to intensify the peak-contraction effect of the movement, and then slowly return to the starting point. Repeat.

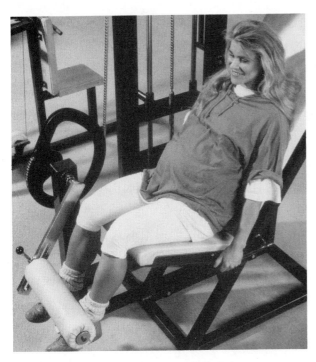

Leg Extensions—start and finish

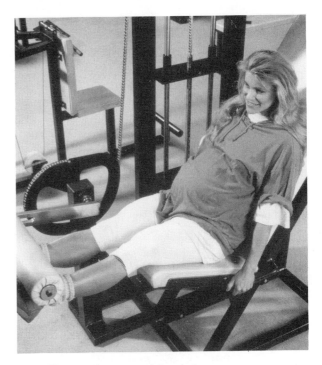

Leg Extensions—midpoint

Common Mistakes—The most common mistake made in leg extensions is performing the movement with too quick a cadence and no static hold at the top point of the exercise. Many bodybuilders also cut their leg extensions short, not performing the entire possible range of motion. Doing less than a full movement gives you less than full benefit from the exercise.

Training Tips—As with leg presses, you can emphasize different sections of your quadriceps by alternating toe angles. Normally leg extensions are done with the feet flexed and toes angled directly upward when in the top position of the movement. This type of exercise works the entire quadriceps muscle complex more or less equally. By angling your toes inward at about a 45-degree angle, you can stress the outer sweep of your quadriceps muscles more. By turning your toes outward at about a 45-degree angle, stress is switched more to the inner sections of your quadriceps, particularly to the teardrop shaped vastus medialis muscle just above your knees.

When you do machine movements for your legs, it is possible to perform the exercise with one leg at a time as well as with both legs simultaneously. Doing one-legged movements has the advantage of making each repetition more intense than if the legs were worked together. This intensity occurs because you don't have to split your mental focus between the two limbs but rather can concentrate all of it on the single working leg.

PULLEY PUSHDOWNS
Areas Emphasized—This movement isolates stress on the triceps muscles at the backs of your upper arms, particularly placing stress on the outer of the three triceps heads.

Starting Position—Attach a short rope with large knots at each end to the end of the cable running through an overhead pulley. Take

Pulley Pushdowns—start and finish

an overgrip on the rope with each hand placed just above the knots. Set your feet together, about 6 inches (20 centimeters) back from the pulley, and pull the weight down so it rests across your upper thighs while your arms are straight down at your sides. Press your upper arms against the sides of your torso and keep them motionless in this position throughout your set. Lean slightly forward at the waist and maintain that torso inclination until you have finished your set.

Movement Performance—Keeping your wrists straight throughout the exercise and mov-

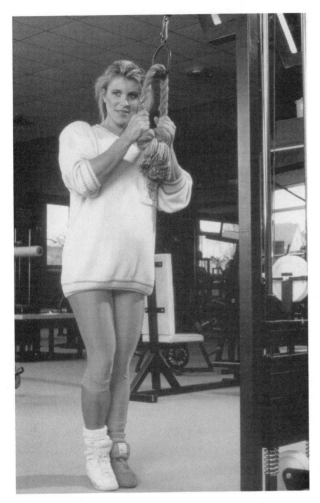

Pulley Pushdowns—midpoint

ing only your forearms, allow the weight to move your hands in a semicircular arc from the tops of your legs to a position against your upper chest in which your arms are completely bent. Reverse the movement and use only triceps strength to push the rope back along the same arc until it again touches your upper thighs. Repeat the movement for the desired number of repetitions.

Common Mistakes—The most common mistake is pushing the handle straight down rather than in a semicircular arc. You should also be sure to avoid letting your elbows move outward to your sides as you execute this move-

ment. If you make either of these mistakes, the weight you are using is probably too heavy and should be reduced.

Training Tips—Over the years I've gotten a lot out of doing this movement with a shoulder-width overgrip on a longer bar handle. It can also be performed with an undergrip, although you'll discover that you can't use as much weight with that grip. Both of these variations were explained and illustrated in detail in previous chapters.

SEATED PULLEY ROWS
Areas Emphasized—This movement not only stresses the lats for both width and thickness but also places a great deal of emphasis on the spinal erectors and trapezius muscles. Secondary stress is placed on the biceps, brachialis, and forearm flexor muscles.

Starting Position—Attach a handle that allows you to use a parallel-hands wide grip to the end of the cable running through a machine pulley. Sit down on the machine seat and place your feet against the restraint bar, with your legs almost completely bent. Incline your torso forward at the waist and straighten your arms. Then straighten your legs to assume the weight attached to the end of the cable. Be sure your legs are kept slightly bent, as illustrated, throughout the movement in order to protect your lower back from harmful stress.

Movement Performance—Starting from a position in which your lats are fully stretched, simultaneously sit erect and pull the handle slowly in to touch the middle of your abdomen. As you pull the handle toward your torso, be sure that you keep your elbows in tightly against your sides. Hold this peak-contracted position for a moment and then slowly return to the starting position. Repeat the movement for the required number of repetitions.

Seated Pulley Rows—start and finish

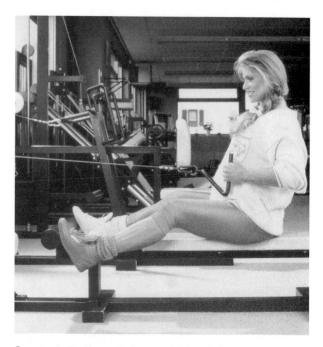

Seated Pulley Rows—midpoint

Common Mistakes—Leaning too far backward, past the point at which your torso is perpendicular to the gym floor, tends to transfer excessive stress to the trapezius muscles, which in turn robs the middle-back muscles of much of the benefit they should be receiving from the movement. Similarly, leaning too far forward at the start of the movement tends to place excessive stress on the erector spinae muscles of the lower back.

Training Tips—A variety of other handles can be used when you perform seated pulley rows. The narrow-grip parallel-hands handle has a somewhat different effect on the middle-back muscles. A straight bar handle is also occasionally used, with which you take a shoulder-width under- or overgrip on the bar. Some gyms have a type of handle that is actually split into two individual loop handles that are in turn attached to the main cable by two shorter cables. Each handle stresses the back differently.

DUMBBELL INCLINE PRESSES

Areas Emphasized—As with barbell incline presses, this dumbbell movement places intense stress on the upper pectorals, the pec-delt tie-ins, the anterior deltoids, and triceps. Significant secondary stress is on the rest of the pectoral muscle complex, the medial deltoids, and the lats and other upper-back muscles.

Starting Position—Grasp two dumbbells and sit down on the incline-bench seat. Sit back to rest your torso against the inclined pad, simultaneously pulling the weights up to your shoulders and pushing them to straight-arm's length directly above your shoulders. Rotate your upper-arm bones in your shoulder joints so your palms face each other at the starting point of the movement. Your feet can either rest on the gym floor, as I've illustrated, to balance your body in position on the bench, or on the bench seat.

Movement Performance—Being sure to keep your elbows back, bend your arms and

Dumbbell Incline Presses—start and finish

Dumbbell Incline Presses—midpoint

slowly lower the weights as far down as possible. As you lower the weights, rotate your wrists so your palms face forward in the bottom position. Without bouncing at the bottom, slowly reverse the movement and press the weights back up to straight-arm's length, rotating your hands again so your palms face inward in the finish position. Repeat the movement for the stated number of repetitions.

Common Mistakes—Be sure the weights don't travel too far out to the sides, or you'll lose one of them and possibly wrench a shoulder. If you rest your feet on the floor, don't use them to bridge your buns off the bench to improve pressing leverage. Never jerk or bounce the weights at any point along their range of motion.

Training Tips—You should experiment with different incline-bench angles. A bench at a 45-degree angle tends to place greater stress on the deltoids at the expense of the upper chest. A bench at 30 degrees is almost ideal. A bench

with a low angle, achieved by merely slipping a block of wood under the head end of a flat exercise bench, tends to shift stress more onto the pectoral muscles themselves.

CABLE CROSSOVERS

Areas Emphasized—Depending on how you move your hands during this exercise, you can affect the entire pectoral muscle complex. Done in the standard manner, which I will describe here, the lower, outer, and inner sections of the pectorals get most of the emphasis, with secondary stress on the balance of the pectoral muscle complex and the anterior deltoids.

Starting Position—Attach loop handles to the ends of cables running through overhead crossover pulleys. Grasp the handle on one side and then grasp the other handle. Position yourself midway between the pulleys and slightly forward of an imaginary line drawn through each pulley. Set your feet a comfortable distance apart, either parallel to each other or with one a bit forward of the other. Bend your arms slightly and keep them rounded like this throughout the movement. Allow the weights attached to the cables to pull your arms up directly toward the pulleys, your palms facing the floor throughout the movement.

Movement Performance—Use pectoral strength to move your hands downward and slightly forward in semicircular arcs from the described starting point to a position at which they meet each other directly in front of your chest. Press your hands together in this position for a moment as you intensely contract your pectorals. Slowly return the pulley handles back along the same arcs to the starting point. Repeat for the suggested number of repetitions.

Common Mistakes—Standing too far forward places excessive stress on your shoulder joints. Doing the movement too rapidly or allowing your hands to gravitate out of their intended arcs of movement takes too much stress off your working chest muscles.

Training Tips—This movement is often performed in a kneeling position directly between the pulleys, something that tends to make the exercise somewhat more strict. You can do it with one arm at a time, holding onto something sturdy with your free hand to brace your body.

SEATED ALTERNATE DUMBBELL CURLS

Areas Emphasized—Since the hands are strongly supinated in dumbbell curls, it should be clear that this is a direct biceps exercise. Minimum secondary emphasis is on the forearm flexor muscles.

Starting Position—Grasp two dumbbells

Cable Crossovers—start and finish

Cable Crossovers—midpoint

and sit down at the end of a flat exercise bench. Place your feet flat on the floor so that your upper body won't rock back and forth as you perform the exercise. Allow your arms to hang straight down at your sides, palms facing inward at the start of each repetition, and be sure to keep your upper arms in tightly against your sides as you do the curls. Slowly curl the weight in your right hand up to your shoulder, supinating your hand as your raise the dumbbell.

Movement Performance—Continue the movement in seesaw fashion, one dumbbell going up as the other descends. As each dumbbell comes down, be sure to pronate your hand so that your palm again faces inward when your arm is down at your side. Be sure to do an equal number of repetitions with each arm.

Common Mistakes—Rushing the exercise so that you begin swinging the weights and letting your upper arms travel outward robs your working biceps of much of the beneficial stress they should be receiving. Don't allow your torso to rock from side to side or forward and backward. Never fail to supinate your hand as completely as possible on each curling repetition, or you will be losing a lot of the effect you should be feeling in your biceps muscles.

Training Tips—I've seen some champion bodybuilders do this exercise a bit differently. They perform all of the reps on a set with one arm continuously, the other arm hanging down at their sides for balance. Then they repeat with the opposite arm. I personally don't have anything against this practice, but doing the exercise in seesaw fashion, as described, makes it significantly stricter. Obviously, you can also do this exercise with both arms simultaneously if you care to, but again a seesaw movement is stricter than curling both weights at the same time.

Seated Alternate Dumbbell Curls—midpoint (right)

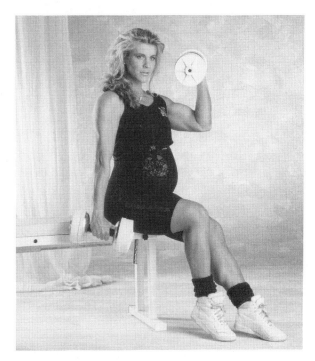

Seated Alternate Dumbbell Curls—midpoint (left)

LUNGES

Areas Emphasized—Lunges can be done in various ways to place intense stress on the quadriceps, buttocks, and hip flexor muscles. In general, you'll be putting the most stress on your glutes on the leg that is in the front and the most stress on your quads and hip flexors on the leg that is in the rear. But this can vary as you try different styles of lunges, since each one feels a bit different from the other in your lower-body musculature.

Starting Position—Essentially, you assume the same starting position as for squats, although there is an alternative arm position. Rather than grasping the bar out near the collars, as I do in performing squats, I wrap my arms around the bar and grasp the edges of the plates to help steady the bar across my shoulders behind my neck. You can either take the weight off a squat rack or merely clean it up to your chest, then push it overhead to rest across your trapezius muscles. Since the weight you will use in lunges is relatively light, you won't have much trouble dispensing with the squat rack. Stand erect, your feet set at about shoulder width and toes angled so your feet are parallel to each other. Look straight ahead during the entire movement and attempt to keep your head up.

Lunges—beginning of movement

Movement Performance—Step forward with your right foot and set it about 3 feet (1 meter) in front of the left one and a bit to the right of center. Bend both legs and lunge forward, as illustrated. Push hard with your right leg and return to the erect position, repeating the movement with your left foot forward. Continue the exercise by alternating legs until you have performed the required number of repetitions with each leg.

Common Mistakes—Not stepping forward enough or merely dipping into a squat between narrowly spread feet places excessive strain on your knees. Keep the movement smooth and steady, even when pushing off with your forward leg to return to the erect position. There is no reason to jerk at any point during the exercise.

Training Tips—Some trainees like to keep their back leg a bit straighter than I do, which transfers a bit more stress to the hip flexors of the rear leg. You can increase the stress on your glutes by lunging up onto a thick block of wood that has been wedged securely against something so it doesn't slide forward as you perform the movement. All variations of lunges can be performed while you are holding a pair of dumbbells in your hands rather than balancing a bar behind your neck.

Lunges—midpoint

ONE-ARM CABLE SIDE LATERALS

Areas Emphasized—This is a truly intense isolation exercise for the medial head of the deltoid. Minimal stress is concurrently placed on the medial head of the working deltoid muscle.

Starting Position—Attach a loop handle to the end of the cable running through a floor pulley. With your left side toward the pulley, grasp the handle with your right hand in such a way that the cable runs diagonally across the front of your body as you do the exercise. Set your feet close together, as illustrated, and brace your body with your free hand so your torso doesn't move during each repetition. Bend your right arm slightly and keep it rounded like this throughout the movement. Start the exercise with your right hand about 6 inches (18 centimeters) directly in front of the middle of your pelvic structure.

Movement Performance—Move the handle in a semicircular arc slightly forward and out to the side and then upward until your hand reaches approximately eye level. Throughout the movement, the palm of your right hand should face toward the floor. Hold this peak-contracted position for a moment to more intensely stress the medial delt and then move the handle along the same arc to the starting point. Repeat the movement for the desired number of repetitions. Repeat the exercise with your left arm. Be sure to complete the same number of sets and reps with each arm.

Common Mistakes—Don't allow your hand to come forward more than about 4 inches (12 centimeters), since going beyond this distance with your hand removes concentrated stress on the medial deltoid and transfers it to the anterior section of the muscle complex. Never jerk or cut a movement short.

One-Arm Cable Side Laterals—start and finish

One-Arm Cable Side Laterals—midpoint

Training Tips—Two distinct variations of this exercise exist, and each stresses the medial head of your working deltoid completely differently from the others. In the first variation, run the cable behind your back rather than diagonally across the front of your body. In the second variation, stand with your working arm toward the pulley, so you pull more directly upward against the weight as you complete the movement.

DUMBBELL KICKBACKS

Areas Emphasized—This is a direct triceps movement that hits the entire muscle complex. It is especially good for using peak contraction, since all of the weight is still on your muscles when the movement has been completed.

Starting Position—Grasp a light dumbbell in your right hand. Place your left knee and left hand on a flat exercise bench, as illustrated, with your right foot on the floor to brace your torso in a position slightly above an imaginary line drawn parallel to the gym floor. Press your right upper arm against the side of your torso and keep it there throughout the entire movement.

Dumbbell Kickbacks—start and finish

Dumbbell Kickbacks—midpoint

Bend your left arm to a bit more than a 90-degree angle, making sure that your hand is oriented so your palm is facing inward toward your body throughout each set.

Movement Performance—Use triceps strength to slowly straighten your arm, moving the dumbbell in a semicircular arc from the aforementioned starting point to a position level with your shoulder joint. Hold this peak-contracted position for a moment before moving the weight along the same arc back to the starting point. Repeat the movement for the correct number of repetitions.

Training Tips—You can also do kickbacks with both arms simultaneously by holding a dumbbell in each hand and standing with your feet close together and your torso held parallel to the gym floor.

A well-balanced diet and a light training routine will keep you and your baby healthy during pregnancy and make getting into shape after delivery a breeze.

11
Nutrition and Diet

Following a diet is a necessity for any body-builder. That means that you have to follow a conscious, specific diet in order to build the foundation needed to realize your full physical potential. Weight or fat reduction is only a small part of "dieting." Not every diet is suitable for every person. There are specific diets for specific purposes, such as gaining weight, fighting skin irritations, and preventing diseases of the organs. You need to find the diet that's right for you.

You should consult your family doctor before starting any diet. Evaluate your physical, psychological, and mental condition before embarking on a new regimen. If you are experiencing a great deal of stress in your life, it is probably not a good time to start a diet. However, I found that my new eating habits, and the discipline they required, strengthened my self-confidence. A healthier diet not only has an external effect but can also give you a feeling of security over and above the physical results.

I cannot imagine dieting without a calorie counter, a notebook, and a scale. I suggest that you buy a calorie counter and a notebook for recording your daily intake. This record will help

A healthy diet has a positive effect on both the body and the mind.

you monitor the relationships between calories, proteins, carbohydrates, and fat so that you are in a position to control them. A kitchen scale makes it easy to determine the nutritional values of foods.

Later in this chapter I explain some of my notes and suggestions for menus, but first I will discuss the basics of nutritional values.

The Most Important Nutrients

Your body needs the following nutrients to secure growth and produce energy:

- Proteins
- Carbohydrates
- Fats
- Vitamins
- Minerals
- Water

PROTEIN

Protein serves to build up, re-create, or preserve the muscle fibers. It contains various amino acids. Without all the necessary amino acids, your body is unable to use the protein that you consume. The body itself can synthesize only some of those amino acids. The others, called *essential amino acids*, have to be taken in with the foods you eat.

Some foods contain "full proteins," which provide all the amino acids necessary for the construction of usable protein. Full proteins can be found in milk, eggs, meat, fish, and some vegetables, such as soybeans. Each of these foods contains a different amount of usable protein. For example, one egg contains only 12% protein by weight; however, your body can use 94% of that protein because of the special amino acids in the egg. Soy flour is 42% protein, but the composition of the protein is such that the body can use only 61% of it. As you can see in the table below there is a great difference between the protein content of food and the proportion of protein that can be used to build up muscles:

Eggs are such a good source of high-quality protein that they are used as a comparative base to judge the protein quality of other foods. In the following table, an arbitrary value of 100 was set for eggs.

Food	Protein Quality (Compared to Eggs)
Eggs	100
Fish	70
Low-fat beef	69
Cow's milk	60
White rice	56
Soy beans	47
Wheat grains	44
Peanuts	43
Potatoes	34
Dried beans	34

As you can see, such foods as rice, potatoes, and beans provide the body with considerably

Food	Protein Content in Weight %	Usability
Soy flour	42	61
Cheese	22–36	70
Meat and poultry	19–31	68
Fish	18–25	80
Eggs	12	94
Brown rice	8	70
Milk	4	82

less usable protein than eggs and fish do. You can, however, combine one or two sources of these lower-quality proteins to create "high-quality" proteins. In bodybuilding, these combinations of proteins are useful because lower-quality proteins usually have a lower fat content and therefore provide a high-quality protein that is relatively low in calories. This can be a great advantage if your goal is maximum muscle growth and low body fat.

Since any source of low-quality protein lacks some essential amino acids, you have to combine nutritional elements sensibly in order to receive a high-quality protein. I suggest using the following combinations:

Cereal Plus Seeds:
Bread made with coarsely ground grain
Bread made with sesame seeds or sunflower seeds

Grain Plus Milk Products:
Wheat flakes with milk
Pasta with milk or cheese
Bread with milk or cheese

Combine bread with coarsely ground grains to create a complete protein.

Grain Plus Peas or Beans:
Rice and beans
White bread and baked beans
Corn-soy bread or wheat-soy bread
Pea or bean soup with bread

While you can refer to a nutritional guide to determine which of the eight essential amino acids are missing in particular foods, it is not really necessary. If you keep in mind the food combinations described above, you can consume plenty of usable protein.

CARBOHYDRATES
Carbohydrates consist of carbon, hydrogen, and oxygen atoms that are created by plants during the process of photosynthesis. The most important carbohydrates include the following:

Monosaccharides:
Glucose (blood sugar)
Fructose (fruit sugar)
Galactose (part of milk sugar)

Oligosaccharides:
Saccharose (cane sugar)
Lactose (milk sugar)
Maltose (malt sugar)

Polysaccharides:
Vegetable polysaccharides (starch and cellulose)
Animal polysaccharides (glycogen)

Simple carbohydrates, found in fruit or refined sugar, are quickly metabolized by the body. Complex carbohydrates, especially starch and cellulose, can be found in foods such as potatoes and rice as well as many vegetables. Complex carbohydrates are closer to the metabolism and therefore have a "deposit effect" on the body's energy supply.

Your body converts carbohydrates into energy more easily than it converts any other nutritional elements. The body converts carbohydrates into glucose. The glucose circulates in the bloodstream and provides the body with the energy needed for muscle contractions. Excess glucose is stored for later use in the muscles and liver as glycogen. A sufficient carbohydrate supply is very important for the serious bodybuilder, or athlete of any kind, for several reasons, including the following:

1. Carbohydrates are important suppliers of energy. The carbohydrates stored in the muscles in the form of glycogen allow you to work out intensely and with stamina.
2. The storage of glycogen and water in individual muscle cells enlarge the muscles.
3. If your carbohydrate intake is sufficient, you "save protein," which means that your body will not use excessive amounts of protein to gain energy. (More on that later.)
4. Carbohydrates are the main source of energy for the brain. A carbohydrate deficiency can have serious consequences for your mood, personality, and mental abilities.

FATS
Fats, found in both plants and animals, consist of the same elements as carbohydrates—carbon, hydrogen, and oxygen—but the atoms are bound in a different way. Fat has 3 main functions in our body:

1. It is the main source of stored energy.
2. It upholsters and protects the bigger organs.
3. It serves as insulation, which protects the body from the cold.

Fat contains more calories than any other nutritional element. One gram of fat has 9 calories, while one gram of protein or carbohydrates has only 4 calories. If you exercise and stay within your aerobic capacity (when you are not breathing too hard), your body gets half the energy it needs from fat and half from carbohydrates. The longer you work out, the more your body de-

pends on fat for energy. After approximately three hours of exercising, your body is getting about 80% of its energy from fat.

Fat molecules differ biochemically in their consistency and are either *saturated, unsaturated,* or *polyunsaturated.* (These terms refer to the number of double bonds that are in the molecule.) Health professionals recommend that unsaturated fats should make up approximately two-thirds of your whole fat supply.

The following foods contain saturated fats, which are solid at room temperature.

Beef
Lamb
Pork
Chicken
Crab
Lobster
Egg yolks
Cream
Milk
Cheese
Butter
Chocolate
Pork fat
Vegetable fat

The following foods contain unsaturated fats, which are liquid at room temperature.

Avocados
Cashew nuts
Olives, olive oil
Peanuts, peanut oil, peanut butter

Polyunsaturated fats are found in the following foods:

Almonds
Cottonseed oil
Clarified butter, Margarine
Pecans
Sunflower oil
Corn oil

Fish
Mayonnaise
Thistle oil
Soy oil
Walnuts

VITAMINS

The body needs vitamins, organic substances found in the foods we eat, in very small quantities. Vitamins supply energy without adding to our girth and have a catalytic effect that helps to set off other reactions in the body.

There is a difference between water-soluble and fat-soluble vitamins. Water-soluble vitamins cannot be stored in the body. Surplus supplies are removed in the urine. Fat-soluble vitamins are stored in the fat fibers of the body. Water-soluble vitamins have to be taken daily; fat-soluble vitamins need to be taken less frequently.

Water-Soluble Vitamins

Vitamin B_1 (thiamine)
Vitamin B_2 (riboflavin)
Vitamin B_3 (niacin)
Vitamin B_6 (pyridoxin)
Vitamin B_{12} (cobalamin)
Vitamin C (ascorbic acid)
Pantothenic acid
Biotin
Folic acid

Fat-Soluble Vitamins

Vitamin A
Vitamin D
Vitamin E
Vitamin K

MINERALS

Minerals are inorganic substances that the body needs in small quantities. In your body there are 22 metal elements that make up about 4% of your body weight. Minerals are found in the ground and in water. Plants absorb minerals from the ground and water through their roots. Human beings receive minerals by eating plants or plant-eating animals.

If your diet consists of a variety of meats and vegetables, you should get all the minerals your body needs. Minerals participate in different parts of the metabolic system and support the synthesis of glycogen, protein, and fat.

WATER

Water is an overlooked essential nutritional element. It is, however, one of the main components of the body. Water transports several chemical substances through the body and is the medium through which biochemical reactions between elements take place.

The human body is 40–60% water. While muscle tissue is 72% water, fat cells are only 20–25% water. Thus an excessive loss of liquids due to poor nutrition or physical activity can have a great influence on the size of your muscles.

Calories and Energy

A calorie is a unit used to measure the energy content of food. Different nutrients have different numbers of calories. Proteins and carbohydrates each contain about 4 calories per gram; fats contain about 9 calories per gram. Of all the energy suppliers, fats contain the most calories and are therefore an unwelcome component in food if you are trying to lose weight or to maintain a specific weight.

Your body stores a surplus of calories in the form of fat (fat cells) in the body. Whether the surplus is from protein, carbohydrates, or fat, the excess ends up in the body's fat cells to be stored as reserves in case your body needs more energy than is taken in by food.

If the body receives all the nutrition it requires to function normally and if you supply your body with the minimum amount of several nutritional elements required at a certain time for your digestive system and to win body-owned energy, it is simple to calculate how much energy you need to expend in order to either lose or gain fat: One pound of body fat contains approximately 3,500 calories. Thus, taking in 3,500 calories more than required causes a one-pound gain, and taking in 3,500 calories less causes a one-pound loss.

There are other factors in the picture, however, that this formula does not take into account and can throw off your calculations:

1. Reduction in muscle tissue
2. Problems metabolizing fat
3. Vitamin or mineral deficiencies
4. Restriction of energy production
5. Physical or psychological symptoms

In order to avoid such problems, each diet plan, whether it's to gain or to lose weight, must be well balanced—that is, include a minimum amount of essential nutrients and a variety of foods.

MINIMUM REQUIREMENTS OF NUTRIENTS

To withhold calories from your body is one thing (the body has fat deposits at its disposal that it can use for energy), but to withhold indispensable nutrients from your body is another thing. A nutritional deficiency can have greater consequences for serious bodybuilders—who need to really exert their bodies to achieve the best possible results from training—than for people who do not overexert themselves physically. There are many different points of view regarding the minimum quantities of nutrients for serious athletes and nonathletes, but the following guidelines can be used as a sensible reference.

Protein—One gram of protein per kilogram of body weight (approximately .5 gram per pound)

is generally recommended. Some experts think this amount is too high, even for nonbodybuilders, but most bodybuilders prefer to take in more protein and recommend 2 grams per kilogram of body weight (approximately 1 gram per pound).

If a bodybuilder wants to get into competition shape, he or she has to strive for maximum muscle quantity and the lowest possible amount of body fat. A trainee must consume a sufficient quantity of protein to build up and maintain fat-free body tissue. He or she must not consume any more protein than is necessary, as any surplus will only be converted into fat. So, for the majority of bodybuilders, more than 1 gram of protein per pound is not recommended.

Carbohydrates—As a rule of thumb, I recommend that you take sufficient carbohydrates to get you through training. If you work on refining muscle definition for a championship, the type of carbohydrates you consume is certainly of great importance. Complex carbohydrates supply energy and nutritional elements with a minimum of calories. Fruit, which contains simple carbohydrates, is a good source of quick energy. The items that usually contain sugar, however—cake, confections, lemonade, and processed foods—contain "empty calories" that increase the calorie supply enormously but have little nutritional value.

Fats—It is very difficult to have a fat-deficient diet. Eggs, raw meat, milk products, and oils all have a high fat content. It is not unusual for a food to contain up to 50% fat. For health reasons, it is usually recommended that you limit your fat intake to less than 30% of your diet. Bodybuilders have an easier time bringing up their definition if they cut their fat supply even more, perhaps to 20%.

Vitamins and Minerals—The discussion

over actual vitamin and mineral requirements never ends. Many nutrition scientists believe that correctly prepared food made up of natural nutritional elements contains a sufficient amount of vitamins and minerals, even for competitive athletes.

Nevertheless, most bodybuilders prefer to take additional vitamin and mineral preparations to make sure they get these nutritional elements in sufficient quantities. While there is no clear evidence that such supplements are required, bodybuilders *are* a special case, for they are the only group of athletes that work for maximum muscle capacity combined with an extremely low body-fat rate at the same time.

It is very likely that the combination of intensive workouts and an inadequate diet can result in certain nutritional deficiencies in a lot of bodybuilders. Therefore, it is only reasonable for bodybuilders to consume vitamin and mineral preparations to optimize their training and body development. However, taking "megadoses" of such preparations—100 to 1,000 times the recommended daily supply—is simply a waste of money for water-soluble vitamins, surplus quantities of which are simply removed in the urine. And megadoses of fat-soluble vitamins and certain minerals can put your health at risk.

Some health experts swear on vitamins of "natural origin," but both natural vitamins and synthesized vitamins seem to have identical effects on the body. Most nutrition scientists agree that the body cannot tell the difference between a natural vitamin and its synthetic counterpart. (An exception is vitamin E, which is available in nature in a different and more effective form than the synthetic vitamin E.)

Electrolytes, loose electric-loaded particles, help to regulate the liquid exchange among several distribution zones in the body and thereby maintain a constant and sufficient nutrition supply and eliminate decomposition products.

When bodybuilders work out very hard, huge quantities of electrolyte minerals (calcium, magnesium, potassium, and sodium) are removed with their sweat. A deficiency of these minerals—particularly calcium and potassium—can result in painful muscle cramps. The loss of excessive liquid through perspiration can lead to convulsions or, in serious cases, to heat exhaustion or heat stroke. As a rule, the loss can be replaced by drinking water and taking small amounts of salt. Many bodybuilders preparing for competitions take diuretics (which I do not recommend), which also lead to an increased excretion of minerals. Some users of diuretics are able to prevent convulsions by taking calcium preparations. Too much calcium, however, can cause nausea, which could prevent or impair participation in a competition. For that reason, please think about the fact that too much can be as harmful as not enough.

Vegetables supply your body with energy and nutritional elements with a minimum of calories—a great way to keep your body healthy while you try to lose excess fat.

A BALANCED DIET

Your body works best if you take in nutrition in certain combinations. The necessary "nutrition balance" is approximately the same for a bodybuilder as it is for everyone else. The McGovern Select Committee on Nutrition and Human Needs recommends that you break down your daily intake into the following proportions:

- 12% protein
- 58% carbohydrates
- 30% fat

During my career, I have used a different nutritional breakdown:

- 40% protein
- 50% carbohydrates
- 10% fat

Because my 50% carbohydrates are composed of more nutritious elements than the 58% of the average person, I surely get all the nutrients my body needs. There are bodybuilders who go on the hunt for protein a great deal too often and follow a diet that contains up to 70% protein. Others think that protein is not so important and limit themselves to 10 or 12%. In my opinion, however, neither of these nutrition plans will produce the desired effects. There are also bodybuilders who eat the same foods—for example, tuna fish, chicken, fruit, or salad—for months. This plan may help them lose body fat, but it also prevents them from getting all the nutrients that they need for maximum energy and muscle growth.

If you reduce the intake of one nutritional group too much, there is a danger of a vitamin or mineral deficiency. If you eat predominately fruit (as recommended in the Beverly Hills diet, for example), it would be difficult to get enough protein and the whole range of vitamins and minerals. A vegetarian diet or a special diet that is rich only in carbohydrates cannot supply a

Homemade, whole-grain bread is hearty, full of nutrients, low in fat, and fun to bake!

sufficient amount of protein for the bodybuilder who strives for maximum muscle growth. A diet that contains too much protein, however, can put unhealthy pressure on the kidneys and liver, lead to a loss of calcium, and cause weight gain.

The most common nutritional extreme in bodybuilding is too much protein. Some bodybuilders think that a protein-rich diet will give them maximum muscle growth with a minimum of body fat. But, as I mentioned earlier, a diet that is too rich in protein with too few carbohydrates can lead to a *loss* of muscle quantity instead of growth.

The reason this is true is that carbohydrates supply your body with energy and "take care" of

your protein deposits. As long as your body can get its energy from carbohydrates, the protein is free to build up and maintain muscles. In the absence of carbohydrates, for energy the body relies on the available protein. Thus the protein deposits that you worked so hard to build up are then metabolized into energy. Your appearance is also affected by too few carbohydrates in your system: the muscles shrink when they lose glycogen and the body looks exhausted rather than strong and healthy.

SUGGESTIONS FOR MEALTIMES

Mealtimes should follow a rhythm. I eat four times a day and take care to have a carbohydrate-rich breakfast consisting of whole-grain bread, rolled oats, muesli, and fruit. Most of the time, carbohydrate deposits are used up during the

night and should be replenished to give you energy for the morning workout. Breakfast should be followed by lunch, a snack, and dinner. If you have to get up early in the morning, six o'clock or so, I recommend a midmorning snack as well. Six to seven hours is too long to wait between meals; you should eat something every three to four hours.

Snacks should contain simple carbohydrates—fruit, juice, or yogurt with honey—that quickly supply you with energy. You should take care not to eat food with a high fat or protein content right before training.

Depending on the contents of a meal, it takes three to four hours to complete the first stage of digestion, in which the food has passed through the stomach and has reached the intestines. Therefore you should not constantly interrupt the digestive process by nibbling, as the process

Fruits contain simple carbohydrates and are a quick source of energy—perfect for a snack to get you through the morning or to provide an energy boost for your workout.

has to start again from the beginning. The food is then much more difficult to digest and could cause nausea or vomiting if you exert yourself physically.

Many people don't believe that four meals a day can sustain them and still provide enough energy for training sessions, but I know my staying power and ambition increase when I'm dieting. The reason probably lies in the specific nutrients that immediately transform food into energy and do not put pressure on the system. While dieting, you should definitely feel lighter.

My Year-Long Nutritional Plan

My experiences during my 8 to 10 weeks of dieting before a contest helped me to be conscious of my diet throughout the year. I cannot always resist goodies—chocolate, ice cream, cake, and candy—so I try to satisfy my desire for sweets. If you're always telling yourself, "I may not eat this or that," before long you will have a day when you eat *only* sweets. So, to satisfy this craving, I eat selected sweet goodies such as fruit slices, whole-grain biscuits, homemade fruit salad, and raisin muffins with honey. I use NutraSweet only during my diet, as this sugar substitute is artificial and cannot be healthy in the long run. While baking or cooking, I do not use white sugar. I try to get along with dark cane sugar, honey, treacle, or thickened pear syrup.

A balanced diet means not only a diet low in fats while avoiding sugar and salt but a diet that takes into account the quality of fats (sunflower oil, thistle oil, high-quality butter) and sweeteners. Salt is an important component in our daily nutrition (compared with minerals) and should always be present in small amounts. Even during a diet I add salt to my food as usual so that my system is not forced to adapt to different conditions. By not cutting out salt completely, I can prevent storing water immediately after I stop dieting. For a lot of athletes, the end of a diet means "now I can eat again," which can have disastrous consequences because of the inevitable salt push.

For those who take part in bodybuilding competitions, it is important to get the excess water out of your body—at least from the peel surface—as much as possible in order to achieve the best possible definition. You can also achieve this with strong medication; however, some athletes suffer from heavy convulsions or circulatory collapses that can interrupt the competition. I do recommend to everyone who aspires to competition-level bodybuilding to try natural methods, such as taking in a great quantity of salt four days before the championship.

If your competition is on a Sunday, on Thursday take four times the amount of salt you usually consume and half of that on Friday. During the second part of the day on Friday, immediately stop taking in any salt. Do not eat any foods that contain salt. The shock to your body causes an immediate natural drainage. You can help this reaction by drinking only distilled water, but be careful. Distilled water supports the drainage of your body's own water, which can lead to a loss of important minerals.

During the competition, you can eat some food that contains salt to make your appearance more plastic and to prevent convulsions. It is important to know that your body will experience a counterreaction 36 to 48 hours after totally eliminating salt that results in the body's storing water. Everybody should test this method before a competition to see what kind of reactions are caused.

Figure 11-1, which lists meals and snacks that are part of my diet, should give you some ideas for planning and preparing your daily food intake.

Figure 11-1. Anja's Diet for One Day (Two Suggestions)

SUGGESTION 1
Breakfast
1 slice whole-grain bread
1 slice crispbread
1 egg (with a little salt)
1 teaspoon butter
2 tablespoons low-fat yogurt
1 teaspoon honey
coffee, tea, or mineral water

Lunch
7 oz. (200 g) fish (plaice, cod, or pike)
lettuce salad (as much as you want) with a vinegar, lemon, and onion dressing
7 oz. (200 g) potatoes
mineral water

Snack
5 oz. (150 g) cottage cheese
3½ oz. (100 g) strawberries

3½ oz. (100 g) pineapple
mineral water

Dinner
2½ oz. (70 g) cooked spaghetti
8¾ oz. (250 g) fresh tomatoes in a fresh tomato sauce
¾ oz. (20 g) 20%-fat hard cheese, grated
mineral water

> Approximate total
> calories: 1,310
> protein content: 110 g
> carbohydrate content: 120–130 g

SUGGESTION 2
Breakfast
1¾ oz. (50 g) muesli
½ grapefruit
1 cup low-fat milk
1 teaspoon sunflower oil
coffee, tea, or mineral water

Lunch
7 oz. (200 g) chicken breast or fillet of turkey (with added spices, grilled)
7 oz. (200 g) vegetable (e.g., broccoli)
1 oz. (30 g) boiled rice
mineral water

Snack
8¾ oz. (250 g) low-fat yogurt
3½ oz. (100 g) apple
mineral water

Dinner
1 slice whole-grain bread
big salad (lettuce, tomatoes, peppers, carrots, fennel, etc.) with non-oil dressing
3½ oz. (100 g) turkey breast (with added spices, grilled)
mineral water

> Approximate total
> calories: 1,260
> protein content: 110 g
> carbohydrate content: 120–130

12
The Psychology of Bodysculpting

Training with weights and generally following a bodybuilding lifestyle of proper diet, stretching, and aerobics can be extremely beneficial psychologically for any woman. At the same time, following a few simple and specific psychological principles can improve both the speed and degree of gains in muscle hypertrophy.

Over the years that I've been involved with weight training and bodysculpting, I have seen hundreds of depressed, insecure women come into gyms, train systematically with resistance equipment for a few short months, and improve their bodies so dramatically that their entire psychological outlook changed. They become self-confident, secure, and emotionally better able to handle life's natural ups and downs. They turned themselves from mice into lionesses!

Improved self-image is the key to an improved emotional outlook, and one of the easiest ways to improve self-image is to begin training with weights while supplementing the exercise program with a healthful bodybuilding diet. Let me tell you a true success story about one of my grade school friends who followed this exact path.

Brigitta was 20 years old when she made the decision to join our bodybuilding sisterhood, a decision that ultimately had a profound impact on her life. She was at least 30 pounds overweight and as weak as a kitten. Colds, flu, and bronchitis seemed like a way of life to her, because she was always suffering from one of the three.

Brigitta's pasty-looking skin was blotchy; she thought so little of herself that she seldom took the time to apply makeup, let alone style her hair or choose appropriate clothing to wear each day. She believed in her heart that she was a loser, and as a result of that belief she was.

Nothing ever seemed to work out for her. She couldn't hold down a job, no one had asked her out on a date for five years, and if her parents hadn't allowed her to live at home, she would not have had enough money to even rent a small room in someone else's house. It wasn't a very nice picture. In fact it was downright pathetic.

I had gone to school with Brigitta and remembered her as an attractive, healthy, socially popular child. Where could things have gone so wrong for her? In an effort to help, I invited her to my gym for a workout, but she was too embarrassed to be seen in public in gym attire. So I lugged an adjustable barbell set over to her parents' home, and even brought along some thick rubber floor mats to protect their nice hardwood floors.

Brigitta was reluctant, but I was still able to prod her through a short session of weight training, having her perform one set each of a single exercise for every body part. She actually liked the way she felt after the workout, as endorphins surged through her body. It was a pleasurable physical sensation. She was willing to try a second workout two days later.

Even though I'd purposely made her initial training session very light and easy, Brigitta experienced considerable muscle soreness as a by-product of it. That was alleviated by a series of lovely long hot baths. With all systems set on "go" for a second workout, I had her work a little harder, heavier, and longer this time. Again, my girlhood friend felt great after she'd finished her light session of pumping iron.

Gradually Brigitta grew to like her weight workouts, and she began to see little changes in her body's shape and condition. Small success fed on small success, and Brigitta's self-confidence and self-esteem began to increase. Soon she was full of questions about how to change her diet to hasten the rate of progress she could see as her body developed a new shape.

As had been the case when I took up bodybuilding during my middle teenage years, a change in diet helped Brigitta's body improve by leaps and bounds. Her sense of psychological well-being improved hand-in-hand with the changes she noted in her body. Self-esteem and self-confidence are firmly tied in to a woman's self-image, and Brigitta became living proof that this system of physical and emotional self-improvement works.

Today Brigitta at 25 bears no resemblance to the person I saw struggle into heavy athletic clothing for a first home-gym weight workout. Now she trains every day in a large coed gym, wearing a leotard, tights, and a G-string bikini bottom that would have turned her red with embarrassment had she even thought about such an outfit five years ago. And does she ever have the type of body to wear attire like this!

As startling as Brigitta's physical transformation has been, the personality change she has undergone is even more impressive. No longer a loser, everything she attempts seems to bear fruit. She takes pride in her hair and makeup and exudes a sexy self-confidence that's difficult to ignore. Indeed, she's now married to the gym hunk, and the happy couple are currently planning their family.

Brigitta's case is exceptionally dramatic, but she's typical of the hundreds of mice I've seen turned into lionesses through adopting and maintaining a bodybuilding lifestyle. It's an everyday fact of life that our sport causes these physical and personality changes. This process of self-improvement is one of the best facets of bodybuilding. It's something you automatically receive as a consequence of being an enthusiastic bodybuilder!

Now that you've seen how easily bodybuilding can improve a woman's psychological well-being, let's look at ways in which several well-founded psychological principles can assist you to more quickly improve your bodybuilding results.

Positive Thinking

It's axiomatic in life—and in bodybuilding, which is a microcosm of life—that you are what you think you are. So you might as well think you're someone special, right?

Unfortunately, the way most parents bring up their children tends to make them negative thinkers. If you have fallen into this pattern, you can take some easy steps to break out of the gutter of life and get back on the road to happiness and physical success. Really, the only difference between being in a rut and being dead is that they actually bury you in one of them.

How many times did your mother or father say to you, "Don't do that, because you'll probably hurt yourself" as you were growing up? Probably hundreds and hundreds of times. Parents are naturally concerned about the welfare of their children, and they try to protect them by shooing them away from every conceivable type of problem. In many cases, this is the right thing to do. (How many times do you have to chase a bouncing ball out into the street to learn that you might get hit by a car doing it?) But sometimes it's the sort of comment that sets a child to thinking negatively.

"If I'm supposed to stay away from everything, how am I supposed to explore the world out there?" most kids are asking themselves, at least on a subconscious level. If you don't take some risk here and there, you never do discover the wonderful things that are out there in the world.

Once a child grows up, he or she is used to thinking about everything that could go wrong if something new is tried, rather than what might go right. This type of negative conditioning can keep you from reaching your bodybuilding goals in an expeditious manner. Every time you're confronted with a heavier-than-usual weight in an exercise, you worry about getting hurt rather than just going ahead and using the more substantial poundage that will hasten muscle hypertrophy.

As long as you are fully warmed up and using proper body mechanics to lift a heavy weight, it is functionally almost impossible to injure yourself. Your body has built-in sensory organs called Golgi reflex tendons that will automatically cause you to fail to execute a lift completely if the weight is even close to something that might injure you. So what's the point of even worrying about an injury?

The first step to reconditioning yourself to think in a consistently positive mode is to recognize that you do have negative thoughts. Write down the most common ones in a training journal or notebook so that you can review them periodically to find out what turns you to thinking negatively most frequently.

Once you have identified your negative road signs, consciously start to turn the other direction every time you think a negative thought. Immediately cast out the negative impulse and substitute a positive one. Sounds pretty corny at first, but it really works if you go about it systematically. Within a few weeks you can condition yourself to think in a positive way first.

It takes several months to recondition your mind to think positively consistently, but it can be done quite easily if you go about the process in a systematic manner. Once you're a positive thinker, you'll notice that a lot more in your life, your workouts, and your dietary approach are going right for you. *What you think and can conceive, you can achieve.*

Mental Concentration

An inexperienced trainee will typically have trouble keeping her mind on the working muscle—or muscles—during an exercise. Failing to concentrate on a muscle you are training tends to detract from the value of each set you perform. It's a good practice to learn to concentrate more fully during a workout.

The first step is to learn which muscles or muscle—or even which part of a muscle—is affected by the exercises you perform in your routine. These muscles are pointed out in the exercise descriptions in this book. The topic is also covered in other books and myriad magazine articles that you might read on building up a certain body area.

If you aren't familiar with muscle anatomy, you'll need to consult an anatomy chart. A variety of medical anatomy books is available in libraries that illustrate clearly how the entire muscle system looks beneath the skin.

To practice mental concentration, start out by doing an isolation movement for a particular body part. An isolation exercise stresses a single muscle group—or even part of one muscle complex—in isolation from the rest of the body. Complex movements stress two more groups in concert. Let's say you are going to do seated dumbbell concentration curls for your initial concentration-improving exercise.

Select a dumbbell and get into the correct position to do concentration curls. Focus your mind as completely and intensely as possible on your right biceps, which will be worked by this movement. Slowly begin to curl the weight upward, feeling the biceps muscles begin to tense harder and harder, shortening themselves to curl the dumbbell in a semicircular arc, until the weight touches your shoulder. Hold your biceps fully contracted with the weight in the top position for a moment, trying to make the flex progressively more intense, almost cramping the muscles as you tense them.

Keeping your mind still focused on your biceps, start to lower the dumbbell back along the same semicircular arc to the starting point. This time mentally visualize the muscles slowly extending under the load as you resist the downward pressure of the weight. In the finish position, you should still be focused mentally on your biceps only, before repeating the movement.

Mentally *seeing* the biceps intensely contract and extend under the weight is a key part of mastering mental concentration. From time to time you'll lose this mental focus, and your mind will begin to wander. The instant it does, force your mind back onto the task at hand, concentrating on the working biceps muscle. With time, you'll find that you can go longer and longer

between episodes of mind wandering, and finally you will be able to concentrate intensely and completely on your biceps muscle for an entire set of dumbbell concentration curls.

Eventually you will be able to concentrate so completely that you won't even hear a training partner urging you to finish a particularly difficult repetition at the end of a set. When you get to this point—when you hear nothing and don't even feel the weight in your hand any longer—you will have mastered workout concentration, and you'll be getting the most out of every set you perform for each muscle group.

Visualization

Visualization plays a part in all of bodybuilding and is not just central to learning how to concentrate. The more real you can make the visualized image of the physique you would like to attain, the easier it becomes for you to achieve that level of physical development and conditioning. There's no mystery about why this happens.

To review what I described in Chapter 5: Visualization is the means by which you can program your subconscious mind—which is much more logical than your conscious mind—to help you make decisions that assist you in achieving your bodybuilding goals. It's much like programming an electronic computer—but you're programming a biochemical computer instead.

I practice visualization in a dark room at night when I'm about ready to retire. This is a time when I am almost perfectly relaxed and free from the myriad mental distractions I face during a normal day. Both relaxation and freedom from distraction are requisites for proper mental programming via visualization.

Lie back in a comfortable position and begin to summon up a mental picture of how you want to look. It will seem as if you are projecting that image on the backs of your eyelids.

Make your mental image as realistic and detailed as humanly possible. See every ridge and valley of muscle, every tiny vein and artery that will be visible beneath the skin, and even the glossy appearance of super-healthy skin at contest time.

Naturally, you'll become distracted from time to time, and you'll have to use the same technique as discussed earlier—notice that you have become distracted and force your mental focus back to the task at hand. With time you'll become adept at maintaining this image for long periods.

It's best to keep a perfect mental image of your physique in focus for 10–15 minutes each night before drifting off to sleep. Visualization is one of the most powerful tools in your mental arsenal, so use it wisely and often. Get your biochemical computer programmed to help you become a bodybuilding success, and you'll get to the top much more quickly!

Goal Setting

If you don't know where you're going, how do you intend to get there? That's a pretty good question. It's vitally important that you develop a road map to guide you from where you are now to where you want to go, a detailed map that shows every turn in the road and every dead end.

Your road map is formed by proper use of goal-setting techniques. First you have to decide what your ultimate goal in bodysculpting might be—just to look good, to achieve optimum physical condition and health, or even to become a top competitive bodybuilder. Your goal may change, and that's all right—the important thing is to set a goal.

For the sake of illustration, let's say that you have chosen the same ultimate goal that I did as a teenager—to one day become Ms. Olympia. That's the highest title in women's competitive bodybuilding, so you might as well shoot for the top.

Once you have a goal in mind, write it down in a place where you will see it often. In fact, all of your goals—ultimate, long-term, and short-term—should be written down, either in a diary or on a sign posted in a prominent place in your gym, bathroom, or bedroom. The mere act of writing down a goal tends to fix it more firmly in your subconscious mind. Unfortunately, many serious trainees completely neglect writing down their goals.

Ultimate goals should be broken down into long-term goals that, when accomplished one by one, will lead to the ultimate goal. These long-term goals are best set at the beginning of each year, when average women make New Year's resolutions. The difference is that you'll be much more serious about achieving your long-term goal than they are about keeping their resolutions.

A typical long-term goal for a competitive bodybuilder is to win a progressively higher-level contest each year. Competitions begin perhaps with a club-level contest and go on to city-, state-, regional-, national-, and international-level shows. At the pro level, there are two or three competitions below the highest level—the Ms. Olympia competition.

To keep your enthusiasm up, long-term goals should be broken down into more easily achieved short-term goals. These might be such things as using a heavier exercise weight for a key movement to improve your weakest body part, losing a certain amount of body fat, or adding a predetermined amount of muscle mass each month.

As with long-term goals, short-term goals should be stepping stones toward achievement of an ultimate goal. I like to think of the goal-setting process as a journey from one end of the country to the other. The individual mileposts that you pass can be likened to short-term goals, the various cities at which you stop for the night can be seen as long-term goals, and the metropolis you're hoping to reach could be the ultimate goal. Accomplish enough short-term goals and you reach a city; reach enough cities and you finally get to your paramount goal.

The last thing I need to tell you about goals is that they should always be realistic, something that you can expect to attain if you train hard and consistently enough while maintaining a good diet. Don't pick something that no one could achieve or something that in all likelihood will be impossible for you to achieve. Then you'll find that you can use the goal-setting process to your advantage for as long as you choose to stay involved in bodybuilding.

Motivation

If you aren't motivated to succeed, you won't have enough mental drive to reach your goals. Reaching each goal you set has to be the most important thing in your life, or you won't have the type of motivation you need to succeed, particularly in the competitive bodybuilding arena.

I've learned from experience that the right mental attitude is the foundation of all gains in muscle mass. As long as my mind is in the correct mode, I can achieve anything I want when it comes to sculpting and perfecting my physique.

My approach to achieving proper motivation to succeed begins with self-confidence. I truly believe I'm going to be one of the greatest bodybuilders of all time. I've got good genes, the will to continue improving, and the intense, burning desire to get 110% from my training and diet every day of the year. There are no half measures

when your mind is programmed like this.

With regard to your physique, remember that your mind is like the tiny rudder of a huge ship plowing through heavy seas. The rudder might be small and seemingly insignificant, but when it rotates, it turns that big ship in any direction the captain desires. Similarly, your mind charts your course as a bodybuilder, guiding you to a balanced, muscular physique in the shortest possible amount of time.

Do you truly believe you'll become impressively developed, have optimum proportional balance, and possess great body symmetry? Do you want an aesthetic physique more than anything else in your life? Unless you can answer "yes" to both of these questions, you need more work on your mental motivation to succeed. If you don't put in that mental work, all the training and dietary manipulations in the world won't give you the desired degree of muscular development.

One technique I use to increase motivation is to save back issues of *Flex* magazine and other muscle mags, so I can review them on a regular basis to see how other top women competitors are progressing in their careers. Sitting down with a cup of cappuccino and leafing through these magazines tends to put me in a mental mode in which I have tremendous motivation to excel, to eventually defeat everyone in my path to win the Ms. Olympia title.

Saving magazines also gives you a reference library from which you can learn about all of the new techniques that evolve in bodybuilding. Books like this are great, but their information is locked into a particular time frame. Magazines, on the other hand, come out monthly and can constantly update you about the latest information on bodybuilding.

When you have the correct level of motivation, you will automatically have the mental drive to succeed as a bodybuilder. The two are inseparable. So you should work hard on developing motivation, and you'll be a success at anything you try in the weight room.

Self-Confidence

One great by-product of consistent weight training—as hinted in my anecdote about my friend Brigitta early in this chapter—is self-confidence. Succeeding at building up and sculpting your skeletal muscles gives you the self-confidence to continue trying more and more difficult tasks, both within our sport and out in the arena of life.

The key to developing self-confidence is picking realistic, achievable goals in the activity so it

Training with weights and following a proper diet can be as good for the mind as it is for the body.

is possible to reach them. Failure defeats your ability to develop self-confidence, so choose your goals wisely at all times.

Turning the Mental Dial

If you work at it, you can learn how to turn every negative thing that happens to you into something positive. It's somewhat like changing the channel on your television set. If you don't like the program on Channel 5, switch to Channel 7. It's easy to do—and it's not that much more difficult to accomplish mentally.

If nothing else, every negative thing that happens to you—and which you survive—improves you. The German philosopher Friedrich Nietzsche wrote: "That which does not kill me only serves to make me stronger." Nothing could be closer to the truth, particularly in competitive bodybuilding.

Tell yourself that you will learn from every mistake you make. Don't get down on yourself, but rather learn why you made that particular mistake and then avoid it in the future. It's not that difficult to do if you concentrate on the fact that mistakes can really be positive rather than negative.

Earlier we discussed the topic of positive thinking, which also has a bearing on how you approach life. The entire idea in positive thinking is to change that channel every time you encounter something negative. Make the negative positive if at all possible, or completely ignore it if you can't make it into something positive.

In the long run, the more positive your attitude is each day, the more good things will happen to you throughout that day. So take control of your mental attitude. Keep it positive at all times. You can never go wrong when you expect good things to happen in your life.

13
Contest Bodybuilding

Training and dieting for a bodybuilding show—and successfully participating in it—are a true test of any woman's character. It has been said that bodybuilding is the world's toughest sport, an assertion with which I agree wholeheartedly. We certainly train as hard and consistently as athletes in any other sport, and we have to do it for months at a time when our energy reserves have been severely depleted by a low-calorie precontest diet.

Preparing for a competition is so hard on my mind and body that I don't think I'll ever enter more than one high-level IFBB pro event per year again. In the past I've competed as often as six times per year as an amateur and two or three times yearly as a pro, and I've paid a price for it as far as my health is concerned. For at least a month after a Ms. Olympia competition, I feel ill and listless, and my mental attitude is totally blah. It usually takes a couple of months for me to get back into great shape to start making gains in muscle mass again.

Despite the rigors of our sport, it seems that a budding competitive bodybuilder lurks within the body of nearly every woman who becomes addicted to pumping iron. So in this chapter I'll tell you how to go about getting your act together for a competition. The rest will be up to you.

Perhaps you'll win a trophy your first time onstage, perhaps not. But you should learn from each competitive preparation phase and every appearance at a show. Evaluate your efforts, determine where you made mistakes, decide how to correct your errors, and then start gearing up for another competitive effort. Soon they'll be hanging a gold medal around your neck and calling you a bodybuilding champion!

Cycle Training

Athletes in most modern competitive sports follow training cycles, and bodybuilders are no exception. We work out and diet in two distinctly different ways, depending on how close we are to a competition. If we dieted strictly and trained with all-out effort throughout the year, we would eventually burn out either physically or mentally or both.

Our cycles consist of what we term *off-season* and *precontest*, or *peaking*, phases. During an off-season cycle, diet is somewhat relaxed in comparison to a precontest diet, permitting us to consume extra calories that will fuel heavier workouts aimed at increasing muscle mass in general and the size of any lagging body part in particular. In a peaking phase, the diet is tightened up considerably, training is accelerated and increased in intensity, and aerobic workouts become more frequent—all in an effort to strip away excess stored body fat to reveal the muscles beneath the skin in sharp relief for contest day.

Precontest cycles usually last 6–12 weeks, while off-season phases can vary in length from as few as 3–4 months to as many as 2–3 years, although intelligent competitors prefer to schedule only one or two peaks per year. There are also brief transitional cycles lasting 2–3 weeks in which an athlete will either gear up or gradually relax both training and dietary intensity between the off-season and precontest phases.

Training and diet are an inseparable duo in competitive bodybuilding, but each one changes in its own way before and after a championship competition. Let's look at off-season and precontest cycles separately and in detail.

THE OFF-SEASON CYCLE

As I have already mentioned, your goals during an off-season phase should be to increase muscle mass in general and to improve the mass and conformation of one lagging body part in particular. While you often will have more than one weak muscle group to bring up in the off-season, it's best to specialize on only the one that most needs work, saving improvement in others for succeeding building cycles.

You simply won't be able to gear up to deal with more than one weak area at a time. It would be only during an extended off-season cycle—one that lasts a year or more—that you might shift your focus from one lagging body part to another after a few months. It would be easy to overtrain a weak muscle complex if you gave it specialized attention for more than 4–6 consecutive months, so switching off can make good sense at times.

In Chapter 2 I discussed how you should go about evaluating your physique periodically in order to recognize and then give priority to a weak area when you are in a building cycle. To review: be certain that your evaluation is objective, whether you use someone else (a judge, gym owner, critical friend, training partner) or yourself (via the mirror and/or periodic progress photos) to determine a weak point.

Always focus on your weakest area only in order to gradually perfect the proportional balance of your physique as a whole. As you approach true contest condition and you're working out to develop an adequate level of muscle mass, remember that the one factor that most clearly separates winners from losers in a judge's eye is the presence or lack of balanced physical proportions.

In Chapter 5 I discussed the subject of muscle priority training, which involves working a weaker body part either first in a gym session or by itself in a separate workout. This is the best way to ensure that you have a maximum amount of mental and physical energy to expend in saturation-bombing your weak area until it has no recourse but to grow larger and become better formed.

Specialized training of a weak area should involve such high-intensity techniques as training to failure, working a set past failure (using cheating reps, forced reps, burns, descending sets, and/or negative reps) and use of pre-exhaustion supersets if the laggard is a torso muscle group. These techniques were all examined in detail in Chapter 5, and you undoubtedly have already determined through experimentation in the gym which individual methods or combinations of techniques work best for you.

So now you know how to deal with a weak area during an off-season cycle. Let's take a look at the main goal of each building phase—increasing general muscle mass. While absolute mass isn't as important to female as it is to male bodybuilders, it's still a vital factor in the competitive arena. You should master the process of acquiring muscle mass and put it into practice during each off-season building cycle.

In terms of training, several things characterize an off-season cycle:

• You train significantly heavier than precontest.
• Your workouts are slower, with longer rest intervals between sets.
• You probably work out less frequently, both for each body part and in terms of total weekly gym sessions.
• Repetition ranges are lower than during a peaking phase.
• You do fewer total sets for each muscle group.
• You use proportionately more basic rather than isolation exercises.
• Your form loosens up a little, in most cases, to allow you to lift heavier weights.
• Because you are using heavier poundages in somewhat less strict form, you need to warm up more thoroughly than you would during a peaking cycle.

To summarize the most important points of an off-season building cycle: your workouts are less frequent, heavier, and slower and involve lower reps than when you are peaking. You still need to do aerobics sessions, but they are a lot less frequent and significantly shorter than in the precontest cycle. The combination of a calorie-deficient diet and a large volume of aerobic work is what helps you burn off stored body fat so that the muscular development you worked so long and hard for in the off-season is revealed.

Nutritionally, you are allowed to eat more total calories when you are building up. But these extra calories shouldn't come from fats but rather from those carbohydrate foods that fuel hard, heavy workouts. As pointed out in Chapter 11, it's best to base your diet on complex carbohydrates rather than on simple sugars.

Food supplements also vary from cycle to cycle. In the off-season you can reduce the amount and variety of supplements used; in the precontest cycle you have to gear up for a stage appearance by dramatically increasing your consumption of vitamins, minerals, and particularly free-form and branched-chain amino acids.

Since supplements are costly, you even have to cycle your finances in a way. When using fewer supplements in a peaking phase, save up your extra food money to spend on a large supply of these expensive food products for use when you are peaking.

THE PRECONTEST CYCLE

Your goals during a competition peaking cycle are to strip away all vestiges of body fat while concurrently retaining the maximum possible amount of muscle mass developed in the off-season. This takes a combination of specific weight workouts (as well as plenty of aerobics) and an equally specific diet, which effectively reduces stores of body fat.

The timing of a precontest cycle is crucial and requires experimentation to determine how many weeks you should devote to each peaking phase. If you have a high BMR, have kept fairly close to your contest weight in the off-season, and tend to refine your muscular development quickly, you may need as few as 6–7 weeks in which to peak out. I personally prefer a 12-week precontest cycle even though my own BMR is rather fast, because I don't like to abuse my body with crash diets if I'm coming up short of true contest shape a week or two out. Crash dieting also is a main cause of loss of muscle mass when you are peaking out for a competition.

Twelve weeks works best for me because it allows me to be less extreme in both diet and training, and it gives me a chance to fine-tune my physical appearance over the final 2–3 weeks so that when I step onstage I am in precisely the shape I wanted to achieve. The length of time you might have to spend will be determined only by peaking for several lower-level shows over varying lengths of time, keeping detailed and precise notes of how quickly your body responds, and then gradually evolving your own personal formula.

Even when you know precisely how quickly you can get into shape, you can screw up your formula by carelessly and foolishly allowing yourself to gain too much fatty body weight during a building phase. The more body fat you allow to accumulate in the off-season, the longer you'll be forced to diet for an upcoming competition. It really does make perfect sense to stay relatively close to contest shape year-round.

A small number of women with the metabolism of racehorses can maintain contest condition all year. The only IFBB pro bodybuilder who currently falls into this category is Jackie Paisley, who won the overall U.S. Championships as an amateur and the prestigious Pro Ms. International, held each year as part of the Arnold Schwarzenegger Classic in Columbus, Ohio. But Jackie has to pay a price for having such a fast BMR; it's exceptionally difficult for her to gain muscular body weight.

Most of us gain a little fat with the muscle when building up in the off-season. The trick is to keep your body weight under strict control when you are in a building cycle. My own goal is to keep within 11 pounds (5 kilograms) of my contest weight, which I manage to do all year except for a week around the Christmas holidays. Then I might get as high as 16 pounds (7½ kilograms) over my target off-season weight, much of that water retention rather than actual body fat increases.

You'll also have to experiment with various body fat levels during successive building phases in order to determine what works best for you. I'd suggest going no higher than a body fat percentage that still reveals your abdominal squares under tension, which will probably be less than 10 pounds of excess avoirdupois. Once you learn your target level, discipline yourself so that you never exceed it. Here's an Anja Bodybuilding Maxim for you: *You can't flex fat!*

Low-fat/low-calorie dieting (outlined in detail in Chapter 11) is the way virtually all top competitive bodybuilders ready themselves for a competition. A handful of women still use the old-fashioned low-carbohydrate diet for an entire peaking cycle, while most of us go low-carb for only 3–4 days as part of the carb-loading technique I'll explain to you later in this chapter.

The key to losing fat and not muscle weight is to increase your body's fat set point. Thousands of years of existence have established this fat set point as nature's way of keeping humans from starving to death during a famine.

When you go on an extremely low-calorie diet, your body perceives it as starvation and begins to metabolize muscle even faster than fat to meet survival energy needs. At the same time, your body tries to force stored body fat up to that set point. Even if you lose weight, a large amount of the loss can be muscle in addition to fat.

The best way to raise your fat set point is to gradually *increase* food consumption to fake your body into believing it has no immediate need to store excess fat. You must, however, simultaneously do some type of aerobic exercise for at least 45–60 minutes each day. I personally have done as much as three hours of aerobics a day prior to a competition, breaking it up into 3–4 sessions. Obviously it's much easier to work aerobics into your schedule when you have aerobic equipment (a stationary bike, stair stepper, and/or treadmill) in your home so you don't have to make umpteen trips to the gym each day.

As a competition approaches, the total amount of aerobic training each day should be increased gradually. If you don't like my choices of aerobics, you can take dance classes, run, cycle outdoors, mountain bike, walk (particularly fast and/or uphill), run stadium bleachers, or row a boat.

Extra amounts of good bodybuilding food raise your fat set point, particularly if the food is burned off immediately with regularly performed aerobics. Once your fat set point has been increased in calories, you'll find that you are eating sufficient food to accelerate muscle-mass increases as a consequence of short, hard, and heavy gym workouts, something that is quite the opposite of what most bodybuilders experience when they *lose* muscle during a peaking diet.

The best part about having raised your set point is that you don't have to diet as strictly to reach contest shape. I can currently get sliced on up to 1,800 calories per day; I used to be forced to go under 1,000, and sometimes as low as 500–600 daily. When you can eat this much—and as long as you continue aerobics—you will reach contest shape without losing any of that precious muscle mass you worked so hard for in the off-season!

Another way to fake out your system and increase your fat set point is to oscillate daily caloric levels up and down but *averaging* progressively fewer total calories each successive week. To illustrate, let's say you want to maintain a caloric intake of 1,500 per day over a seven-day period. Here's how you might vary your daily food intake and still average 1,500 calories per day for the week:

Day Number	Total Calories Consumed
1	1,500
2	900
3	2,100
4	1,000
5	1,200
6	2,200
7	1,600

The total number of calories is 10,500, or an average of 1,500 per day. By jerking caloric intake up and down like this, you keep your body from perceiving a particularly low-cal day (e.g., Days 2, 4, and 5) as something akin to starvation. Your system is slow to respond, requiring at least 3–4 days of consistently deficient caloric intake before it goes into a set point protection mode.

Ideally you should be in competitive shape—or very close to it—at least a week before each show so you can fine-tune your condition by manipulating food intake and aerobic levels. I personally like to be a bit below my contest weight 3–4 days before the competition so I can cease aerobic training and eat more calories from complex carbohydrates, a technique that allows my muscles to fill out and reach a temporary peak of muscle mass.

While I don't mess around with eccentric last-minute dietary manipulations, some top bodybuilders will use carbohydrate depletion-loading or sodium loading-depletion, or both over the final week in order to (they believe) make their muscles appear fuller and to eliminate unnecessary body water.

My own experiments with carbohydrate and sodium manipulation before a competition have been unsatisfactory, but because this technique may well work for you, I'll explain how it's done. You'll then be able to conduct your own experiments to determine whether this is something you wish to use for an actual competition.

Carbohydrate loading is based on two principles. The key principle is that muscle glycogen holds extra water in your muscles if you can force a lot of glycogen into your muscles at the right time. You can induce your muscles to hold greater-than-normal amounts of glycogen on contest day—and thus make your muscles appear fuller than they actually are—by severely depleting your body's stores of carbohydrates for a few days and then loading up on carbs for a few more. This induces the body to "supercompensate" by cramming more glycogen than usual into the muscles. At least that's the theory. Carb loading just makes me appear flat and unimpressive.

Start your carb loading process 5–6 days before your competition by strictly limiting carbohydrate intake for three days while at the same time exhausting yourself with a lot of aerobics. Some bodybuilders go as close to zero carbohydrate intake as possible over these three days. Others limit it to anything between 10 and 60 grams per day. This is the depletion phase.

For the next two or three days (the length of time necessary seems to vary from one individual to another), you should load up on complex

The free-posing round gives bodybuilders a chance to show their grace, power, and ability to dance.

carbohydrates. Eat at least 250–300 grams of rice, potatoes, pasta, and other complex carbohydrate foods each day, spacing your carb intake out over at least six small meals per day. This is the loading phase, which should fill your muscles with more glycogen than they can usually hold.

Sodium loading is also based on a water-retention factor, although it's the opposite of carb loading. Sodium outside the muscle cells will retain a huge amount of water, thereby blurring out your best cuts if the water is not eliminated. The theory here is to load up on sodium for 3–4 days (taking in up to 10 grams per day, which will make your body look positively bloated), and then you completely eliminate sodium from your diet for the final 48–60 hours prior to competing. This completely rids your body of retained water, at least in theory.

Be sensible and conduct experiments with varying carb- and sodium-loading formulae during the off-season so that you won't blow an entire peaking effort should the techniques fail to work as predicted for you. You'll need plenty of will power over the final precontest week in order to survive these processes, however, because they will cause you to look like death warmed over early in the final week leading up to your competition. When they kick in, you hope you will look like Superwoman. It's tough for anyone with less than an iron will to want to compete when she looks as bad as you will early in the week, particularly when your mind is fogged by the lack of blood sugar that the carbohydrate depletion process will cause.

Your training program should be progressively and markedly intensified over your peaking cycle, with absolute maximum intensity maintained for at least the last 3–4 weeks. As with aerobic training, you'll look best onstage in terms of combined muscle fullness and cuts if you cease weight workout sessions 3–4 days before your prejudging. I've personally discovered that I have to cut out heavy squats and leg

presses two weeks earlier—doing only light, high-rep leg extensions up to the weight cut-off point—in order to maximize quadriceps, glute, and hamstring muscularity.

Once you cease weight workouts, it's important to double up on your posing practice until about 24 hours before you step onstage for your prejudging. This will not only even out your free-posing routine but also sharpen up your general muscularity a bit more, giving your physique a final polish that will help you shine like a ten-karat diamond onstage.

In general, your precontest training programs should incorporate the following:

- Train significantly lighter than in the off-season.
- Do faster and faster workouts, with progressively shorter rest intervals between sets.
- Work out in the gym more frequently than you do in the off-season, at least six times per week and sometimes more than once per day.
- Increase repetition ranges (12–20 reps per set precontest as compared to 5–8 in the off-season).
- Perform more total sets per muscle group.
- Use proportionately fewer basic exercises (but retain at least one per muscle group) and do more isolation movements in your body-part routines.
- Use stricter exercise form than in the off-season.
- Include a wide variety of intensification techniques (e.g., peak contraction, continuous tension, quality training, and ISO-tension, which will be discussed later in this chapter) specifically aimed at inducing maximum onstage muscularity.

Precontest workouts get pretty insane in terms of training intensity, but it's easy to train so intensely because your mental intensity is automatically increased by the prospect of looking bad onstage if you don't work out as hard as possible. Most women will find that their workouts just automatically become longer, quicker, and more intense as a competition approaches, and they become progressively more hysterical (well, at least *concerned*) about embarrassing themselves in front of their friends if they fail to achieve peak condition.

As I hinted earlier in this chapter, it takes incredible character, self-discipline, and drive to keep training hard when your energy reserves are depleted by your precontest diet and increased aerobics program. But this is how champions are made. The Russians have a saying for it: The strongest piece of steel is the one that has passed through the hottest flame. Keep that in mind when the going gets tough, and then get going yourself!

Quality Training
. . . .

I have already talked about progressively decreasing the length of rest intervals between sets during a peaking cycle. In bodybuilding lingo, this process is called *quality training*, and to some degree most champions use the technique. A few women, however, never vary the pace of their workouts—nor sometimes even the workouts themselves—from off-season to precontest cycles.

In general, training resistance intensity can be increased in the following four ways:

1. Increase the amount of weight used in an exercise.

2. Use the same weight but increase the number of sets performed of a particular exercise.

3. Do a consistent number of reps with a set weight in a movement but increase the number of sets performed of that exercise.

4. Keep the weight, sets, and reps consistent, but progressively decrease the amount of rest taken between sets.

All bodybuilders increase resistance intensity by combining the first two rules, increasing reps with a set weight until an upper guide number for repetitions has been reached and then increasing the weight and decreasing reps only to gradually work the reps up again. For the first year or so of steady training, you will gradually add to your training load by increasing the total number of sets performed for each body part. But only advanced, contest-level bodybuilders use the quality training method of increasing intensity.

Obviously, decreased energy reserves during a peaking cycle will make it virtually impossible to keep training poundages consistently high as you gradually reduce the length of rest intervals between sets. But as long as you keep your weights as relatively high as possible—an action that will require terrific mental drive and willpower—you'll get the most out of using the quality training principle.

Continuous Tension
. . . .

One common means of increasing intraset intensity during a peaking cycle is to use continuous tension on various exercises, particularly isolation movements. It's tougher to use this technique on incline presses than on pec-deck flyes, for example, because heavier weights are clumsy to handle in the type of slow-motion style demanded by the continuous tension training principle.

Let's use seated dumbbell concentration curls to illustrate continuous tension in a gym setting. Take the dumbbell in either hand, sit down at the end of a flat exercise bench, set your feet solidly on the gym floor about 2 feet (60 centimeters) apart, brace your working elbow against the inside of your knee on the same side, and fully straighten your arm. Rotate your wrist so your hand is completely supinated from the start of the movement, maintaining supination throughout each set.

Now tense your biceps and its antagonistic muscle group—the triceps—intensely and then slowly curl the weight from straight-arm's length up to your shoulder, being careful to keep both triceps and the working biceps tensed to the limit over the full range of motion of the exercise. Continue to keep all of your upper-arm muscles tensed as you lower the weight back to the starting point somewhat more slowly than you raised it. Moving the weight slowly up and down like this over a full range of motion, while keeping both the working muscle group and its antagonist tightly flexed, is called continuous tension.

The main advantage of continuous tension is that it stresses a muscle more intensely than usual by completely eliminating the effect of bar momentum. Usually, you'll curl the dumbbell up and down somewhat more quickly, which causes the weight to become ballistic. This means it would continue to coast upward a bit on its own, even if you abruptly stopped contracting your biceps. That, in turn, means that you're robbing your bis of some of the stress they should have been receiving if you had done something to keep bar momentum out of each repetition. That something is continuous tension, which you should seriously consider including in your overall training philosophy, particularly during a precontest cycle.

Peak Contraction

It's a physiological fact that more muscle cells are contracted when you have your biceps—or any other muscle group—maximally contracted and shortened to its limit. This phenomenon depends on a concept called the all or nothing principle, and you'll have to understand how a muscle complex like the biceps is formed from individual muscle cells in order to understand it. I'll try to keep my explanation as simple as possible.

Individual muscle cells look like oblong rectangles when viewed under a microscope, and they are arranged end to end like beads on a string to form long muscle fibers. These fibers are, in turn, bundled together to form the skeletal muscles you can see beneath your skin when your body-fat percentage is particularly low.

An individual muscle cell never contracts partially in order to lift a weight and shorten the skeletal muscle. It either contracts completely (which is the "all or nothing" part of the model), or it doesn't contract at all. When a skeletal muscle has been completely contracted and shortened, it has been made that way by many, many individual cells contracting completely. This also bunches the muscle up, as is the case when you pose your biceps onstage at a competition. Again, the shorter the muscle becomes when it's contracted completely, the more individual cells you will have had to "fire off" to get it that way.

Bodybuilders have discovered that placing a maximum weight on a muscle group when it is completely contracted gives skeletal muscle development a significant boost. But there are unfortunately a large number of weight-training movements that place little or no weight on a fully contracted muscle group.

Let's stick with the biceps to see what I mean. When you are doing standing barbell curls, the maximum amount of weight is placed on the muscles only when your forearms are at a right angle with your upper arms, or when they run parallel to the gym floor. This is the only time that the weight is pulling directly downward against your hands as they briefly travel directly upward on the semicircular arc from the movement's starting point at your thighs to the finish position beneath your chin.

At the starting point of the movement, very

little stress is on the biceps. Stress increases as you curl the weight upward and is at its maximum when your forearms are parallel to the gym floor. The stress begins to fall off as you continue and complete the curling movement by bringing your hands up to shoulder level.

Unfortunately, the biceps are fully contracted only in the finish position, when the weight has reached shoulder level. There is virtually no resistance on the biceps in this position; the weight is actually supported by the shoulder, upper-back, and upper-chest muscles.

So how can you ensure that you have maximum resistance on the biceps when they are fully contracted? The best way I know of with free weights is to take a narrow undergrip on the barbell (there should be about 5–6 inches, or 12–15 centimeters, of space showing between your little fingers when you have the correct width of grip). Bend over at the waist until your torso is parallel with the gym floor, hanging your arms directly down from your shoulders. In this position, you can do a movement called barbell bent-over concentration curls in which you keep your upper arms motionless as you curl the weight slowly up to your shoulders. Try this exercise and you'll discover immediately that you have to really fight hard to finish each repetition, since maximum resistance is definitely placed on the working biceps at the top point of each movement.

Fortunately, for every body part there are free-weight exercises that place a peak-contraction effect on your working muscles. These movements are listed in Figure 13-1.

Figure 13-1. The Best Peak Contraction Exercises

Quadriceps—leg extensions
Hamstrings—lying/seated/standing leg curls
Glutes/Lumbars—back hyperextensions
Lats—chins, pulldowns, all types of rowing movements
Traps—all variations of shrugs and upright rows
Delts—side/front/bent-over laterals, upright rows
Biceps—barbell concentration curls, various machine curls
Triceps—dumbbell kickbacks
Forearms—standing barbell behind the back wrist curls
Calves—all types of calf raises
Abs—crunches, hanging leg raises

Earlier I talked about combining two or more training intensification techniques to maximize the stress you place on a working muscle. One great combination along these lines is peak contraction and continuous tension—useful particularly before a competition, when you're trying very hard to sculpt your muscles to the hardness of a marble statue. I've often combined these two techniques in one set, and they're murder on the working muscles when used together. But they really do the job when it comes to adding detail to your muscles.

ISO-Tension

It's a well-known fact among top bodybuilders that practicing posing a lot tends to make the muscles appear harder. This has led to the development of a technique called *ISO-tension*, which consists of doing repeated poses of each muscle group on an almost daily basis over the final few weeks leading up to a competition. I personally find this technique to be a little boring to use, so I reserve it for only the last 2–3 weeks, when I'm putting the finishing touches on my physique.

This time let's use the quadriceps muscles to give you an example of ISO-tension in action. Stand in front of a mirror so you can be sure you are bringing out every facet of your quads as you tense them (you'll be able to see this much more easily than you'll be able to feel it at first). Then arrange your legs in a favorite pose and tense your quads as hard as you can for 8–10 seconds. Rest for 10–15 seconds to catch your breath a bit, and then repeat the 8–10 seconds of tensing. Alternate tenses and relaxations until you have done between 20 and 30 reps of a pose. Do 2–5 of these poses for each muscle group as your show approaches.

The more ISO-tension you use, the more intramuscular details you'll be able to bring out in your quadriceps and other muscle groups. This happens simply because you gain greater control over each muscle mass by more firmly establishing a mind-to-muscle link. And the more detail you can show onstage, the better your chances of coming home with a gold medal the next time you compete.

Another way to use ISO-tension, and the method I personally favor, is to hold each compulsory pose you'll need to do at a prejudging for 30–60 seconds at a time, attempting to bring out more details each second you hold it. Start out with about 30 seconds per pose and gradually work up to a full minute. Over a period of time, you can learn to go through mandatory poses 10 or more times, holding each one for 60 seconds.

It's important to master holding the compulsory poses for an extended period of time without either shaking like a leaf in a high wind or passing out, because you'll have to hold them quite a while during competition prejudging. Attend a contest or two and you'll notice many women who just haven't mastered this skill. They end up winded or feeling faint, and they have to relax the poses before the judges have looked down the entire lineup. If you have this problem yourself, practice the 60-second pose routine mentioned, and the deficiency will soon be a thing of the past.

Onstage Personal Appearance

The way you appear physically onstage for a competition is one thing, and the way your suit, hair, skin color, and makeup look is quite another. One is controlled by what you do in the gym and at the dining room table, while the other is a result of careful planning and preparation. Let's take a look at what you must consider when it comes to optimizing onstage personal appearance.

SKIN COLOR

If you have fair skin, you will have to do something to darken the color of your skin before a competition. Pale skin just doesn't take light the way a tan skin does, and it won't show your development at its best.

The best combination for a mahoganylike tan is a natural one from the sun or a sunbed to build up a good base, supplemented by several coats of makeup. Of course, a completely natural tan would be ideal, but most non-national-level competitions are held over the winter and early spring, when there isn't enough sun available in many areas to induce a deep tan.

A few of the more affluent competitors will travel somewhere tropical for a few weeks to get a tan, but the cost of this type of trip is prohibitively high for most of us. And in many tropical areas, training facilities are below par, and it's chancy to count on the availability of properly prepared precontest fare.

When working on a natural tan, start out as long before your show as possible (10–12 weeks is not excessive); stay in the sun for only a short time at first, gradually building up exposure time. Remember, sunburned skin is counterproductive. A burned skin will become bloated with water, and the burn will set you back a week or more in your tanning program. Wearing a sunscreen of correct strength will protect your skin from harmful rays while letting the beneficial rays through to tan you at the same time.

Sunbed sessions can be costly—particularly here in Europe—but using sunbeds is often the only way to induce a naturally deep skin color during the winter. As with lying in the sun, start out with short periods of exposure and gradually work them upward. In both the natural sun and sunbeds, you'll have to shift body positions periodically in order to achieve an even tan all over your body, particularly under your arms and down the sides of your torso. Be sure to tan either nude or while wearing a competition suit so that there won't be pale areas where you don't want them at contest time.

"Instant tan" products are widely available through ads in bodybuilding magazines and at gym pro shops. Experiment with as many brands as possible, because some of them may give your skin a color other than what I'd call naturally tan. Choose the one that gives you the best and darkest color.

You'll need someone to "paint" you the night before and the morning of your show. It will take several coats of makeup to yield the correct color density, between 3–6, depending on the brand. Be patient when the coats are being put on; they must be applied evenly and allowed to dry thoroughly before you sit or lie down. Usually these preparations have acetone as a base, and that chemical evaporates very quickly. But a few dry more slowly, and those are the ones with which you have to be the most careful.

Put less makeup over thick-skinned areas such as knees and elbows, because these will turn darker than the rest of your skin. After you have practiced at a couple of lower-level shows, you'll soon get the hang of this technique. Be sure to leave your face free of painted-on makeup— make up your face separately with standard cosmetics.

Take an old set of bed linens with you to the show if it's out of town, because the makeup stains sheets beyond the point where they can be washed clean. These days hotels are charging a small fortune to replace stained sheets and pillow cases.

The last skin-tone factor you'll need to consider is the body oil used to highlight your muscularity onstage. Vegetable oils like almond and avocado are far preferable to petroleum-based oils such as baby oil. Vegetable oils sink into the skin and then are exuded out of the pores to give your skin a nice glow as you begin to perspire onstage. Petroleum-based oils, in contrast, lie on the skin and tend to make you look like you're swathed in plastic freezer wrap!

You'll need a friend or fellow competitor to help you oil up backstage—particularly by putting oil on your back—prior to competing or posing at the evening show, plus to even up and renew your oil between judging rounds. You'll have to watch more experienced competitors the first time out to see how much oil to apply, because it's impossible for me to tell you what amounts to use. In any case, be sure the oil is put on uniformly all over your body, including under your arms and on the inner sides of your legs.

SUIT CHOICE

The choice of style and color of your posing suit is an individual matter that will probably require some experimentation and trial-and-error judgments. As with skin coloring agents, a variety of suits can be purchased via mail-order ads in muscle magazines and at gym pro shops, as well as at beachwear boutiques. In North America, I'd suggest calling Andreas Cahling, a former IFBB Pro Mr. International winner, at (619) 753-8000 during business hours for help if you're stuck. He has a terrific variety of styles and colors of both women's and men's suits and will give you next-day service if you have a credit card to which you can charge your order.

Current IFBB rules dictate that women's posing suits cover a conservative area of the buttocks, so don't buy something too briefly cut, only to find that you can't wear the suit once you're at your contest. Otherwise, find one that fits you like a glove and is cut so it displays a maximum amount of your muscular development.

Cut excessively long shoulder and bra strings shorter so that they don't dangle over half of your back during your posing routine. Very few other things will make you look as amateurish as dangling strings, so take care of them.

Suits should definitely be of a single color, since patterns tend to distract the judges from your physique, which after all is what you're onstage trying to display. The color should be harmonious with your own skin and hair coloring. Most bodybuilding federations prohibit the use of shiny cloth—so forget about the sequins.

Once you have picked out the perfect suit for your physique and coloring, purchase 1–2 extra ones if your funds permit it. All suits become oil-spotted and otherwise soiled (usually by skin makeup running into the edges of the fabric), so it's nice to have a spare suit or two available to replace a soiled one. Some women like to wear a color at the night show that's different from the one they wore at the prejudging, while others like to stick to a single favorite color all of the time.

HAIR AND MAKEUP

Hairstyle is important in that your hair must look stylish but must not in any way obscure your upper back and shoulder musculature. It doesn't require a professional hairdresser to do your hair correctly. I style my own hair for shows, getting

my ideas from leafing through fashion magazines and observing what other top competitors have done with their own hair. If you can't actually attend a show or two, you can at least observe the hairstyles of various women in contest photos run in *Flex* and other bodybuilding magazines.

Because stage lights are very bright, you'll have to make up your face more heavily and boldly for a contest than for normal social circumstances. If you don't opt for the depth of makeup used by stage actresses (and serious competitive bodybuilders), the lighter your skin the more washed out your face will look when you are onstage.

The best tip I can give you is to get yourself backstage at a higher-level show somewhere to see how much makeup the women use and how they apply it. Make good mental notes, copy what you've seen for your initial competitive effort, and then make adjustments according to how trusted friends said you looked onstage the first time out. After a contest or two, you'll be using your makeup like an IFBB pro!

HOW TO ACT ONSTAGE

There's a definite pattern to how a prejudging is conducted, so nothing can replace attending a couple of them and learning how they're run before you make your maiden competitive effort. But whether you already know the drill or have never even seen a prejudging before you are in one yourself, stay very alert to the commands of the head judge. You'll look like a complete novice if the head judge tells the lineup to make a quarter turn to the right and you're the only one onstage who makes a quarter turn to the left.

At both the prejudging and evening presentation, do your best to appear happy and self-confident onstage. Sometimes this is difficult to accomplish—particularly when it's obvious that

At both the prejudging and the evening
presentation, do your best to appear happy
and self-confident onstage.

you're totally outclassed by some of your competitors—but try hard anyway to keep your composure. Onstage charisma is an elusive and very valuable quality, and it starts with a look of complete self-confidence.

Never show any disappointment if you fail to place as high as you feel you deserve. You'll be judged frequently by the same individuals at each competitive level, and they have the memories of elephants when it comes to recalling

some sourpuss who smashed her trophy to bits because she disagreed with their decisions.

A much better approach is to try to talk calmly and courteously with as many judges as possible after your show, attempting to identify which areas they feel you'll need to improve before you give competition another try. This not only helps you identify weak points but also leaves a favorable impression with each judge you personally encounter.

Pumping Up

You've no doubt already noticed in the gym mirror that a pumped-up muscle group appears larger and better contoured than it does when it's cold. You can take advantage of this fact by pumping up a weak body part or two prior to stepping onstage. Stick with pumping up only 1–2 areas, however, because there isn't enough blood volume in your body to pump up everything.

Most contest promoters these days provide barbells, dumbbells, and benches in a backstage pump-up room. Start about 15 minutes before you will have to go onstage and do several light, high-rep sets of different exercises for your weak areas. Each time you leave the stage you'll need to pump up again, because a pump will only last 15–20 minutes at a time.

In the event that you attend a show where they don't provide weights for pumping up, you'll need to work out a series of calisthenics and partner-assisted exercises to replace the weight work. Don't panic if you have trouble coming up with these beforehand, however, because the more seasoned competitors backstage will know them all, and you can mimic these women's actions to get your own pump.

Posing Secrets

To me, one of the most exciting things about bodybuilding is that it's both an art and a sport. The sport part—the hard, consistent training we undergo throughout the year and the dietary regimens we maintain—is always on view in *Flex* and other bodybuilding magazines. In this book I've written a lot about the training and dietary part. Now it's time to begin discussing the artistic part of the sport: onstage physique presentation, or posing.

At lower-level competitions, you will frequently see well-developed bodybuilders who place lower than they should because of poor posing skills. They seem to have spent all of their time in the gym, all of their self-discipline in avoiding those high-calorie foods that might have prevented them from having optimum onstage muscularity. In the process, they have spent little or no time on posing practice. They pose so poorly in a competition that they place below lesser athletes.

You'll seldom see this type of thing at a national or international amateur competition, and certainly never at the IFBB pro level. Those bodybuilders who survive the rigors of climbing the competitive ladder—let's call this process bodybuilding Darwinism—invariably have practiced sufficiently on their presentation. The ones who didn't were weeded out early in the struggle for survival of the fittest. I know that I personally put in progressively more time and effort into perfecting my posing skills as I moved rung by rung up the ladder of competitive success.

Before moving on to a discussion of how to pose, I have to caution readers against expecting to get away with simply copying the routines of top champions. Every physique is unique, and every serious bodybuilder must learn to pose uniquely in order to succeed. This can easily be demonstrated. Cut out front double-biceps pose photos from bodybuilding magazines and line them up against a wall or on the floor and compare them. No two will be alike. I certainly do that pose differently from Juliette Bergmann, who does it differently from Diana Dennis, and so on. Similarly, the transitional movements between poses will vary widely from one bodybuilder to the next.

It's also necessary to resign yourself to the fact that you'll need to reserve plenty of time and energy year-round (if you want to be good!) for posing practice. I don't think it's excessive to spend 30 minutes per day on posing in the off-season, and as many hours each day before a show as you spend pumping iron in the gym. You might be able to gradually reduce posing-practice time once you've mastered the art form, but most people don't because they're afraid their routines will become stagnant if they fail to work on them consistently. I agree with this assertion.

I divide my time about equally between the mandatory poses used in Rounds I and II and the free-posing routine used in Round III of the IFBB judging system. Your free-posing program will be built around the five compulsory poses, just as those mandatories are based upon the four semirelaxed stances you'll need to master. I personally feel you should spend more than the expected amount of time on the semirelaxed stances at first, because you'll be seen onstage at a prejudging most frequently in the front version of this series. You never know when a judge might glance back into the lineup and notice you, so you always have to be "on" and perfectly composed when you're in the lineup.

If the gym where you train doesn't have a posing room, you'll need to set one up in your home. You must have two mirrors, one large main mirror on one side of the room and a smaller one on the other side that is angled so you can see your entire physique when doing straight-on back shots. In order to keep from deluding yourself about the relative excellence of your physical condition, don't settle for flattering lighting in your posing area. The harsher the light, the more it shows, and the more it shows, the better off you'll be in the long run.

I begin each posing practice session with about a 10-minute warm-up similar to the one most bodybuilders do prior to a session of pumping iron. I do various aerobic, calisthenic, and stretching exercises—with no rest between movements—until I'm well warmed up and have broken into a light sweat. Only then do I feel ready to get down to the nitty-gritty of posing practice.

Usually I start with the four semirelaxed stances, changing from one to another every minute or so. If you think these poses are *performed* relaxed, forget it! You have to learn how to use a judicious amount of tension in various muscle groups, most particularly in the leg and abdominal areas. Almost everyone keeps abs tensed at about 90% of max, legs at about 75%. The remainder of the body might be at about 50% of full flex throughout the time you are onstage. Obviously, this can be exhausting, which is one good reason why you have to practice these techniques.

The other main reason for so much practice is that it will make you come across at your best—in total comfort—once you're onstage. Don't underestimate the fright factor of having a thousand or more fans in the audience, because it can be quite intimidating the first couple of times out. With experience, however, you'll almost master the fear; it'll always be there to a small degree—at least it is for me—but you'll have it under control with sufficient practice and experience. When you really know your free-posing routine and your mind goes on automatic pilot, it's those hundreds of hours in front of the mirror that you have to thank as you perform magnificently.

When you practice the four semirelaxed stances, constantly experiment with various leg, torso, arm, and head positions. Each small change will make the stance look different, and you can work out what's best for you only through continual experimentation and observation. Just be sure that you've read the rules for executing each of these stances in the IFBB rule book first. You don't want to transgress when it comes to one of them and have to change a well-practiced stance on the spur of the moment.

As you know, the five mandatory poses for women are the front double biceps, side chest, back double biceps, side triceps, and front abdominal and thigh stances. I practice them for a minimum of 20 minutes at a time after I've thoroughly worked out my semirelaxed positions. Again, I constantly experiment with different body positions in each pose in an attempt to gradually evolve the ideal position. Although my compulsory poses are widely admired, I'm still working on them all of the time, occasionally changing one a bit to improve it even more.

Onstage, as the judges compare various small groups of bodybuilders, you'll find that you are forced to hold each mandatory pose for 15–30 seconds at a time. This is the reason I earlier suggested that you hold your practice poses for 30–60 seconds. Posing hard like this will have the beneficial side effect of making your physique appear significantly harder onstage.

The compulsory poses that are done onstage are designed to allow fair comparisons of athletes in standardized positions, which means it's very difficult to emphasize strong areas and camouflage weak points. But you aren't this confined in your free-posing program, which can be chosen precisely to make you look your best by hiding weak areas and prominently displaying stronger ones.

Many young bodybuilders—even some professionals—work with choreographers when they are putting together a free-posing program. These choreographers are either experienced competitive bodybuilders known for their own posing expertise or dance professionals who are willing to work with a bodybuilder in an area that might be challenging to them. If you have access to and can afford to engage a choreographer, I recommend it.

It's definitely possible to develop an exciting and effective free-posing routine on your own with the aid of videotape facilities. By watching enough videos of various champions going through their routines, you'll learn effective transitions between poses, and you can gradually work them into a routine of your own. Then by taping your own free-posing program to music, you can see it just as the judges and audience

will, allowing you to gradually improve your presentation without direction from a choreographer.

With my extensive dance background, I'd be the first to tell you that being a good dancer can come in quite handy when you're working up your free-posing routine. Viewing various bodybuilding and gymnastics competitions, either in person or via television, will also give you ideas, as will reviewing bodybuilding books and magazines.

As your physique improves, it's natural to spend more and more time in front of a mirror evaluating it. In the process, you will begin to imitate the poses of various stars you've seen published in *Flex* and other magazines. You unconsciously adapt these individual poses to suit your own physique, perhaps even coming up with poses so unusual and effective that they are considered part of your signature as a bodybuilder. "Oh, that's the Diana Dennis pose, and that's the Anja pose." The first time you hear this for one of your own originals, it'll make your day.

Music establishes the mood of your routine, so don't settle on some piece of music overnight. Listen to various instrumental and vocal pieces for days and weeks before choosing one to work with. Make sure that you have several copies made of the tape, with the selection edited so it's the correct length for your level of competition. A local disc jockey may be able to help you select and produce a special mix.

You can usually learn to string poses together through trial and error, or you can use a more mechanical process. If you're having any trouble, try having Polaroid shots taken of each potential pose for your routine, and then shuffle them around on the living room floor in order to come up with a logical sequence. This is mechanical, but the technique works quite well.

As you grow more experienced as a poser, don't fear taking a chance on new poses and transitions from time to time—that is the only way growth occurs. It's very easy to sit in one place but difficult to take risks; the risktakers in bodybuilding, however, are the winners in our sport. They are the athletes who invariably have the most exciting and effective free-posing routines onstage during Round III.

Decide from the beginning what you most want to project in your free-posing program and then keep those factors firmly in mind as you work on your routine. Do you want to project grace? Power? Sensuality? What else? Merely keeping these things mentally prominent will transfer them automatically into your routine, and you actually end up projecting them!

For me, the free-posing round is a time to flow, a time to show grace and power and the ability to dance to music. When I have a good routine and great music—to say nothing of optimum physical condition—I'm really in my element during my free-posing program. It's the most exciting and fulfilling feeling in bodybuilding, akin to being able to fly!

My Personal Training Program
· ·

Since I became an IFBB professional bodybuilder in 1987 and began to receive publicity in various international bodybuilding magazines, there has been considerable interest in precisely how I train. Indeed, I've given hundreds of bodybuilding seminars all over the world, and the first question I'm always asked is, "How do you actually train?"

Many sample body-part training programs have been published in *Flex, Muscle & Fitness*, and a variety of international muscle magazines, but this will be the first time I have revealed my exact day-by-day weight workout routine. It can be found in Figure 13-2. Everything in this program has been personally evolved by me over a

long period of time with systematic experimentation. It works perfectly for me, and I'm sure that sections of it will also work well for almost any advanced bodybuilder.

Figure 13-2. Anja's Personal Training Program

Day 1
Program A
Chest

Exercise	Sets	Reps
Barbell Incline Presses	4–5	15–6*
Dumbbell Incline Presses	3–5	15–6*
Cable Crossovers	3–4	15–25

Triceps

Exercise	Sets	Reps
Lying Barbell Triceps Extensions	4	15–6*
UnderGrip Pulley Pushdowns	3–4	10–25
One-Arm Pulley Pushdowns	3–4	15–20

Biceps

Exercise	Sets	Reps
Standing Barbell Curls	4–5	15–6*
Seated Alternate Dumbbell Curls	4	8–15
One-Arm Cable Curls	3–4	15–25

Program B
Chest

Exercise	Sets	Reps
Barbell Decline Presses	4–5	15–6*
Dumbbell Decline Presses	3–5	15–6*
Pec-Deck Flyes	3–4	15–30

Triceps

Exercise	Sets	Reps
Pulley Pushdowns	4	15–8*
Rope Triceps Extensions	3–4	10–20
Dumbbell Triceps Extensions	3–4	10–15

Biceps

Exercise	Sets	Reps
Barbell Preacher Curls	4–5	15–5*
Standing Barbell Curls	3–4	8–12
Barbell Reverse Curls	3–5	10–20

Day 2
Program A
Legs

Exercise	Sets	Reps
Squats	4–6	15–3*
Hack Squats	4–5	15–5*
Leg Extensions	3–4	10–25

Hamstrings

Exercise	Sets	Reps
Lying Leg Curls	4–5	25–8*
Standing Leg Curls	3–4	15–25

Adductors

Exercise	Sets	Reps
Adduction Machine	4–6	15–30

Calves

Exercise	Sets	Reps
Seated Calf Machine Toe Raises	3–5	15–30
Standing Calf Machine Toe Raises	3–5	15–20

Program B
Legs

Exercise	Sets	Reps
Angled Leg Presses	4–6	20–8*
Squats or Hack Squats	4–5	8–12
Lunges	3	20–30

Hamstrings

Exercise	Sets	Reps
Seated Leg Curls	4–5	20–8*
Standing Leg Curls	3–4	15–30

Adductors

Exercise	Sets	Reps
Adduction Machine	4–5	8–20

Calves

Exercise	Sets	Reps
Donkey Calf Raises	3–5	15–20

	Sets	Reps
Calf Presses (on angled leg-press machine)	3–4	20–35

Day 3
Program A
Abdominals

Exercise	Sets	Reps
Leg Raises	3–4	20–25
Sit-Ups	3–4	20–30

Back

Exercise	Sets	Reps
Chins	3–4	15–8*
Lat Machine Pulldowns Behind Neck	4–5	10–20
Seated Low-Pulley Rose	4–5	25–8*
Back Hyperextensions	4	15–25

Shoulders

Exercise	Sets	Reps
Seated Dumbbell Bent-Over Laterals	3	10–20
Cable Bent-Over Laterals	3	15–25
Dumbbell Side Laterals	4–5	15–8*
Machine Side Laterals	4–5	15–8*

Program B
Abdominals

Exercise	Sets	Reps
Floor Crunches	3–4	20–25
Elbow Pedestal Leg Raises	3–4	20–30

Back

Exercise	Sets	Reps
Chins	3	15–8*
Barbell Bent-Over Rows	4–5	20–8*
Deadlifts	3–4	15–5*
One-Arm Dumbbell Bent-Over Rows	3–4	10–15
Back Hyperextensions	3–4	15–25

Shoulders

Exercise	Sets	Reps
One-Arm Cable Bent-Over Laterals	4	10–25

Seated Barbell Presses Behind Neck	3–4	15–8*
Dumbbell Side Laterals	3–4	15–8*
Dumbbell Alternate Front Raises	3–4	10–15

Day 4
Rest

*Pyramid all exercises marked with an asterisk in this program, increasing the weight and decreasing reps with each succeeding set.

There are several things you should understand about this routine. It's almost always a three-on/one-off program during both off-season and precontest cycles, although in the off-season I might occasionally take an extra day of rest between repetitions of the routine if I feel I'm not fully recovering. Close to a show, it's a strict three-on/one-off program with no deviations whatsoever allowed.

I alternate the A and B parts of the routine, doing the A section the first four-day cycle and the B part the second four-day period, before starting back with A again. I like to vary my program in this manner so that it remains fresh and interesting to me, and I tend to make much better gains under these circumstances.

Usually I stick pretty much to the routine as it is listed, but on some days I don't feel that I'm completely up to par. Then I'll create an entirely different training schedule according to my instinct for what my body wants and needs on that particular day. Some of these instinctive programs are relatively short, while others are about the same length as the ones listed in Figure 13-2.

About every three months, I'll give myself a break during the off-season and switch off for 2–3 weeks to a three-day-per-week split routine, training Monday, Wednesday, and Friday only. This sounds like a common beginners' training schedule, but I do it differently, working only part of my body each of the three days. Actually, during such a cycle I'll work a muscle group only once per week, splitting it up over three distinctly different workouts. I'll also tend to train lighter and faster during this "active rest" cycle.

If you're curious, here's the way I typically split up my body parts for the three-day-per-week program:

Monday—chest, delts, biceps
Wednesday—legs, hamstrings, calves, abs
Friday—back, triceps, forearms

I find that I need to back off in training frequency and intensity for 2–3 weeks at a time like this to give my body a rest before I again begin to attack each muscle group with peak intensity on my normal three-on/one-off program. This period of active rest allows my joints to recover from the heavier, harder, and more frequent workouts. I don't want to end up with the chronically sore joints that some bodybuilders experience.

I hope you learn something from my training programs and can incorporate this new knowledge into your own training philosophy. And I hope you have a lot of success training for your first competition!

Glossary of Bodybuilding Terms

....

Aerobic Exercise. Prolonged, moderate-intensity work that uses up oxygen at or below the level at which the cardiorespiratory (heart-lung) system can replenish oxygen in the working muscles. *Aerobic* literally means *with oxygen*, and it is the only type of exercise that burns body fat to meet its energy needs. Bodybuilders engage in aerobic workouts to develop additional cardiorespiratory fitness, as well as to burn off excess body fat to achieve peak contest muscularity. Common aerobic activities include running, cycling, swimming, dancing, and walking. Depending on how vigorously you play them, most racquet sports can also be aerobic exercise.

AMDR. An abbreviation for the Adult Minimum Daily Requirement of certain nutrients as established by the United States Food and Drug Administration (FDA).

Anabolic Drugs. These drugs, also called anabolic steroids, are artificial male hormones that aid in nitrogen retention and thereby add to a male bodybuilder's muscle mass and strength. These drugs are not without hazardous side effects, however, and they are illegal in most states. Steroids are available in most gyms via the black market, but it is very dangerous to use these substances. Very few women resort to using steroids; in all national- and international-level women's competitions, contestants are tested for drug use.

Anaerobic Exercise. Exercise in which oxygen is used up more quickly than the body can replenish it in the working muscles. It is of much higher intensity than aerobic work. Anaerobic exercise eventually builds up a significant oxygen debt that forces an athlete to terminate the exercise session rather quickly. Anaerobic work (the kind of exercise to which bodybuilding training belongs) burns up glycogen (muscle sugar) to supply its energy needs. Fast sprinting is a typical anaerobic form of exercise.

Androgenic Drugs. Androgens are drugs that simulate the effects of the male hormone testosterone in the human body. Androgens can be used to build a degree of strength and muscle mass, but they also stimulate secondary sex characteristics such as increased body hair, a deepened voice, and high levels of aggression. As such they are completely inappropriate for use by women.

Balance. A term referring to pleasing and even relationship between body proportions in a bodybuilder's physique. Perfectly balanced physical proportions are a much-sought-after trait among competitive bodybuilders.

Bar. The steel shaft that forms the basic part of a barbell or dumbbell. These bars are normally about one inch thick, and they are often encased in a revolving metal sleeve.

Barbell. Barbells, most of which measure between four and six feet in length, are the most basic piece of equipment used in weight training and bodybuilding. Indeed, you can train every major skeletal muscle group in your body using only a barbell. There are two major types of exercise barbells in common use: adjustable sets (in which you can easily add or subtract plates by first removing a detachable outside collar held in place on each side by a set screw) and fixed barbells (in which the plates are either welded or bolted permanently in place). Fixed weights are arranged in a variety of poundages on long racks in commercial bodybuilding gyms, the approximate poundage for each one painted or etched on the bar. Fixed weights relieve you of the necessity of changing plates on your barbell for the various exercises. While fixed barbells and dumbbells are normally found in large commercial gyms, adjustable barbell and dumbbell sets are more frequently used at home.

Basic Exercise. A bodybuilding movement that stresses the largest muscle groups of the body (e.g., the thighs, back, chest), often in combination with smaller muscles. Heavy weights are used in basic exercises in order to build great muscle mass and physical power. Typical basic movements include squats, bench presses, and deadlifts. (You should also see the glossary entry *Isolation Exercise.*)

Benches. The most common type of bench is the flat exercise bench; other types are incline and decline benches (which are angled at about 30–45 degrees). A wide variety of exercise benches is available for use in barbell and dumbbell exercises that are performed either lying down or seated.

Biomechanics. The scientific study of body positions or body form in sports. In bodybuilding, biomechanics is the study of form when a person exercises with weights. When you have good biomechanics in a bodybuilding exercise, you will be safely placing maximum beneficial stress on your working muscles.

BMR. Basal metabolic rate, or the speed at which a resting body burns calories to provide for its basic survival needs. You can elevate your BMR and more easily achieve lean body mass through consistent exercise, and particularly through aerobic workouts.

Bodybuilding. A type of weight training applied in conjunction with sound nutritional practices to alter the shape or form of a human body. In the context of this book, bodybuilding is a competitive sport recognized nationally and internationally in both amateur and professional categories for women. A majority of those in the sport, however, use bodybuilding methods merely to lose excess body fat or to build up a too thin part of the body.

Burn. A beneficial burning sensation in a muscle that is being trained. The burn is caused by a rapid buildup of fatigue toxins in the working muscle and is a good indication that the muscle is being optimally trained. The best bodybuilders consistently forge past the pain barrier erected by muscle burn and consequently build massive, highly detailed muscles.

Burns. A training technique used to push a set past the normal failure point, thereby stimulating a muscle to greater hypertrophy. Burns consist of short, quick, bouncy reps that extend 4–6 inches in range of motion. Most bodybuilders do 8–12 burns at the end of a set that has already been taken to failure. This technique generates a terrific burn in the muscles, hence the name.

Cardiorespiratory Fitness. Physical fitness of the heart and lungs, which is indicative of good aerobic fitness.

CBBF. The Canadian Bodybuilding Federation, the sports federation responsible in Canada for administering amateur bodybuilding for men, women, and mixed pairs. The CBBF is one of the more than 120 national bodybuilding federations affiliated internationally with the IFBB.

Cheating. A method of pushing a muscle to keep working far past the point at which it would normally fail to continue contracting because of excessive fatigue buildup. In cheating, a self-administered body swing, jerk, or otherwise poor exercise form is used once the failure point is reached to take some of the pressure off the muscles and allow them to perform two or three repetitions past failure.

Chinning Bar. A bar attached high on the wall or on the gym ceiling on which chins, hanging leg raises, and other movements for the upper body are performed. A chinning bar is analogous to the high bar that male gymnasts use in national and international competitions.

Circuit Training. A special form of bodybuilding through which aerobic conditioning, muscle mass, and strength are simultaneously increased. In circuit training, a series of 10–20 exercises is performed in a circuit around the gym. The exercises chosen should stress all parts of the body. There is an absolute minimum of rest between exercises. At the end of a circuit, a rest interval of 2–3 minutes is taken before the circuit exercises are begun again. Three to five circuits constitute a circuit training program.

Clean. The movement of raising a barbell or two dumbbells from the floor to your shoulders in one smooth motion to prepare for an overhead lift. To properly execute a clean movement, you must use the coordinated strength of your legs, back, shoulders, and arms.

Collar. A cylindrical metal clamp that is used to hold plates securely in place on a barbell or dumbbell bar by means of a set screw threaded through the collar and tightened securely against the bar. Inside collars keep plates from sliding inward and injuring hands, while outside collars keep plates from sliding off the end of the barbell.

Couples' Competition. A relatively new form of bodybuilding competition in which teams composed of a man and a woman compete against each other with particularly appealing posing routines featuring adagio and other dance movements and lifts. More frequently called Mixed Pairs Competition, this event is rapidly gaining popularity with the bodybuilding community and general public. It is held in amateur World Championships.

Cut Up (or Cut). Terms used to describe a bodybuilder who has an extremely high degree of muscular definition because of a low degree of body fat.

Definition. The absence of fat over clearly delineated muscles. Definition is often referred to as muscularity. A highly defined bodybuilder has so little body fat that very fine grooves of muscularity, called striations, are clearly visible over each major muscle group.

Density. Muscle hardness, which is also related to muscular definition. A bodybuilder can be well defined and still have excess fat within each major muscle complex. But when she has muscle density, even this intramuscular fat has been eliminated. A combination of muscle mass and muscle density is highly prized among male competitive bodybuilders, but it is less sought by females.

Dipping Bars. Parallel bars set high enough above the floor to allow dips, leg raises, and a variety of other exercises to be performed between them. Some gyms have dipping bars that are angled inward at one end; the angled section is useful when changing grip width on dips.

Diuretics. Sometimes called water pills.

These drugs and herbal preparations are used to remove excess water from a bodybuilder's system just before a show so that greater muscular detail will be revealed. Harsh chemical diuretics can be harmful to your health, particularly if they are used on a consistent basis. Two of the side effects of excessive chemical diuretic use are muscle cramps and heart arrhythmias (irregular heartbeats).

Dumbbell. For all intents and purposes, a dumbbell is a short-handled barbell (usually 10–12 inches in length) intended primarily for use in one hand. Dumbbells are especially valuable for training the arms and shoulders, but they can be used to build up almost any muscle.

Exercise. An individual movement (e.g., a seated pulley row, barbell curl, or seated calf raise) that is performed in bodybuilding workouts.

EZ-Curl Bar. A special type of barbell used in many arm exercises but particularly for standing EZ-bar curls, during which it removes strain from your wrists. An EZ-curl bar is also occasionally called a cambered curling bar.

Failure. The point in an exercise at which the working muscles are so fully fatigued that they can no longer complete an additional repetition of a movement in strict form. Post–warm-up sets should be taken at least to the point of momentary muscle failure, and frequently past that point.

Flexibility. A suppleness of joints, muscle masses, and connective tissues that lets you move your limbs over an exaggerated range of motion, a valuable quality in bodybuilding training, since it promotes optimum physical development. Flexibility can be attained only through systematic stretching training, which should be the cornerstone of your overall bodybuilding philosophy.

Forced Reps. Forced reps are frequently used to extend a set past the point of failure to induce greater gains in muscle mass and quality.

With forced reps, a training partner pulls upward on the bar just enough for you to grind out two or three reps past the failure threshold.

Form. This is simply another word to indicate the biomechanics used during the performance of any bodybuilding or weight-training movement. Perfect form involves moving only the muscles specified in an exercise description, while moving the weight over the fullest possible range.

Free Weights. Barbells, dumbbells, and related equipment. Serious bodybuilders use a combination of free weights and such exercise machines as those manufactured by Nautilus, Hammer Strength, and Universal Gyms. In workouts, primarily free weights are used.

Giant Sets. Series of 4–6 exercises done with little or no rest between movements and a rest interval of 2–3 minutes between sets. You can perform giant sets for either two antagonistic muscle groups or for a single body part.

Hypertrophy. The scientific term denoting an increase in muscle mass and an improvement in relative muscular strength. Hypertrophy is induced by placing an overload on the working muscles with various training techniques during a bodybuilding session.

IFBB. The International Federation of Bodybuilders, the gigantic sports federation founded in 1946 by Joe and Ben Weider. With more than 120 member nations, the IFBB proves that bodybuilding is one of the most popular of all sports on the international level. Through its member national federations, the IFBB oversees competitions in each nation, and it directly administers amateur and professional competitions for men, women, and mixed pairs internationally.

Intensity. The relative degree of effort that you put into each set of every exercise in a bodybuilding workout. The more intensity you place on a working muscle, the more quickly it will increase in hypertrophy. The most basic methods of increasing intensity are: 1) to use heavier weights in good form in each exercise, 2) to do more reps with a set weight, or 3) to perform a consistent number of sets and reps with a particular weight but progressively reducing the length of rest intervals between sets.

Isolation Exercise. In contrast to a basic exercise, an isolation movement stresses a single muscle group (or sometimes just part of a single muscle) in relative isolation from the remainder of the body. Isolation exercises are good for shaping and defining various muscle groups. For thigh development, squats are a typical basic movement; leg extensions are the equivalent isolation exercise.

Judging Rounds. In the universally accepted and applied IFBB system of judging, bodybuilders are evaluated in three distinctly different rounds of judging, plus a final posedown round for only the top five competitors after the first three rounds have been adjudicated. In Round I, women bodybuilders are first viewed in groups and then individually in five well-defined compulsory poses (men do seven poses). In Round II, they are viewed from the front, both sides, and back; they are in semirelaxed postures. In Round III, which lasts 60 seconds on the amateur level and up to 4 minutes on the pro level, they perform their own uniquely personal free-posing routines to their choice of music. In general, the three rounds of judging and the posedown round result in a very fair choice of the final winners of a bodybuilding championship.

Juice. A slang term for anabolic steroids (e.g., "being on the juice").

Layoff. Most intelligent bodybuilders occasionally take a one- or two-week layoff from bodybuilding training. A layoff after a period of intense precompetition preparation is particularly beneficial as a means of allowing the body to completely rest and recuperate. Minor training injuries that might have cropped up during the peaking cycle are thus given time to heal

Lifting Belt. This is a leather or synthetic-fabric belt 4–6 inches wide at the back that is fastened tightly around the waist in the performance of squats, heavy back work, and overhead pressing movements. A lifting belt adds stability to the midsection, preventing lower back and abdominal injuries.

Mass. The relative size of each muscle group or of the entire physique. As long as there is a high degree of muscularity and good balance of physical proportions, muscle mass is a prized quality among competitive bodybuilders, particularly among the men.

Mixed Pairs Competition. Also called couples' competition. A relatively new form of bodybuilding competition in which man-woman teams performing particularly appealing posing routines featuring adagio and other dance movements compete against others.

Muscularity. An alternative term for "definition" or "cuts."

Nautilus. A brand of exercise machine in common use in large gyms.

NPC. The National Physique Committee, Inc., which administers men's and women's bodybuilding competitions in the United States. The NPC National Champions in each weight division are annually sent abroad to compete in the IFBB World Championships.

Nutrition. The applied science of eating to foster greater health, fitness, and muscular gains. Through correct application of nutritional practices, you can selectively add muscle mass to your physique or totally strip away all body fat, revealing in bold relief the hard-earned muscles lying beneath your skin.

Olympian. A term reserved only for bodybuilders who have competed in the Mr. Olympia or Ms. Olympia contests.

Olympic Barbell. A special type of barbell used in weightlifting and powerlifting competitions but also used by bodybuilders in heavy basic exercises such as squats, bench presses, barbell bent-over rows, standing barbell curls, and deadlifts. An Olympic barbell without collars weighs 45 pounds (20 kilograms), and each collar weighs five pounds (2.5 kilograms).

Olympic Lifting. The type of weightlifting competition contested at the Olympic Games for men every four years as well as at national and international competitions each year. Currently women compete nationally and internationally, but not in the Olympics. Two lifts (the snatch and the clean and jerk) are contested in a wide variety of weight classes.

Overload. The amount of weight a muscle is forced to use over and above its normal ability to lift. Applying an overload to a muscle forces it to increase in hypertrophy.

Peak. The absolute zenith of competitive condition achieved by a bodybuilder. To peak out optimally for a bodybuilding show, you must intelligently combine bodybuilding training, aerobic workouts, diet, mental conditioning, tanning (for fair-skinned women), posing practice, and a large number of other preparatory measures.

PHA. An abbreviation for peripheral heart action, a system of circuit training in which 4–6 short exercise circuits are performed in order to stimulate cardiorespiratory conditioning and further physical development.

Plates. The flat discs placed on the ends of barbell and dumbbell bars to adjust the weight of the apparatuses. Although some plates are made from vinyl-covered concrete, the best and most durable plates are manufactured from metal.

Pose. Each individual stance that a bodybuilder does onstage in order to highlight her muscular development.

Poundage. The amount of weight used in an exercise, whether that weight is on a barbell, dumbbell, or exercise machine.

Powerlifting. A second form of competitive weightlifting (not contested in the Olympics, however) featuring three lifts: the squat, bench press, and deadlift. Powerlifting is contested both nationally and internationally in a wide variety of weight classes for both men and women.

Progression. The act of gradually adding to the amount of resistance used in each exercise. Without consistent progression in workouts, muscles are not sufficiently overloaded to promote optimum increases in hypertrophy.

Pump. The tight, blood-congested feeling in a muscle after it has been intensely trained. Muscle pump is caused by a rapid influx of blood into the muscles to remove fatigue toxins and replace supplies of fuel and oxygen. A good muscle pump indicates that you have optimally worked a muscle group.

Quality Training. A type of workout used just prior to a bodybuilding competition in which the lengths of rest intervals between sets are progressively reduced to increase overall training intensity and help further define the physique.

Repetition (or Rep). Each individual count of an exercise that is performed. Series of repetitions are called sets, and are performed on each individual exercise in your routine.

Resistance. The actual amount of weight that is used in any exercise.

Rest Interval. The brief pause lasting 30–90 seconds between sets that allows your body to partially recuperate prior to the initiation of the succeeding set.

Ripped. The same as "cut up."

Routine. Also called a training schedule or program. A routine is the total list of exercises, sets, and reps (and sometimes weights) used in one training session.

Set. A grouping of repetitions (usually in the range of 6–15) that is followed by a rest interval and usually another set. Three to five sets of each exercise are usually performed.

Sliced. The same as "cut up" or "ripped."

Sleeve. The hollow metal tube that fits over the bar on most exercise barbell and dumbbell sets. This sleeve makes it easier for the bar to rotate in your hands as you do an exercise.

Spotters. Training partners who stand by to act as helpers when you perform such heavy exercises as squats and bench presses. If you get stuck under the weight or begin to lose control of it, spotters can rescue you and prevent needless injuries. A spotter or two is also necessary in the performance of forced reps.

Steroids. Prescription drugs that mimic male hormones but without most of the androgenic side effects of actual testosterone. Many bodybuilders acquire these dangerous drugs on the black market and use them to help increase muscle mass and strength. Possession of these drugs is illegal in most states.

Sticking Point. A stalling out of bodybuilding progress.

Stretching. A type of exercise program in which you assume exaggerated postures that stretch muscles, joints, and connective tissues; hold these positions for 30–90 seconds; relax; and then sometimes repeat the postures. The regular performance of stretching exercises promotes body flexibility and suppleness and also helps to prevent injuries.

Stretch Marks. Tiny tears in a bodybuilder's skin caused by poor diet and too rapid increases in body weight. If you notice stretch marks forming on your own body (usually around your pectoral-deltoid tie-ins), increase zinc intake and rub vitamin E cream over them two or three times per day. Also try lowering your body weight by reducing body fat levels.

Striations. Tiny grooves of muscle across major muscle groups in a highly defined bodybuilder.

Supersets. Series of two exercises performed with no rest between sets and a normal rest interval between supersets. Supersets increase training intensity by reducing the average

length of rest intervals between sets.

Supplements. Concentrated vitamins, minerals, proteins, and amino acids used by bodybuilders to improve the overall quality of their diets. Many bodybuilders believe that food supplements help promote quality muscle growth, although no scientific evidence exists to support this assertion.

Symmetry. The shape or general outline of a person's body, as when seen in silhouette. If you have good symmetry, you will have relatively wide shoulders, flaring lats, a small waist-hip structure, and generally small joints.

Testosterone. The male hormone primarily responsible for the maintenance of muscle mass and strength induced by heavy training. Since women produce less testosterone than men, they have proportionately smaller muscles. Testosterone is also responsible for the development of such secondary male sex characteristics as a deep voice, body hair, and male pattern baldness.

Training Partner. A person who works out along with you, duplicating your routine. A good training partner is essential when you are pushing hard prior to a competition, because he or she helps keep rest intervals between sets to a minimum. A training partner functions as a spotter to help you with forced reps, keeping your workouts safe.

Trisets. Series of three exercises performed with no rest between movements; there is a normal rest interval between trisets. Trisets increase training intensity by reducing the average length of rest between sets.

Vascularity. A prominence of veins and arteries over the muscles and beneath the skin of a well-defined bodybuilder. Prominent vascularity usually comes out only when a woman is in contest shape and fully carbed up just before an appearance onstage.

Warm-Up. The 10–15-minute session of light calisthenics, aerobic exercise, and stretching undertaken prior to the performance of heavy bodybuilding training movements. A good warm-up helps prevent injuries and actually allows you to get more out of your training than if you went into a workout totally cold.

WBF. The World Bodybuilding Federation, formed in 1990. To date, this professional federation has promoted only men's competitions.

Weight. The same as "poundage" or "resistance."

Weight Class. In order for bodybuilders to compete against women of similar size, the IFBB has instituted weight classes for all amateur competitions. The normal women's classes are under 114 pounds (52 kilograms), between 114 and 124 pounds (52 and 56 kilograms), and over 124 pounds (56 kilograms).

Weightlifting. The competitive form of weight training in which each athlete attempts to lift as much as she can in well-defined movements. Olympic lifting and powerlifting are the two types of weightlifting competitions.

Weight Training. An umbrella term used to categorize all acts of using resistance training. Weight training can be used to improve the body, rehabilitate the body after injuries, and improve sports conditioning. It is also a competitive activity in terms of bodybuilding and weightlifting.

Workout. A bodybuilding or weight-training session.

Suggested Reading

Training

Combes, Laura, with Bill Reynolds. *Winning Women's Bodybuilding.* Chicago: Contemporary Books, 1983.

Francis, Bev, with Bill Reynolds. *Bev Francis' Power Bodybuilding.* New York: Sterling, 1989.

Grymkowski, Peter, Ed Connors, Tim Kimber, and Bill Reynolds. *The Gold's Gym Training Encyclopedia.* Chicago: Contemporary Books, 1984.

McLish, Rachel, with Bill Reynolds. *Flex Appeal by Rachel.* New York: Warner Books, 1984.

Pirie, Dr. Lynne, with Bill Reynolds. *Getting Built.* New York: Warner Books, 1984.

Reynolds, Bill, Peter Grymkowski, Ed Connors, and Tim Kimber. *Gold's Gym Mass Building Training and Nutrition System.* Chicago: Contemporary Books, 1992.

Reynolds, Bill, Peter Grymkowski, Edward Connors, and Tim Kimber. *Solid Gold: Training the Gold's Gym Way.* Chicago: Contemporary Books, 1985.

Sprague, Ken, with Bill Reynolds. *The Gold's Gym Book of Bodybuilding.* Chicago: Contemporary Books, 1983.

Weider, Betty, and Joe Weider. *The Weider Body Book.* Chicago: Contemporary Books, 1984.

Weider, Betty, and Joe Weider. *The Weider Book of Bodybuilding for Women.* Chicago: Contemporary Books, 1981.

Weider, Joe, with Bill Reynolds. *Competitive Bodybuilding.* Chicago: Contemporary Books, 1984.

Weider, Joe, with Bill Reynolds. *Joe Weider's Ultimate Bodybuilding.* Chicago: Contemporary Books, 1989.

Nutrition

Kimber, Tim, Bill Reynolds, Peter Grymkowksi, and Edward Connors. *The Gold's Gym Nutrition Bible.* Chicago: Contemporary Books, 1986.

Reynolds, Bill, and Negrita Jayde. *Sliced: State-of-the-Art Nutrition for Building Lean Body Mass.* Chicago: Contemporary Books, 1991.

Reynolds, Bill, and Joyce L. Vedral, Ph.D. *Supercut: Nutrition for the Ultimate Physique.* Chicago, Contemporary Books, 1985.

Mental Approach

. . . .

Garfield, Charles, Ph.D., and Hal Z. Bennett. *Peak Performance: Mental Training Techniques of the World's Greatest Athletes.* Los Angeles: Tarcher, 1984.

McDonald, Kathleen. *How to Meditate: A Practical Guide.* London: Wisdom Publications, 1984.

Reynolds, Bill. *Freestyle Bodybuilding.* New York: Perigee Books, 1988.

Siegel, Peter C. *Supercharged!: The Secrets to Personal Power.* Dallas: Taylor Publications, 1992.

Tutko, Thomas A., and Umberto Tosi. *Sports Psyching: Playing Your Best Game All of the Time.* Los Angeles: J.P. Tarcher, 1976.

Index

orthotics for, 121
and pre-exhaustion sets, 177–78
and stretching, 246
and training intensity, 88
See also Injuries; Soreness
Paisley, Jackie, 294
Partners, 8, 14, **24**, 59, 87, 317
and cheating form, 89
for critiquing form, 37
for descending sets, 91–92
for pre-exhaustion sets, 177
for safety, 176
See also Injuries
Peak contraction, 90–91
for advanced training, 185–86,
299–300
dumbbell kickbacks for,
210–212
See also Muscles
Pec Deck machine
pec deck flyes for, 61, 171
See also Machine exercises
Physical exam, for beginners, 9
Physician
for dietary advice, 271
for pregnancy advice, 253, 257
for workout advice, 9
See also Podiatrist
Physique
for bodybuilding success, 169
and bone structure, 169
and competition appearance,
301–5
cross-training for, 29–30
and drugs, 187
flexibility for, 221
individualized routines for,
118–19
muscle priority training for, 9,
100–102
and nutrition, 17
quality training for, 11
and self-evaluation, 27, 165–66
squats for, 38–40
training modes for, 116–18
Plates, **7**–8, 316
See also Barbells
PNF. *See* Proprioceptive Neural
Facilitation
Podiatrist, for knee pain, 121
Posing
and ISO-Tension, 300–301
practice for, 297–98
secrets for, 305–8

and skin color, 301–2
suit choice for, 302
See also Competition; Training
cycles
Positive movement, in repetitions,
12
Positive outlook on life
and bodybuilding, 2, 283–84
for stress management, 179–81
See also Mental attitude;
Visualization
Powerlifting, 6, 316
Powerlifting USA, 120
Precontest cycles, 293–98
See also Training cycles
Pre-exhaustion supersets
and isolation exercises, 95–97
See also Sets; Training cycles
Pregnancy
and bodybuilding routine,
249–50
nutrition for, **250**–51
stretches for, 254–57
training in, 251–53
See also Exercises, in pregnancy
Program. *See* Workout
Progressive resistance training. *See*
Resistance progression
Pronation
in exercise form, 69
See also Muscles
Proprioceptive Neural Facilitation
(PNF), dangers of, 222–23
Protein
in balanced diet, 278
digestive enzymes for, 19
in food supplements, 21–22
minimum requirements for, 276
in pregnancy diet, 250–51
qualities of, **272**–73
in weight-gain diet, 17–19
See also Diet
Psychology
and bodybuilding, 283–84
See also Mental attitude; Positive
outlook
Pulleys
muscle groups for, 8
See also Exercises; Muscles
Pump. *See* Muscle pump

Q

Quality training. *See* Training

R

Racks, for exercise bench, 8
Range of motion (ROM), in calf
raises, 90
Recovery cycles, and sleep needs,
12
Repetitions, 7, **10**, 12, 16–17, 172
for break-in procedure, 22–23
and cheating form, 88–90
and holistic training, 117–18
positive and negative, 12, 92–93
in pre-exhaustion sets, 177–78
for warm-ups, 23
See also Training intensity;
Workouts
Resistance equipment, 6, 8
See also Equipment
Resistance progression, **10**–11,
316
Rest interval, 7, 11, 186
decreasing, 83, 94
in off-season cycle, 293
for pre-exhaustion sets, 177–79
and split routines, 98–99
and training circuits, **175**–76
Revolving sleeve, for barbell, **7**
Reynolds, Bill, 167
RICE, for injury treatment, 109
ROM. *See* Range of motion
Routines. *See* Workouts
Running, for aerobic training, 32

S

Safety rules, for weight training,
24
Salt. *See* Sodium
Schwarzenegger, Arnold, 91, 103,
117, 123, 172
Self-confidence, and mental
attitude, 289
Self-image
and bodybuilding, 283
for onstage appearance, 301–4
Sets, 7, **10**, 316
descending, 91–92, 172
and holistic training, 117–18
for off-season cycle, 293
supersets, 93–94, 177–78, 317
and training circuits, **175**–76
trisets and giant sets, 184–86,
314, 317
See also Exercises; Repetitions;
Workouts

Water
   and diuretics, 313–14
   and nutrition, 275
   in training routine, 173
   for weight training, 17
   See also Diet; Sodium
Weak points
   specialized training for, 169
   and training cycles, 292–93
Weight
   for barbells, 7–8
   in break-in procedure, 22
   for dumbbells, 8, 177
   gaining, 5, 18–19
   losing, 19–20
   records for, 27

Weight training, 5–11, **7**, **10**, 318
   and aerobics, 6, 33–35, 83,
      175–76
   appreciating gains in, 165–68
   basic vs. isolation exercises for,
      95–97, **96**
   biomechanical positions for, 23,
      24
   break-in procedures for, 22–23
   and circuit training, **175**–76
   clothing for, 14–16
   correct forms for, 11, **24**, 37–38
   and cross-training, 33–35
   warm-ups for, 23–24
Weightlifters, and bodybuilders,
   170–72

Workouts, 6–7, 12, 32–33, 116–19
   for beginners, **80–81**
   calorie consumption in, 19
   and changing routines, 102–3
   and cross-training, 33–35
   diary for, 16
   maximizing, 176–79
   in off-season cycle, 293
   outdoors, 122–23
   in precontest cycle, 297–98
   and pregnancy, 251–53
   and training circuits, **175**–76
   See also Exercises; Split routines

Y

Yoga, for flexibility, 220